Profiles
of the
Presidents

Profiles
of the
Presidents

Revised Edition

Emerson Roy West

Deseret Book Company   Salt Lake City, Utah   1980

Library of Congress Cataloging in Publication Data

West, Emerson Roy.
   Profiles of the presidents.

   Bibliography: p.
   Includes index.
   1. Church of Jesus Christ of Latter-day Saints—
Biography.   2. Church of Jesus Christ of Latter-day
Saints—Government.   I. Title.
BX8693.W47   1980   289.3'3 [B]   80-10455
ISBN 0-87747-800-7

To Gloria, my eternal companion,
and to our children,
Jerry, Jennifer, Julie Ann,
Janelle, and Jonathan

CONTENTS

ACKNOWLEDGMENTS

Grateful appreciation is expressed to all the people who have contributed to this book.

To my loving wife, Gloria, whose love, counsel, encouragement and personal sacrifices made this book possible. She typed the manuscript, helped research, write, edit, and proofread, and offered constructive criticism and suggestions during its preparation. She helped to make the period of time spent in writing this book a happy and rewarding one.

To my father, Roy A. West, who saw the need for this type of book and gave extensive guidance, encouragement, and help in countless ways in the preparation and in seeing it to completion. To my father-in-law, Golden K. Driggs, for his genial counsel and encouragement.

To Church scholars Roy W. Doxey, James B. Allen, Russell R. Rich, Glen R. Stubbs, T. Edgar Lyon, Milton M. Backman, Jr., Reed C. Durham, Jr., Leonard J. Arrington, and Hyrum L. Andrus for reading and evaluating the material and offering helpful suggestions.

To Nancy Wudel, Francia Stephens, and Edward L. Kimball for their editorial assistance.

To Lowell M. Durham, Jr., Eleanor Knowles, and Emily Bennett Watts of Deseret Book Company for their professional contributions.

To Junius E. Driggs for his generous financial support, which helped to make this book possible.

To the Church Historical Department for providing important information and assistance and for photographs provided.

To the Division of Health, State of Utah, which provided information on causes of death for presidents who died in Utah.

To Joseph Anderson, Harold Glen Clark, Loren Cluff, Don W. Driggs, J. Robert Driggs, Kathy Gilmore, Steven Gossman, Judy Hill, Gloria Kemker, Rae Ann Merrill, Dianne Montgomery, Sterling Nelson, Max Parker, Glen N. Rowe, Henry Smith, Leonard C. Smith, Kay B. Stubbs, and Patricia Tate for their helpful assistance.

INTRODUCTION

Profiles of the Presidents introduces the men who have presided over the restored Church of Jesus Christ from its organization in April 1830 to the present. These sketches do not attempt to offer exhaustive biographies, but rather to highlight selected incidents from the lives of the prophet-leaders of this great and last dispensation.

This new, revised edition is replete with examples of loyalty, obedience, humanity, courage, faith, steadiness in trial, and purity of life. These examples provide worthy patterns for the reader while standing as testimonies of the prophets and of the divinity of their callings.

The presidents of the Church were not spared from the problems of life that beset us all. But their special ways of handling these problems and the evidences of divine intervention in their behalf help to point them out as men whom God has called and prepared and brought forth to accomplish specific missions in his kingdom.

These profiles will be especially helpful to readers who do not have time for extensive reading and research, but wish to get a perspective of the latter-day prophets, their times, their contributions, and the events that characterized their administrations. Studying the words, the testimonies, and the lives of these great men can help every reader understand both the generalities of the eternal, unchanging gospel and the very specific nature of the counsel that each prophet has given to his own time.

"The men who have presided over this Church from the beginning have been men raised up by the Lord for the particular time during which they served, men prepared and qualified for the service they were to render and for the leadership they were to give. These men are not mediocre men; they are giants of the Lord, chosen and ordained before they came here to perform the work they have done and will do. Each is different from the others, but all are men of inspiration, of revelation, of devotion, and of faith—prophets of the living God."

—Elder Joseph Anderson, *Improvement Era*, May 1970, p. 8

PROFILE OF A PROPHET

"We thank thee, O God, for a prophet, to guide us in these latter days. . . ." (*Hymns,* no. 196.)

It is no accident that this hymn is one of the most loved in Mormondom, one whose sentiments always ring true no matter which man is occupying the holy position of prophet. Not only is it sung in tribute to the prophet in his presence, but it is also sung in many tongues, in congregations all over the world, comforting people with the reassurance of divine guidance as they face the confusion, violence, and insecurity of the world around them and linking them to the hundreds of thousands of saints, both living and dead, who have borne that same testimony in song.

When Amos assured his own recalcitrant people that "surely the Lord God will do nothing, but he revealeth his secret unto his servants the prophets" (Amos 3:7), he was simply giving voice to a universal theme of both the Old Testament and the New Testament. In his day, as in ours, one man was called of God to become a spokesman to receive the revelation of His will and to announce it to the world. Obedience to the teachings of this prophet inevitably brought inner peace, happiness, and love for others.

When the Lord reforged that long-broken chain in 1830 by designating the young Joseph Smith as his prophet, he recognized the crying need for continual revelation—not only individual, but institutional—to maintain the purity, purpose, and direction of his restored church.

1

President Ezra Taft Benson points out the orderly succession of that prophetic calling: "The Lord's mouthpiece and prophet on the face of the earth today received his authority through a line of prophets going back to Joseph Smith, who was ordained by Peter, James, and John, who were ordained by Christ, who was and is the head of the Church." (*God, Family, Country*, p. 159.)

The Lord himself instructed members of the Church: "Thou shalt give heed unto all his words and commandments which he shall give unto you as he receiveth them, walking in all holiness before me; For his word ye shall receive, as if from mine own mouth, in all patience and faith." (D&C 21:4-5.)

Who are these men who speak to us with authority from our Lord himself? Just as the Savior was reared in a mortal environment and experienced both the joys and the sorrows of earth life, so these prophets have experienced mortality: learning obedience, struggling with temptations and challenges, loving their families, and suffering grief as the inevitable losses come. Yet they have met life's hardships with courage and strength. They have been victors over their environments because they have centered their lives upon the greatest source of spiritual strength, Jesus Christ. Sometimes as children, certainly as young men, they recognized their God-given self-worth and centered their energies on becoming committed servants of the Lord. Thus each prophet qualified himself early in life to become the Lord's spokesman.

What else do they have in common? Although each prophet in our dispensation has had the unique gifts of his own personality, and differs even from his own brothers and sisters, still within the mantle of the sacred calling that has come to each, they share certain vital characteristics.

A prophet is ordained of God, called by God himself, to act as God's messenger and watchman and as interpreter of God's will to man. He learns the desires of God under the inspiration of the Holy Spirit. President Harold B. Lee said: "A prophet, then, does not become a spiritual leader by studying books about religion, nor does he become one by attending a theological seminary. One becomes a prophet, a divinely called religious leader, by actual spiritual contacts. He gets his diploma, as it were, directly from God." (*Improvement Era*, [IE], Feb. 1970, p. 94.)

A prophet declares that God speaks to him. He has the right, the power, and the authority to speak the mind and will of God to his people, saying, "Thus saith the Lord." He holds all the keys of priesthood authority. He bears witness that he knows by personal revelation from the Holy Ghost that God lives and that Jesus Christ is the Son of God, "For the testimony of Jesus is the spirit of prophecy." (Rev. 19:10.)

A prophet often foretells future events. Although he warns of impending judgments, he offers hope and a way to salvation for those who repent.

A prophet is a preacher of righteousness. He calls men to repentance and declares his message courageously, without compromising gospel standards. His mission is to fellowship people, to purify their minds and souls, to direct them back to God.

A prophet is an interpreter of the scriptures. He declares their meaning and application. His words and writings may become scripture when he speaks under the influence of the Holy Ghost.

A prophet is an instructor in Church policy. Well-versed, he directs and instructs others in it.

A prophet is humble. He readily admits his limitations. He is human with imperfections common to mankind in general, but his "humanness" never overpowers his ability to give divine direction and example. His life demonstrates commitment, courage, moral excellence, knowledge, patience, humility, temperance, and godliness.

A prophet is charismatic. He has a special endowment and holds special powers, such as those held by Ezekiel. He has love, compassion, and mercy, as did Moses and John the Beloved.

A prophet is self-denying, even to the point of enduring great suffering or even death for the gospel message.

3

When these trials come, he is loyal, courageous, and faithful.

A prophet is a leader actively involved in bettering mankind. He teaches the way by which war, depression, unemployment, ignorance, poverty, illness, and sin can be eliminated.

President Spencer W. Kimball, long before he became president of the Church, declared:

> To be a prophet of the Lord, one . . . must understand the divine language and be able to receive messages from heaven. . . .
>
> What the world needs is a prophet-leader who gives example— clean, full of faith, godlike in his attributes with an untarnished name, a beloved husband, a true father.
>
> A prophet needs to be more than a priest or a minister or an elder. His voice becomes the voice of God to reveal new programs, new truths, new solutions. I make no claim of personal infallibility for him, but he does need to be recognized of God, to be an authoritative person. He is no pretender, as numerous persons are who presumptuously assume position without appointment and authority. He must speak like his Lord: "as one having authority, and not as the scribes." (Matthew 7:29.)
>
> He must be bold enough to speak truth even against popular clamor for lessening restrictions. He must be certain of his divine appointment, of his celestial ordination, and of his authority to call to service, to ordain, to pass keys that fit eternal locks. He must have commanding power like prophets of old. (*Faith Precedes the Miracle*, pp. 318-19.)

A prophet is known by the fruits of his message. He may possess all other qualifications, but if his message does not stand up under this test, he cannot justify a claim to the divine call. The prophet Jeremiah identified the test of a true prophet: "When the word of the prophet shall come to pass, then shall the prophet be known, that the Lord hath truly sent him." (Jer. 28:9.)

Elder Orson Hyde, an apostle of this dispensation, pointed out:

> . . . it is invariably the case, that when an individual is ordained and appointed to lead the people, he has passed through tribulations and trials, and has proven himself before God, and before His people, that he is worthy of the situation which he holds . . . that when a person has not been tried, that has not proved himself before God,

and before His people, and before the councils of the Most High, to be worthy, he is not going to step in to lead the Church and people of God. It has never been so, but from the beginning some one that understands the Spirit and counsel of the Almighty, that knows the Church, and is known of her, is the character that will lead the church. (*Journal of Discourses* [JD] 1:123.)

Elder Marvin J. Ashton of the Council of the Twelve asks a revealing question pertaining to the prophet of the Church: "Are we not within our rights as members of The Church of Jesus Christ of Latter-day Saints to regard our Prophet, Seer, and Revelator as a close, personal friend as he leaves us improved daily by his willingness to reprove, admonish, love, encourage, and guide according to our needs?" (*What Is Your Destination?*, p. 142.)

To members of The Church of Jesus Christ of Latter-day Saints, a prophet is indeed that. From Joseph Smith, whom Jesus personally called as the first prophet of the restored church, to today's prophet, members acknowledge prophets as men called of God to perform a holy work.

SUCCESSION IN THE PRESIDENCY

We may not know the name of the next president of the Church, but there is no question who he will be. When newscasters interrupted holiday programming on December 26, 1973, to announce the death of President Harold B. Lee, members felt shock and grief—but they felt no confusion, doubt, or distress about who his successor would be and how he would be chosen.

The principle of succession, established by Brigham Young as president of the Council of the Twelve after the death of the Prophet Joseph, was disputed only in 1844—never since. Faithful members of the Church have known since then that the keys of the presidency reside with the Twelve, and have taken comfort in the Lord's plan, articulated by Heber J. Grant, the seventh president of the Church: "You need have no fear . . . that any man will ever stand at the head of the Church of Jesus Christ unless our Heavenly Father wants him to be there." (IE, Dec. 1937, p. 735.)

No political maneuvering, no popular following, no aspirations will ever lead a man to the presidency of the Church. In fact, as long as life and death are in the Lord's hands, even speculation is fruitless.

God makes his will known in the selection of a new president according to a system described clearly by President Joseph Fielding Smith:

The Prophet [Joseph Smith], in anticipation of his death, conferred upon the Twelve all the keys and authorities which he held. He did not bestow the keys on any one member, but upon them all, so that each held the keys and authorities. All members of the Council of

Sustaining of Spencer W. Kimball as the twelfth president of the Church

the Twelve since that day have also been given all of these keys and powers. But these powers cannot be exercised by any one of them until, if the occasion arises, he is called to be the presiding officer of the Church. The Twelve, therefore, in the setting apart of the President do not give him any additional priesthood, but confirm upon him that which he has already received; they set him apart to the office, which it is their right to do. . . .

There is no mystery about the choosing of the successor to the President of the Church. The Lord settled this a long time ago, and the senior apostle automatically becomes the presiding officer of the Church, and he is so sustained by the Council of the Twelve which becomes the presiding body of the Church when there is no First Presidency. The president is not elected, but he has to be sustained both by his brethren of the Council and by the members of the Church. (*Doctrines of Salvation* 3:155-56.)

The Lord gives us insight into the vital role of the twelve apostles:

"For unto you, the Twelve, and those, the First Presidency, who are appointed with you to be your counselors and your leaders, is the power of this priesthood given, for the last days and for the last time, in the which is the dispensation of the fulness of times.

"Which power you hold, in connection with all those who have received a dispensation at any time from the beginning of the creation;

"For verily I say unto you, the keys of the dispensation, which ye have received, have come down from the fathers, and last of all, being sent down from heaven unto you." (D&C 112:30-32.)

Members of the first Council of the Twelve were chosen in 1835 by the Three Witnesses. At that time Joseph Smith arranged the Council of the Twelve according to their ages (birthdates in parentheses):

1. Thomas B. Marsh (Nov. 1, 1799)
2. David W. Patten (Nov. 14, 1799)
3. Brigham Young (June 1, 1801)
4. Heber C. Kimball (June 14, 1801)
5. Orson Hyde (Jan. 8, 1805)
6. William E. M'Lellin (1806)
7. Parley P. Pratt (April 12, 1807)

8. Luke S. Johnson (Nov. 3, 1807)
9. William B. Smith (March 13, 1811)
10. Orson Pratt (Sept. 19, 1811)
11. John F. Boynton (Sept. 20, 1811)
12. Lyman E. Johnson (Oct. 24, 1811)

Thomas B. Marsh and David W. Patten preceded Brigham Young in seniority. In 1838, Elder Patten was killed by mobbers. Elder Marsh, senior member and president of the Twelve, apostatized and was excommunicated in 1839. Brigham Young was then the senior member of the Council of the Twelve.

In a meeting of the Twelve in Preston, England, Brigham Young was unanimously sustained as president of the Twelve, an action sanctioned by Joseph Smith.

On August 7, 1844, after the death of the Prophet, Brigham Young met with the Council of the Twelve, the high council of Nauvoo Stake, and the high priests. Speaking of the Twelve, he said: "Joseph conferred upon our heads all the keys and powers belonging to the Apostleship which he himself held before he was taken away, and no man or set of men can get between Joseph and the Twelve in this world or in the world to come. How often has Joseph said to the Twelve, 'I have laid the foundation and you must build thereon, for upon your shoulders the kingdom rests.'" (*Millennial Star* [MS] 25:215-16.)

Following Joseph Smith's death in 1844, the procedure was established that the senior member and president of the Council of the Twelve would be the new president of the Church unless otherwise directed by the Lord. John Taylor, the third president, said this about succession in the presidency: "I occupied the senior position in the quorum, and occupying that position, which was thoroughly understood by the quorum of the twelve, on the death of President Young, as the twelve assumed the presidency, and I was their president, it placed me in a position of president of the church." (*Gospel Kingdom*, p. 192.)

In 1887, shortly before John Taylor's death, while

Wilford Woodruff was the president of the Twelve, Elder Heber J. Grant of the Twelve asked if the president of the Twelve would become the next president of the Church and if this would always be the procedure. On March 28, 1887, President Woodruff replied in writing:

. . . When the President of the Church dies, who then is the Presiding Authority of the Church? It is the Quorum of the Twelve Apostles (ordained and organized by the revelations of God and none else). Then while these Twelve Apostles preside over the Church, who is the President of the Church? It is the President of the Twelve Apostles. And he is virtually as much the President of the Church while presiding over Twelve men as he is when organized into the President of the Church, and presiding over two men.

As far as I am concerned it would require . . . a revelation from the same God who had organized the Church and guided by inspiration in the channel in which it has traveled for 57 years, before I could give my vote or influence to depart from the paths followed by the Apostles since the organization of the Church and followed by the inspiration of Almighty God, for the past 57 years, by the apostles, as recorded in the history of the Church. (Matthias F. Cowley, *Life of Wilford Woodruff*, p. 560-61.)

Since the time of Brigham Young there has been no deviation from this procedure.

Appointment of the senior apostle as president places at the head of the Church the apostle who has been longest in service and is thus most familiar with Church government. It also eliminates any politics from operating within the council. President Spencer W. Kimball said: "We may expect the Church President will always be an older man; young men have action, vigor, initiative; older men, stability and strength and wisdom through experience and long communion with God." (IE, June 1970, p. 93.)

The Lord revealed to Joseph Smith specific guidelines pertaining to Church leadership:

Of the Melchizedek Priesthood, three Presiding High Priests, chosen by the body, appointed and ordained to that office, and upheld by the confidence, faith, and prayer of the church, form a quorum of the [First] Presidency of the Church.

The twelve traveling councilors are called to be the Twelve Apostles, or special witnesses of the name of Christ in all the world—

11

thus differing from other officers in the church in the duties of their calling.

And they form a quorum, equal in authority and power to the three presidents previously mentioned. (D&C 107:22-24.)

President Spencer W. Kimball explains why there are no politics in succession: "The moment life passes from a President of the Church, a body of men become the composite leader—these men already seasoned with experience and training. The appointments have long been made, the authority given, the keys delivered. . . . The kingdom moves forward under this already authorized council. No "running" for position, no electioneering, no stump speeches. What a divine plan! How wise our Lord, to organize so perfectly beyond the weakness of frail, grasping humans!" (*Faith Precedes the Miracle*, p. 314.)

President N. Eldon Tanner, first counselor to President Kimball in the First Presidency, explained:

exactly what took place following the unexpected death of President Harold B. Lee on December 26, 1973. I was in Phoenix, Arizona, to spend Christmas with my daughter and her family when a call came to me from Arthur Haycock, secretary to President Lee. He said that President Lee was seriously ill, and he thought that I should plan to return home as soon as possible. A half-hour later he called and said: "The Lord has spoken, President Lee has been called home."

President Romney, who in my absence was directing the affairs of the Church, was at the hospital with President Spencer W. Kimball of the Council of the Twelve. Immediately upon President Lee's death, President Romney turned to President Kimball and said, "You are in charge." Not one minute passed between the time President Lee died and the Twelve took over to preside over the Church.

Following President Lee's funeral, President Kimball called a meeting of the apostles for Sunday, December 30, at 3:00 p.m. in the Salt Lake Temple council room, President Romney and I had taken our respective places of seniority in the Council, so there were fourteen of us present. Following a song, and prayer by President Romney, President Kimball, in deep humility, expressed his feelings to us. He said that he had spent Friday in the temple talking to the Lord and had shed many tears as he prayed for guidance in assuming his new responsibilities and in choosing his counselors.

Dressed in our temple robes, we held a prayer circle. President

Kimball asked me to conduct it and Elder Thomas S. Monson to offer the prayer. Following this, President Kimball explained the purpose of the meeting and called on each member of the Quorum in order of seniority, starting with Elder Ezra Taft Benson, to express his feelings as to whether the First Presidency should be organized that day or whether we should carry on as the Council of the Twelve. Each said, "We should organize now," and many complimentary things were spoken about President Kimball and his work with the Twelve.

Then Elder Ezra Taft Benson nominated Spencer W. Kimball to be the President of the Church. This was seconded by Elder Mark E. Petersen and unanimously approved. President Kimball then nominated his counselors: N. Eldon Tanner as first counselor, and Marion G. Romney as second, each of whom expressed a willingness to accept the position and devote his whole time and energy in serving in that capacity. They were unanimously approved. Then Elder Mark E. Petersen, second in seniority in the Twelve, nominated Ezra Taft Benson as President of the Quorum of the Twelve. This was unanimously approved.

At this point all members present laid their hands upon the head of Spencer W. Kimball, and President Ezra Taft Benson was voice in blessing, ordaining, and setting apart Spencer W. Kimball as the twelfth President of The Church of Jesus Christ of Latter-day Saints. Then, with President Kimball as voice, N. Eldon Tanner was set apart as first counselor and Marion G. Romney as second counselor in the First Presidency of the Church. Following the same procedure, he pronounced the blessing and setting apart of Ezra Taft Benson as President of the Quorum of the Twelve. (*Ensign*, April 1978, pp. 72-73.)

After a new president of the Church is selected, it is necessary for him to be sustained by the membership of the Church, in the procedure known as the law of common consent. This means that the people must accept him as president of the Church and promise to support him in his position and to follow his direction. Agreement is demonstrated by raising the right hand. A solemn assembly is held, usually at a session of general conference. Each quorum votes separately, then the entire congregation votes.

In several revelations to the Prophet Joseph Smith, the Lord instructed him to "call your solemn assembly." (D&C 95:7; see also sections 88 and 109.)

This voting pattern has been used since the sustaining

of President John Taylor (third president) in the 1880 general conference. The appointment and sustaining of a new president is done not secretly but publicly at a general or special conference. For example, special conferences were held (1) when Lorenzo Snow died on October 10, 1901, and Joseph F. Smith was sustained in November 1901; (2) when Joseph F. Smith died on November 19, 1918, and Heber J. Grant was sustained in June 1919 (the delay was due to a flu epidemic that year).

At the death of Joseph Smith, the Twelve under Brigham Young administered the affairs of the Church for three and a half years before a new First Presidency was organized. John Taylor also presided over the Church for three years in the same capacity, as did Wilford Woodruff for two years. In this calling, each was just as much a prophet and spokesman for the Lord as he was when he later presided as president of the Church with two counselors.

President Woodruff, prior to his death, received a revelation and instructed not only Lorenzo Snow but also other leaders that after his death the First Presidency should be organized as soon as possible. Since then, no more than a few days have separated the death of a president and the setting apart of the next.

In summary, then, here is the procedure that has developed from Joseph Smith to the present:

1. When the president of the Church dies, the First Presidency is dissolved, and the counselors are automatically released and returned to their former quorums of priesthood activity.

2. The presiding power resides in the Council of the Twelve, and during that interim period they are virtually the presidency of the Church, the presiding quorum.

3. To become president of the Church, a man must be an apostle and a member of the Council of the Twelve, called of God, approved by the Council of the Twelve, and sustained by members of the Church in the solemn assembly.

4. Seniority begins automatically when a man be-

comes a member of the Council of the Twelve, and is based on length of service, not age.

5. The new president, who is the senior apostle and usually president of the Council of the Twelve, is selected "by prophecy and by the laying on of hands by those who are in authority." This is done in a meeting in the temple, where members of the Council of the Twelve are assembled in prayer and fasting. Each man, guided by inspiration, declares his belief, judgment, and testimony as to whom the Lord has chosen.

6. With the approval and the sustaining vote of the Twelve, the senior apostle is ordained and set apart as president by the laying on of hands by the Council of the Twelve. The new president of the Twelve is the voice of the council during this sacred occasion. Later, in solemn assembly, the membership of the Church votes.

7. The person who has held apostleship longest (next to the president of the Church) is appointed and sustained as the president of the Council of the Twelve. He officiates in this position unless he is called into the First Presidency and is excused from these duties. If this occurs, he still retains his apostleship, seniority, and presidency of the Council of the Twelve.

8. If the new president of the Church selects the senior member of the Twelve—the president of the Council of the Twelve—as his counselor, the next member of the Twelve in seniority usually becomes the acting president of the Twelve.

9. The president of the Church selects his own counselors. They need not be apostles, but must be high priests. It is essential that they be approved and sustained by the Council of the Twelve and the Church membership. Usually he selects two counselors.

10. This procedure of succession has been followed in every instance, with no deviation since the Church was organized, and will continue to be the order of the Church unless the Lord changes the procedure by revelation to the senior apostle or to the president before his death.

But there is more than procedure behind this principle

of succession. The late John A. Widtsoe wrote: "Men are called to the prophetic office of the President of the Church through inspiration from God. The call does not come by chance, or merely by attaining seniority in the councils of the Church. There must be fitness in the man, to be placed in the foremost office in God's latter-day Church." (IE, May 1948, p. 224.)

Line of Authority

THE LORD JESUS CHRIST

PETER, JAMES, AND JOHN
were ordained apostles by the Lord Jesus Christ.
(John 15:16.)

JOSEPH SMITH, JR., and
OLIVER COWDERY
received the Melchizedek Priesthood in 1829 under
the hands of Peter, James, and John.

THE THREE WITNESSES
were called by revelation to choose the Twelve
Apostles and on February 14, 1835, they were "blessed
by the laying on of the hands of the Presidency,"
Joseph Smith, Jr., Sidney Rigdon, and Frederick G.
Williams, to ordain the Twelve Apostles.
(*Documentary History of the Church*, vol. 2, pp. 187-88.)

BRIGHAM YOUNG
was ordained an apostle February 14, 1835, under the
hands of the Three Witnesses, Oliver Cowdery,
David Whitmer, and Martin Harris.

GEORGE Q. CANNON
was ordained an apostle August 26, 1860, by
Brigham Young.

HEBER J. GRANT
was ordained an apostle October 16, 1882, by
George Q. Cannon.

SPENCER W. KIMBALL
was ordained an apostle October 7, 1945, by
Heber J. Grant.

THE ROLE OF THE PRESIDENT

". . . to be a seer, a revelator, a translator, and a prophet, having all the gifts of God. . . ." (D&C 107:92.)

The immense duties, responsibilities, and blessings so quietly enumerated in this verse of scripture describe the role of the president of the Church. The previous verse calls him the "President of the office of the High Priesthood," emphasizing that the Church is not just another corporation, club, or organization that requires a president to lead it, but is the visible entity through which the priesthood of God operates with its saving ordinances. As president of the high priesthood, the president of the Church is "to preside over the whole church, and to be like unto Moses." The Lord, in summarizing those duties, comments tellingly, "Behold, here is wisdom." (D&C 107:91-92.)

As presiding officer, the president is the oracle of the Lord, lawgiver, judge, prophet, and the Lord's representative on earth—duties for which he has been trained through a long spiritual education. As J. Reuben Clark, Jr., counselor to three Church presidents, observed: "God . . . has fashioned every man whom he has ever called to lead his people. . . . No man ever comes to lead God's people whom he has not trained for his task." (*Deseret News*, May 15, 1945.)

Because of the president's link with the divine head of the church over which he presides, he has the necessary authority and wisdom to "set in order all the affairs of this church and kingdom." (D&C 90:16.)

Elder John A. Widtsoe explained that this authority

comes because each president "holds all the keys of authority of the Priesthood and of the Church." This enables him to act "as the earthly head of the Church of which the Lord Jesus is the Eternal Head. There is only one man at a time upon the earth who holds these keys. He is the Prophet, Seer and Revelator of the Church, the only one authorized to receive revelation for the Church." (*Priesthood and Church Government*, p. 131.)

At another time Elder Widtsoe explained in more detail the meaning of those three terms: "A prophet is a teacher of known truth; a seer is a perceiver of hidden truth, a revelator is a bearer of new truth. In the widest sense, the one most commonly used, the title, prophet, includes the other titles and makes of the prophet, a teacher, perceiver, and bearer of truth." (*Evidences and Reconciliations*, pp. 258-59.)

The president of the Church receives three types of revelation:

1. Revelation pertaining to the organization of the Church. President Kimball's reconstitution of the First Quorum of the Seventy in October 3, 1975, was such a revelation. Another was Lorenzo Snow's revelation, in a personal visitation from the Savior the night after President Woodruff died, instructing him to organize the Presidency of the Church immediately. (See Thomas C. Romney, *The Life of Lorenzo Snow*, p. 421.)

2. Revelation of Church doctrine. Joseph Smith stands preeminent in this regard since he restored the fullness of the gospel, including all of the essential ordinances and principles for the salvation of mankind. The Lord, however, gives additional revelations as he deems appropriate and "in case of difficulty respecting doctrine or principle, if there is not a sufficiency written to make the case clear to the minds of the council, the president may inquire and obtain the mind of the Lord by revelation." President Kimball's revelation that all worthy male members of the Church were eligible for the priesthood, announced June 9, 1978, is an example of such revelation. (*Ensign*, July 1978, p. 75.)

3. Continuous revelation pertaining to the welfare and progress of the Church given because of current problems and the need for current solutions. The recent emphasis on combatting pornography and abortion is an example.

Official prophetic declarations to the Church by the president are usually spoken at the general conferences or appear in signed statements.

In addition to receiving revelation, the president of the Church has the following general duties:

1. He holds the "keys of the kingdom" (D&C 65:1-2), the governing power and authority to administer in all spiritual and temporal affairs of the Church. By delegation, other General Authorities, temple presidents, mission presidents, regional representatives, stake presidents, bishops, patriarchs, and others receive keys pertaining to specific offices in their own areas. Thus, through the president's authority, salvation becomes available to the people of the world.

2. As sole spokesman for the Lord to the Church, he receives revelation and sets policies.

3. He has the gift of the Holy Ghost and of prophecy.

4. He has full responsibility for the welfare of the Church, authorizes and receives reports pertaining to its progress and problems, and preserves order in the Church.

5. He is the only one who holds keys to the sealing ordinance and temple, and he must delegate them personally to sealers. Only he can grant cancellation of sealing. All temples are under his direct supervision.

6. He is trustee-in-trust for the Corporation of the President, which holds or may hold title to all properties of the Church.

7. He is the president of Zion's Securities Corporation, the legal entity that holds title to and operates properties that are subject to taxation, such as investment property.

8. He acts as chairman or president of some of the businesses in which the Church has major interests. For example, he is president of the Church Board of Education.

9. He is responsible for the preparation and procedures of general conference.

Joseph F. Smith, sixth president of the Church, summarized his powers and duties:

I have the right to bless. I hold the keys of the Melchizedek Priesthood and of the office and power of patriarch. It is my right to bless; for all the keys and authority and power pertaining to the government of the Church and to the Melchizedek and Aaronic Priesthood are centered in the presiding officers of the Church. There is no business, nor office, within the Church that the President of the Church may not fill, and may not do, if it is necessary, or if it is required of him to do it. He holds the office of patriarch; he holds the office of high priest and of apostle, of seventy, of elder, of bishop, and of priest, teacher and deacon in the Church; all these belong to the Presidency of the Church of Jesus Christ of Latter-day Saints, and they can officiate in any and in all of these callings when occasion requires. (*Conference Report* [CR], Oct. 1915, p. 7.)

With the exception of Joseph Smith and Brigham Young, all the men who have become presidents of the Church have done so at an advanced age. In order to bear the heavy burdens of the office, these men must be sustained by the Lord. The nature of the president's work is demanding and unrelenting. He nourishes his own spirituality by spending many hours in prayer, meditation, and study of the scriptures so that he will be attuned to the prompting of the Spirit. His work requires him to attend many meetings, read and answer a great deal of correspondence, and prepare many speeches and articles.

Official letters from the president and the First Presidency are personally signed by the president. In addition, he signs calls to full-time missionaries, letters approving appropriations for properties and building projects, and letters to regional representatives, stake presidents, and bishops. He answers questions on points of doctrine and policy and signs letters dealing with sealing cancellations and approvals for the divorced to reenter the temple. To these and other matters the president of the Church gives his personal attention.

The president is assisted by at least two counselors; together they form the First Presidency. They meet regularly with the Council of the Twelve in the Salt Lake Temple, usually on Thursdays, to make decisions concerning the affairs of the Church. For the most part, the president acts in concert with his two counselors and the Council of the Twelve, and his decisions are thus usually quorum decisions. (See D&C 90:12-18; 107:22, 79.) Before he became president, Spencer W. Kimball described this meeting:

When in a Thursday temple meeting, after prayer and fasting, important decisions are made, new missions and new stakes are created, new patterns and policies initiated, the news is taken for granted and possibly thought of as mere human calculations. But to those who sit in the intimate circles and hear the prayers of the prophet and the testimony of the man of God; to those who see the astuteness of his deliberations and the sagacity of his decisions and pronouncements, to them he is verily a prophet. To hear him conclude important new developments with such solemn expressions as "the Lord is pleased;" "that move is right;" "our Heavenly Father has spoken," is to know positively.

. . . The Lord definitely calls prophets today and reveals His secrets unto them; as He did yesterday, as He does today and as He will do tomorrow—that is the way it is. (*Instructor*, Aug. 1960, p. 257.)

President N. Eldon Tanner, first counselor to President Kimball, states: "Some of the things administered directly by the First Presidency: area conferences; solemn assemblies; Budgeting, Educational, Historical, and Personnel departments; temples; auditing; the Coordinating Council; and the Welfare Services." (*Ensign*, April 1978, p. 74.)

The president's schedule normally requires him to give many addresses. He speaks at general conferences, general priesthood meetings, area conferences, solemn assemblies, regional representative seminars, stake conferences, firesides, funerals, youth conferences, missionary meetings, civic, governmental, and patriotic assemblies, and universities, colleges, and schools.

He dedicates chapels, temples, and other Church buildings. He ordains and sets apart various Church officers. He meets with many people in his extensive travels and greets the notables of the world who come to

Salt Lake City. He also meets with educators and with civic and government leaders.

When the president of the Church gives conference addresses today, millions of people throughout the world may hear and see him by radio and television. Furthermore, his messages are translated into seventeen languages and printed in Church publications throughout the world. Harold B. Lee as president of the Church emphasized the importance of learning and following the prophet's directions: "If you want to know what the Lord has for this people at the present time, I would admonish you to get and read the discourses that have been delivered at this conference, for what these brethren have spoken by the power of the Holy Ghost is the mind of the Lord, will of the Lord, the voice of the Lord, and the power of God unto salvation." (*Ensign*, July 1973, p. 74.)

Perhaps one of the greatest responsibilities of the president is to unite Church members worldwide and to build brotherhood. Thus he oversees the preaching of the gospel to "every nation, kindred, tongue and people," and teaches members that each convert enters the Church as an equal.

And finally, the president lives to be an example of total commitment to the work of the Savior. He bears testimony of divine truths. He exercises kindness, patience, long-suffering, charity, and love. In short, he manifests all the godly virtues prompted by the Spirit of the Lord for the blessing and advancement of all mankind.

JOSEPH SMITH, JR.
First President of the Church

Born: December 23, 1805, Sharon, Vermont
Died: June 27, 1844 (martyred), Carthage, Illinois (age 38)
First Elder of the Church: April 6, 1830, to January 25,
    1832 (1 year, 9 months; age 24-26)
President of the Church: January 25, 1832, to June 27, 1844
    (12½ years; age 26-38)
Ancestry: English, Scottish
Education: Grammar schools, heavenly tutors, School of
    the Prophets, self-educated
Occupation: Farmer
Missions: 1831-32: Missouri; 1833: Canada; 1835:
    Michigan; 1836: Eastern States
Apostle: Ordained May 1829
General Authority: 15 years
Church callings prior to presidency: Apostle, First Elder,
    missionary
Selective works of teachings: *History of the Church* and
    Teachings of the Prophet Joseph Smith
Physical characteristics: Six feet tall, 200-210 pounds,
    athletic build, military carriage, light brown hair, blue
    eyes, distinguished appearance
Family: Son of Joseph and Lucy Mack Smith; married
    Emma Hale; eleven children; practiced plural
    marriage. Complete list of wives and children is not
    available.

Profile of Joseph Smith

Brigham Young, second president of the Church, said, "I feel like shouting hallelujah, all the time, when I think that I ever knew Joseph Smith." (JD 3:51.)

Josiah Quincy, the mayor of Boston, observed Joseph's noble bearing and noted that only one other man among his acquaintances possessed "the kingly faculty" to the same degree. (*Figures of the Past*, p. 381.)

Amasa M. Lyman, the only member of his family to join the Church, traveled some six hundred miles to see Joseph and remembered, "When he grasped my hand in that cordial way (known to those who have met him in the honest simplicity of truth), I felt as one of old in the presence of the Lord . . . and the still small voice of the spirit whispered its living testimony in the depths of my soul, where it has ever remained, that he was the Man of God." (*Deseret News,* Sept. 8, 1858.)

Sariah Workman, an associate of the Prophet, recorded, "I always felt a divine influence whenever I was in his presence." (*Young Woman's Journal* 17:542.)

Among his friends were Orson Pratt, scientist; Orson Spencer, scholar; Brigham Young, carpenter; Frederick G. Williams, physician; Lorenzo Snow, teacher; Wilford Woodruff, Oliver Cowdery, and Heber C. Kimball, all honorable men and all intimately acquainted with his character. Orrin Porter Rockwell, his frontiersman-bodyguard, who was imprisoned for nearly nine months, traveled for twelve days after his release to reach the Prophet's house dirty, ragged, with bleeding feet, long hair, and a shaggy beard. When the Prophet recognized him, he embraced him with tears in his eyes. (M. Lynn Bennion, *Oil for Their Lamps*, pp. 192-97.)

Yet during one of the first revelations he received, Joseph Smith heard the angel Moroni warn him that his "name should be had for good and evil among all nations, kindreds, and tongues, or that it should be both good and evil spoken of among all people." (*History of the Church* [HC] 1:11-12.)

A poor farm boy and day laborer, he rose to lead what has become one of the fastest-growing churches in America today, to become mayor of a city that challenged Chicago in size, and to act as lieutenant general of the Nauvoo Legion and as a candidate for the presidency of the United States. Passionately loved, he was also unreasoningly despised and hated.

The remarkable story of Joseph Smith began December 23, 1805, in Sharon, Vermont, where he was born—the fourth of eleven children—to Lucy Mack and Joseph Smith, Sr. His early home life was an important factor in preparing him for what was to come. His father, a farmer who taught school for a few years during the winter months, exposed his children to the hard work of the farm but also to an atmosphere of study, inquiry, thinking, and discussion.

When Joseph was about seven, he developed a severe infection in his leg. A team of doctors concluded that the leg would have to be amputated. When the family refused to give permission for the amputation, the doctors decided to operate instead. During the painful surgery, Joseph would not be bound as the doctors had ordered, nor would he take whiskey to dull the pain. Instead he chose to have his father hold him. Later his leg healed so well he was able to wrestle and play in the most rigorous of sports, although that leg was one quarter of an inch shorter than his other leg. In fact, his athletic ability became widely known. A friend once said of Joseph, "I've seen the Prophet wrestle, and run, and jump, but have never seen him beaten. In all that he did he was manly and almost godlike." (*Young Woman's Journal* 17:537-38.)

Perhaps the Lord foresaw the physical trials in store for Joseph Smith and provided through the Prophet's parentage and his youth a foundation of strength and endurance. Standing at least six feet tall and weighing about 200 pounds, he walked hundreds of miles in the Lord's work. When he was imprisoned for his beliefs, he suffered great physical abuse. Yet, despite these physical hardships, he remained generally healthy.

Favorite reading in the Smith family was the Bible, which was discussed on a regular basis. His parents were God-fearing people who, though reluctant in some ways to affiliate with a church, felt it important to seek divine guidance and obey God's commandments. They often could be seen walking to nearby villages to attend Sunday "preaching services."

During Joseph's early life, his family moved often in attempts to find financial success. Finally arriving in upstate New York, they became involved in a current re-

Young Joseph studying the Bible

ligious revival, and several brothers and sisters joined different faiths. But young Joseph could not decide which church was right.

He later recorded in a letter that even at age twelve, he was starting to feel "important concerns for the welfare of my immortal soul which led me to searching the Scriptures. . . ."

By age fourteen, he was deeply troubled by inconsistencies in the interpretation of scriptures around him. It was this personal turmoil that led young Joseph to a grove of trees one morning in 1820 to seek an answer from God. Prompted by a passage in the Bible, "If any of you lack wisdom, let him ask of God, that giveth to all men liberally, and upbraideth not; and it shall be given him" (James 1:5), he uttered his first vocal prayer and asked which church to join.

The answer to that simple question came in a form that was to change the world. Joseph records:

". . . I saw a pillar of light exactly over my head, above the brightness of the sun, which descended gradually until it fell upon me.

". . . When the light rested upon me I saw two Personages, whose brightness and glory defy all description, standing above me in the air. One of them spake unto me, calling me by name and said, pointing to the other—*This is My Beloved Son. Hear Him!*" (Joseph Smith—History 1:16-17.)

Then Joseph received the specific answer to his prayer—that none of the existing churches was the true church of Jesus Christ and that he should join none of them.

Later angelic messengers came with more information and instructions: If Joseph remained faithful he would be the instrument in God's hands to bring His truths back to earth. He was to be the prophet of the restoration of the Church of Jesus Christ.

Ultimately he would receive the Aaronic Priesthood from John the Baptist and the Melchizedek Priesthood with keys from Peter, James, and John. This would be all the priesthood authority he needed to preside over the restoration of Christ's church.

That was still in the future. He began first telling the story to his family. His brother William recalled hearing seventeen-year-old Joseph tell them "how the angel appeared to him, what he had told him. . . . He continued talking to us [for] some time. The whole family melted to tears, and believed all he said." (*William Smith on Mormonism*, pp. 9-10.)

In 1830, Joseph Smith published the Book of Mormon, a translation of ancient records of the early inhabitants of the American continent. In the same year, he became prophet-leader of the restored Church of Jesus Christ.

A precious part of Joseph's life and a contributing factor to his spiritual strength was his relationship with his family. They, too, passed through much physical and spiritual hardship for his sake. In 1827, before the publication of the Book of Mormon, Joseph married a loyal and capable woman, Emma Hale. Later he would write of her:

". . . with what unspeakable delight, and what transports of joy swelled my bosom, when I took by the hand . . . my beloved Emma—she that was my wife, even the wife of my youth, and the choice of my heart. Many were the reverberations of my mind when I contemplated for a moment the many scenes we had been called to pass through, the fatigues and the toils, and sorrows and sufferings, and the joys and consolations, from time to time, which had strewed our paths and crowned our board. Oh what a commingling of thought filled my mind for the moment, again she is here, even in the seventh trouble—undaunted, firm, and unwavering—unchangeable, affectionate Emma!" (HC 5:107.)

Joseph and Emma had nine children, including eight boys and one girl, and adopted two others, twins—a boy and a girl. Of these children, only five lived to maturity. Emma gave birth to their last child five months after the Prophet's death.

In his journal Joseph talked about taking his family to concerts, the theater, circus performances, and excursions on Mississippi River boats. The family often enjoyed what we would call home evenings around the fireside, playing games, reading and studying together. Despite the many duties and persecutions that took Joseph away from home, his family was very important in his life. His personal journal records entries such as these:

"In the morning I took my children [on] a pleasure ride in the carriage." (HC 5:369.)

"Enjoyed myself at home with my family, all day . . ." (HC 2:345.)

"At four in the afternoon, I went out with my little Frederick, to exercise myself by sliding on the ice." (HC 5:265.)

One historian states that Joseph's children

regarded their father with mixed feelings of awe and affection. At this time, all of them were old enough to take note of the deferential respect most people paid to their famous parent. And while they were shielded, to a large extent, from the ugly hatred of their father's enemies, they were aware of the controversy that surrounded him. This aspect of their father, however, was of relatively minor importance to the Smith children. What counted most with them was the unfailing kindness and love he showed toward them, as well as his exuberance, his athletic interests, and his friendly nature. Most important, however, they were touched by his profoundly spiritual nature. They had heard him pray in their family circle with a fervor and humility that thrilled them. They had been blessed under his hands and had felt the spiritual power which emanated from him as he had rebuked disease or had given comfort or made promises. (Francis M. Gibbons, *Joseph Smith: Martyr, Prophet of God*, p. 308.)

Time spent with his family was doubly precious because there were so many other demands on it, and the very development of the Church meant that mobility, not stability, was the pattern. In the fourteen years between the organization of the Church and Joseph's martyrdom in 1844 the Church moved from New York to Ohio, from Ohio to Jackson County and later to Caldwell County, Missouri, from Caldwell County, Missouri, to Nauvoo, Illinois. The unceasing efforts of missionary work brought in a constant stream of new members to be fellowshipped, taught, and sent out as missionaries in their turn. In addition to his translation of the Book of Mormon, published

33

in 1829, Joseph also translated the Pearl of Great Price, which includes the writings of the patriarch Abraham and revelations of Moses and Enoch; a third volume of sacred scripture, the Doctrine and Covenants, is composed largely of the revelations he received from the Lord.

The Prophet preached in public gatherings sometimes several times a week and frequently taught small groups of people. He was a powerful and inspiring speaker and teacher who deeply moved thousands of people to commitment and action by the truth and power of his testimony. He motivated people to live good lives. His articles and writings appeared in the Church periodicals—*The Times and Seasons, The Evening and Morning Star, Messenger & Advocate, The Wasp, Nauvoo Neighbor, Millennial Star,* and *Elder's Journal*—and in newspapers as far away as Philadelphia, Washington, New York, and St. Louis. Thousands of copies of his *Views of the Powers and Policy of the U.S. Government* were distributed throughout the United States in his 1844 campaign for the presidency.

In March 1842, at the request of John Wentworth, editor and proprietor of the *Chicago Democrat,* Joseph Smith wrote a letter of nearly six pages in which he told of the rise, progress, persecution, and faith of the Church members. Near the end of the letter, he stated in simple but concise terms the religious creed that has since become known as the Articles of Faith.

A theologian, educator, and author, Joseph Smith was also a builder of Zion. His plans were used as the basis for the laying out of Nauvoo, "the city beautiful," and as a model for many of the western cities established by the members of the Church.

In 1834 he led a group of 205 Mormon men on a 1,000-mile march from Kirtland, Ohio, to Independence, Missouri. This group, known as Zion's Camp, sought to reestablish the Saints in the homes from which they had been driven by mobs. He also participated in a movement in which the western frontier was opened for settlement.

An active proselytizer in Canada, he set forth the basic principles and organization for a worldwide missionary

Profile of Joseph Smith, taken from a lithograph published in New York

system. He helped lay the foundation and gave impetus to the cause of massive genealogical research.

Charismatic and compelling, he could have easily become wealthy had he so desired. Instead, while his personality and its power attracted those with less-than-pure motives, his intense spirituality and personal purity claimed the loyalty of those who knew him best. George Q. Cannon, later a member of the Council of the Twelve and of the First Presidency, said, "His face possessed a complexion of such clearness and transparency that the soul appeared to shine through." (*The Life of Joseph Smith*, p. 19.) Wilford Woodruff, describing the last address Joseph ever gave to the Council of the Twelve, recalled its power: "He was clothed upon with the Spirit and power of God. His face was clear as amber. The room was filled as with consuming fire. He stood three hours on his feet." (CR, April 1898, p. 89.)

Because he had access to the gifts of the Spirit and used them freely in the service of others, his people loved and trusted him and testified to his kindness as well as to his righteousness.

One time he called at a house to see a man on business and found a child with a swollen sore throat and in much pain. With consecrated oil he anointed the throat and then administered to the child. The child was healed. (Leonard J. Arrington, *Ensign,* Jan. 1971, p. 37.)

Newly arrived in Illinois, the Saints were stricken by illness as they camped along the banks of the Mississippi River. Wilford Woodruff, an apostle, church historian and later Church president, wrote: Joseph "went through among the sick lying on the bank of the river, and he commanded them in a loud voice, in the name of Jesus Christ, to come up and be made whole, and they were all healed. . . . They crossed the Mississippi river and came to Brother Elijah Fordham's house who was nigh unto death. The "Prophet of God spoke with a loud voice, . . . 'Elijah, I command you, in the name of Jesus of Nazareth, to arise and be made whole!' . . . Elijah Fordham leaped from his bed like a man raised from the dead." (Woodruff, *Leaves from My Journal,* pp. 62-63.)

On one occasion a visitor asked the Prophet Joseph how he managed to control the people of Nauvoo, recognizing that they had come from many walks of life. His answer reflected his greatness and deep religious understanding: "I teach them correct principles, and they govern themselves." (As quoted by John Taylor, MS 13:339.)

Joseph Smith had an overwhelming love for people, and there was nothing so dear to his heart as friendship. During the Nauvoo period, when he was in hiding, some of his friends visited him. After their departure he wrote, "How good and glorious it has seemed unto me, to find pure and holy friends, who are faithful, just, and true, and whose hearts fail not; and whose knees are confirmed and do not falter." (HC 5:107.) As he prayed for them, rejoicing in their kindness, the still, small voice whispered to his soul, "These, that share your toils with such faithful hearts, shall reign with you in the kingdom of their God." (HC 5:109.)

His capacity to love was often revealed in his capacity to forgive. Once Joseph was kidnapped by two sheriffs who brutally bruised his flesh with their guns. When they arrived in Nauvoo his release was ordered, and he immediately invited the two sheriffs to join him for dinner. When the meal was ready, the Prophet placed them in the position of honor at the head of the table, and served them with the best in the house. He said: "I have brought these men to Nauvoo, . . . not as prisoners in chains, but as prisoners of kindness. I have treated them kindly. I have had the privilege of rewarding them good for evil." (HC 5:467.)

Another example of his ability to forgive concerned William W. Phelps. During the bitter days of persecution in Missouri, Phelps apostatized and turned against the Church. He signed his name to a false affidavit that brought much suffering to the members and imprisoned Joseph. This resulted in his excommunication on March 17, 1839. Phelps soon recognized what a terrible thing he had done and asked for forgiveness and readmission into the Church. He wrote the Prophet Joseph and among other things said: "I have seen the folly of my way, . . . I have done wrong and I am sorry. . . . I ask forgiveness in the name of Jesus Christ of all the Saints, . . . for I will do right." (HC 4:142.)

Joseph's answer revealed the quality of love and forgiveness for the wayward: "Believing your confession to be real, and your repentance genuine, I shall be happy once again to give you the right hand of fellowship, and rejoice over the returning prodigal. . . . 'Come on, dear brother, since the war is past, for friends at first, are friends again at last.' " (HC 4:162.)

William Phelps came back into the Church in 1841 and became very active. He served a mission and made many valuable contributions, particularly to the music of the Church. He wrote many hymns, including "The Spirit of God Like a Fire is Burning" and "Praise to the Man."

The devotion of Joseph's people was reinforced by their thirst for the long-lost doctrines that he explained and revealed to them, even though believing in such things as visions, the visitation of angels, new scriptures, and restored priesthood alienated him from other religious leaders. He taught a consistent, authoritative theology, a theology that he revealed line upon line, and he was urgent in his haste to provide it in the short time that remained.

Donna Hill, author of a biography of Joseph Smith, notes: "Religion was to him a matter of total commitment and every aspect of life was a part of the Lord's plan. He

The Prophet liked to rock in this chair

felt himself to be chosen of the Lord to reveal the true gospel in the latter days and he was keenly aware of his responsibility. He was anxious for salvation not only for himself, his family and his followers, but for his country, and for the world. God's plan was meant for all. For those who rejected it, there was nothing ahead but disaster. Time was short; the millennium was fast approaching. Zion, the refuge for the righteous, must be built. The message must be carried as fast as possible to everyone who would listen." (*Joseph Smith, the First Mormon,* pp. 107-8.)

Joseph Smith's contributions to mankind bear witness of his divine calling. Undoubtedly one of the greatest among them was his insight into the physical nature of Deity. His first vision in 1820, one of the most important events in the history of the world, revealed that God the Father and Jesus Christ are two separate beings. Joseph saw the Savior on that occasion and again on February 16, 1832, at Hiram, Ohio. He and Oliver Cowdery also saw the Savior in the Kirtland Temple on April 3, 1836. He counseled the Saints concerning this doctrine: "You have got to learn how to be Gods yourselves, and to be kings and priests to God, the same as all Gods have done before you, namely, by going from one small degree to another, and from a small capacity to a great one; from grace to grace, from exaltation to exaltation, until you attain to the resurrection of the dead, and are able to dwell in everlasting burnings, and to sit in glory, as do those who sit enthroned in everlasting power." (*Teachings of the Prophet Joseph Smith*, pp. 346-47.)

John Taylor, third president of the Church, reported the extent of Joseph's heavenly contacts: "When Joseph Smith was raised up as a Prophet of God, Mormon, Moroni, Nephi and others of the ancient Prophets who formerly lived on this Continent, and Peter and John and others who lived on the Asiatic Continent, came to him and communicated to him certain principles pertaining to the Gospel of the Son of God." (JD 17:374.)

"Other writings record the appearance to the Prophet of John the Baptist, Peter, James, and John, Moses, Elias, Elijah, and others. So intimate was Joseph's knowledge of these personages that he related not only what they said but also how they looked and acted." (Francis M. Gibbons, *Joseph Smith: Martyr, Prophet of God*, p. 38.)

Joseph Smith received keys of authority from these resurrected prophets. He received the Aaronic Priesthood from John the Baptist; the Melchizedek Priesthood from Peter, James, and John; the sealing powers from Elijah; and keys to gathering Israel from Moses.

Through these visions and revelations and by direct commission from Jesus Christ, Joseph Smith organized Christ's church with all its original offices and powers, including the same offices, powers, ordinances, and doctrines that had existed in ancient times. He was also given the correct name that the church should bear, and was told that the followers of Christ's church were and should be called "saints." He laid the foundation for the "restoration of all things" spoken of by the holy prophets. So important was his mission that holy prophets spoke of him by name thousands of years before his mortal birth. (See JST, Gen. 50:25-28, 31-33; Mal. 3:1; 2 Nephi 3:14-16.)

Among the doctrinal teachings Joseph restored to the world was that which concerns man's true relationship with deity—the true knowledge of God, Christ, and the Holy Ghost. This knowledge allows man to understand the purpose of his life—his past, present, and future estates. The Prophet also clarified important doctrine relating to the fall of Adam, the atonement, resurrection, judgment, exaltation, salvation for the dead, degrees of glory, priesthood, tithing, salvation of little children, and the doctrine of eternal marriage and continued family associations in the resurrection of the righteous. He revealed the law of consecration and stewardship, providing for the establishment of a divine economic system. He gave the world the Word of Wisdom, a health code that points out the spiritual significance of a healthy body.

Joseph Smith received divine instruction on saving ordinances for both the living and dead. He gave instructions for correct procedures for the blessing of infants, baptism, confirmation, priesthood ordination, bestowal of the gift of the Holy Ghost by the laying on of hands, anointing the sick, the consecration of oil for the administration of the sick, and partaking of the sacrament. He revealed the temple endowment and the rite and covenant of eternal marriage.

Joseph Smith's vision of the celestial kingdom, received in 1836, was approved for addition to the scriptures on April 3, 1976, by the general conference of the Church and is now section 137 of the Doctrine and Covenants. In other scriptures restored through him appear such major philosophic statements as: "For behold, this is my work and my glory—to bring to pass the immortality and eternal life of man" (Moses 1:39), and "It is impossible for a man to be saved in ignorance" (D&C 131:6).

Stephen L Richards, a member of the First Presidency from 1951 to 1959, wrote: "The world's enlightenment of the century following his [Joseph's] life has not disclosed a single error in his theological and philosophical pronouncements, and the society which he established is without question the peer, and many students not belonging to it maintain it is the superior, of all social systems on the earth." (*Contributions of Joseph Smith,* p. 7.)

But perhaps Joseph Smith's most significant contribution in religion was the reestablishment of the doctrine and practice of continuous revelation. He taught that every obedient and righteous person may receive personal revelation. "No man can receive the Holy Ghost without receiving revelations," the Prophet said. "The Holy Ghost is a revelator." (*Teachings of the Prophet Joseph Smith,* p. 328.) Many of Joseph Smith's revelations and visitations were witnessed by other living men who were regarded by contemporaries as trustworthy individuals and men of integrity. Joseph prophesied of the Civil War, the westward movement of the Saints, and his own martyrdom. He envisioned by prophecy conditions of the last days, including the coming of Christ.

The Prophet's desire to know and understand divine truths was matched by his desire for secular education. Even though his formal education did not go beyond the early elementary grades, he studied Hebrew, German, law, and many other subjects. He read widely and taught the principle that the glory of God is intelligence and that men cannot be saved in ignorance. He established the School of the Prophets, one of America's early schools for adults. He argued for freedom of slaves and the elimination of social classes. He appreciated the nobility of womanhood and authorized the 1842 organization of the Relief Society.

From the age of fourteen, Joseph had been persecuted with an intensity difficult to comprehend today. He was slandered, libeled, vilified, scorned, ridiculed, terrorized,

Engraving depicting Joseph Smith's last public address in the spring of 1844

and repeatedly torn away from his family and friends. He was forced to live in exile from his home, was robbed, beaten, tarred, illegally imprisoned for months at a time in dirty and uncomfortable prisons, and was mercilessly hounded with lawsuits and false arrests. Once on a trumped-up charge he spent four winter months in a dungeon with a dirt floor, little light, and no sanitation. His family was in such poverty that Emma could not afford to send him a blanket.

Even more serious was the combination of internal disunity and persecution from without. The national economic depression in 1837 led to the failure of the Kirtland Bank, established by Church leaders, and Joseph was blamed. In 1838, Joseph and the Saints moved to Missouri, where trouble arose from the state's slave-owning majority. Later the Church was forced to leave Missouri and settle in Illinois.

The Lord revealed to the Prophet Joseph the doctrine of plural marriage at Kirtland as early as 1831. Most non-Mormons and many Mormons disagreed with this practice. In 1844, some dissidents set up a highly critical newspaper in Nauvoo and the Mormon town council ordered its destruction. Hostility heightened when, within a few weeks, Joseph Smith opened a campaign for the presidency of the United States.

In June 1844, enemies of the Church demanded the arrest of the Prophet. At the urging of those who taught that perhaps this time he would be given a fair trial, the Prophet and the town councilmen rode to Carthage to meet the charges, even though Joseph was personally convinced this journey meant his death. The Lord had spared Joseph's life on previous occasions but, at last, his work was sufficiently completed that others could carry on, and he said he no longer had the Lord's promise of protection.

It was on the hot, muggy Friday afternoon of June 27, 1844, that a mob of about one hundred fifty self-styled vigilantes descended upon Carthage Jail, where Joseph, his brother Hyrum, John Taylor, and Willard Richards were imprisoned. Some circled the building and others forced their way through the doors and ran upstairs, firing as they came. Hyrum was killed first. Joseph was shot and fell out the window to the ground. An examination of his body showed that he had been hit four times, twice in the front and twice in the back. Accounts differ as to whether he was dead before he hit the ground. The assault lasted for about three minutes and was over by about 5:15 P.M.

It was significant—even suitable—that Hyrum Smith laid down his life as the second witness for the gospel. Hyrum had always guarded his younger brother, and he accepted Joseph's mission in a sacred and loyal spirit. He was one of the eight witnesses to handle the gold plates and one of the six founding members of the Church in 1830. Hyrum's greatest honor, however, was to succeed Oliver Cowdery as the Second Elder, or associate president, of the Church. Joseph once said of Hyrum, "I love Hyrum with a love that is stronger than death."

John Taylor, gravely wounded in the Carthage assault, expressed the feelings that filled the hearts of the Saints who had loved Joseph and Hyrum so much: "I felt a dull, lonely, sickening sensation. . . . When I reflected that our noble chieftain, the Prophet of the living God, had fallen, and that I had seen his brother in the cold embrace of death, it seemed as though there was a void or vacuum in the great field of human existence to me, and a dark gloomy chasm in the kingdom, and that we were left alone." (Daniel Tyler, *A Concise History of the Mormon Battalion in the Mexican War*, pp. 51-52.)

"The murder of Joseph and Hyrum Smith at Carthage, Illinois was not a spontaneous, impulsive act by a few personal enemies of the Mormon leaders, but a deliberate political assassination, committed or condoned by some of the leading citizens in Hancock County. As such it falls within the brutal but familiar American tradition of vigilante activity, and formed but one episode in a long series of anti-Mormon depredations in New York, Ohio, Missouri, and Illinois." (Dallin H. Oaks and Marvin S. Hill, *Carthage Conspiracy*, p. 6.)

Joseph's contemporaries who knew him best were to comment as President Wilford Woodruff did: "When I look at the history of Joseph Smith, I sometimes think that he came as near following the footsteps of the Savior . . . as anyone possibly could." (John A. Widtsoe, *Joseph Smith: Seeker After Truth*, p. 348.)

One historical evaluation is made by Donna Hill. She states:

As Joseph saw it, he had the truth, and the truth was for the whole world. His urgent mission was to spread the gospel and to call the faithful to Zion. . . . Joseph soon learned that he could not fulfill his destiny unless he made his people invincible, but his difficulties only increased when he tried to combine spiritual with worldly leadership, adding to his responsibilities as prophet, seer and revelator the duties of real estate agent, city planner, banker, businessman, architectural consultant, journalist, social reformer, lieutenant general of militia and politician. Most of his followers saw nothing improper in this. It semed only wise and expedient that their prophet, whose inspiration came directly from the Lord, should lead them in all things. (*Joseph Smith, the First Mormon*, p. viii.)

Elder Parley P. Pratt wrote shortly after the martyrdom:

President Joseph Smith was in person tall and well built, strong and active; of a light complexion, light hair, blue eyes, very little beard, and of an expression peculiar to himself, on which the eye naturally rested with interest, and was never weary of beholding. His countenance was ever mild, affable, beaming with intelligence and benevolence; mingled with a look of interest and an unconscious smile, of cheerfulness, and entirely free from all restraint or affectation of gravity; and there was something connected with the serene and steady penetrating glance of his eye, as if he would penetrate the deepest abyss of the human heart, gaze into eternity, penetrate the heavens and comprehend all worlds.

He possessed a noble boldness and independence of character; his manner was easy and familiar; his rebuke terrible as the lion; his benevolence unbounded as the ocean; his intelligence universal, and his language abounding in original eloquence peculiar to himself—not polished—not studied—not smoothed and softened by education and refined by art; but flowing forth in its own native simplicity, and profusely abounding in variety of subject and manner. He interested and edified, while, at the same time, he amused and entertained his audience; and none listened to him who were ever weary with his discourse. I have even known him to retain a congregation of willing and anxious listeners for many hours together, in the midst of cold or sunshine, rain or wind, while they were laughing at one moment and weeping the next. Even his most bitter enemies were generally overcome, if he could once get their ears. (*Historical Record* 7:575-76.)

In view of his divinely inspired record and the everaccumulating evidence of his prophetic powers, it is easy to understand why his rapidly increasing numbers of followers around the world join in saying: "Praise to the

Statue of the Prophet by Mahonri Young

man who communed with Jehovah! Jesus anointed that Prophet and Seer. Blessed to open the last dispensation, Kings shall extol him, and nations revere." (*Hymns*, no. 147.)

Monuments have been built to him, poets sing of him, authors have written books about him. Who was this man, Joseph Smith?

The answer to that question lies in the honest, prayerful study of the things he taught and did. Yes, he was an instrument in the hands of the Lord in opening a new gospel dispensation. He was in every deed what he claimed to be—a prophet of the living God.

His testimony of the Lord and Savior Jesus Christ stands today as one of the most beautiful and powerful scriptural passages in the Doctrine and Covenants. Speaking of a vision he and Sidney Rigdon had witnessed, he said:

"And now, after the many testimonies which have been given of him, this is the testimony, last of all, which we give of him: That he lives!

"For we saw him, even on the right hand of God; and we heard the voice bearing record that he is the Only Begotten of the Father—

"That by him, and through him, and of him, the worlds are and were created, and the inhabitants thereof are begotten sons and daughters unto God." (D&C 76:22-24.)

As Joseph Smith bore testimony, so many others testified of him. From the hearts of his mourning people came what might have been his epitaph, but which is a testimony that thousands have reechoed since: "Joseph Smith, the Prophet and Seer of the Lord, has done more, save Jesus only, for the salvation of men in this world, than any other man that ever lived in it." (D&C 135:3.)

Important Dates and Events
in the Lifetime of Joseph Smith

Church Membership: 1844: 35,000 (est.)
1844   Stakes: 9   Missions: 3   Temples: 2
         Number of General Authorities: 29
         Missionaries Called in 1844: 586 (est.)

1805   Joseph Smith was born December 23 in Sharon, Windsor County, Vermont.
1808-10 Moved to Royalton, Vermont.
1811   Moved to Lebanon, New Hampshire.
1812-13 Was stricken with typhus fever. Had an operation due to infection in his leg. The operation was successful, but Joseph had to use crutches for several years and limped for life.
1813   Moved to Norwich, Vermont, for three summers. Family was unsuccessful in farming.
1816   Moved to Palmyra, Ontario County (now Wayne),New York.
1818   Moved a couple of miles south of Palmyra to a farm in Manchester.
1819-20 Religious revivals. Joseph became interested in religion.
1820   Joseph's first vision. He had prayed for guidance in response to a religious revival in the area when he heard the Reverend George Lane quote James 1:5 in a sermon titled "What Church Shall I Join" (age 14).
1823   Joseph was visited three times during the night of September 21 by the angel Moroni. Moroni told him of ancient metal plates and instructed him in his role in restoring the gospel and translating the Book of Mormon. Joseph was unable to work in the fields, having been kept awake all night by angelic visitations. Moroni appeared again and commanded Joseph to tell everything to his father, which he did. Joseph found the record's location the next day in the Hill Cumorah near the Smith farm, but was told he could not have the records.
1824   Joseph was visited again by the angel Moroni.
1825   Was visited again by the angel Moroni, September 22. Was

employed by Josiah Stowell (Stoal) in search of old Spanish mines in Harmony, Pennsylvania. Resided at the home of Isaac Hale. Met Emma Hale.

1826   Was visited again by the angel Moroni, September 22. Farmed for Joseph Knight, Sr., November.

1827   Married Emma Hale in South Bainbridge, New York, January 18 (age 21). Left Stowell to work on his father's farm in New York. Received the golden plates of the Book of Mormon from Moroni. Also received the Urim and Thummim, which was used to assist in translation. After much harassment, Joseph left Manchester and went to the home of his wife's father, Isaac Hale, in Harmony, Pennsylvania. Commenced translation of the plates. Moved to a smaller house near the Hale farm.

1828   Martin Harris took copies of characters from the plates to New York City, where Charles Anthon and Samuel E. Mitchell pronounced them authentic, February. Martin Harris borrowed and lost 116 pages of the completed manuscript. Joseph visited New York, June 14. Joseph returned to Harmony and operated a small farm he had purchased, July.

1829   Joseph continued translating with Oliver Cowdery as scribe. John the Baptist appeared and conferred the authority of the Aaronic Priesthood on Joseph and Oliver, May 15. The two baptized each other. Peter, James, and John conferred the apostleship and Melchizedek Priesthood, May or June. Joseph left Harmony for Peter Whitmer's farm, Fayette, New York. Finished translation of the Book of Mormon, June. Three Witnesses saw the angel Moroni and the plates. Eight Witnesses were shown the plates by Joseph shortly after the Three Witnesses had seen them at Smith home in Manchester.

1830   First copies of the Book of Mormon were available for sale in March. E. B. Grandin printed 5,000 copies. Joseph organized the "Church of Jesus Christ" at Peter Whitmer, Sr., home in Fayette, New York, April 6. Joseph and Oliver ordained each other to the office of elder, June. First conference of the Church was held in Fayette, New York. Joseph was arrested for disorderly preaching, tried, and acquitted twice. Joseph commenced a revision of the English Bible. "Visions of Moses," later incorporated in Pearl of Great Price, were revealed to Joseph. The "Writings of Moses" were added to the revelations. Joseph moved to Fayette, New York.

1831   Moved to Kirtland, Ohio, January. Revelation was given on law of consecration. First bishop was ordained, February. Emma lost twin babies at birth; Joseph and Emma adopted a set of twins. Church headquarters were moved to Kirtland. First high priests were ordained, June. Zion was founded at Independence, Missouri. Joseph worked on revising and clarifying the Bible. Church membership was divided into main bodies in Ohio and Missouri.

1832   Was sustained as president of the High Priesthood at conference at Amherst, Ohio, January 25. He received the vision of glories (D&C 76) at Hiram, Ohio, February 16. Was tarred and feathered by mob, March 24. Recorded first part of personal history. Met Brigham Young, Joseph Young, and Heber C. Kimball, November 8. Received the revelation known as "Revelation and Prophecy on War," concerning the Civil War, December 25.

1833   The Word of Wisdom was given to the Church, February. The First Presidency was organized March 18, with Joseph Smith as president and Sidney Rigdon and Frederick G. Williams as counselors. Joseph Smith, Sr., was ordained as patriarch, December 18. The Prophet completed his first translation and review of the New Testament. Started the School of the Prophets in Kirtland. Served a mission to Canada, October 5-November 4. The saints were driven from Jackson County, Missouri, by a mob.

1834   First stake and high council were organized in Kirtland, February 17. May-June: The Prophet led Zion's Camp march from Kirtland to Clay County, Missouri, to assist the exiled Missouri Saints. Served mission to the eastern states with Hyrum Smith, Sidney Rigdon, and Oliver Cowdery.

1835   Organized the Council of the Twelve Apostles on February 14 and the First Quorum of Seventy on February 28. Received a revelation on priesthood (D&C 107). Michael A. Chandler exhibited mummies with rolls of papyrus covered by hieroglyphics in Kirtland, July. The Prophet commenced to translate these records (Book of Abraham). Book of Commandments was approved by general assembly of Church. Joseph Smith and the Saints labored on the Kirtland Temple.

1836   The Prophet received a vision of the celestial kingdom concerning the redemption of the dead (D&C 137). Dedicated the Kirtland Temple, March 27. The Savior, along with Moses, Elias, and Elijah, appeared to Joseph and Oliver Cowdery in the Kirtland Temple, April 3. (See D&C 110.)

1837   The Kirtland Safety Society Bank failed. The British Mission, first permanent mission, was opened. This was a period of apostasy for the Church. The Prophet traveled to Canada and Missouri, July to November.

1838   Adam-Ondi-Ahman, near Grand River, Missouri, was

named. The Prophet fled from Kirtland, Ohio, to Caldwell County, Missouri, to escape mob violence. He and five companions were imprisoned in Liberty Jail for six months; they escaped April 16, 1839. The Church of Jesus Christ of Latter-day Saints was officially named. (D&C 115.) The Prophet began dictating his personal history (*History of the Church*).

1839   The Prophet was moved as a prisoner to the Gallatin jail in Daviess County, Missouri. Was indicted by a Daviess County grand jury, presumably for "treason and murder," and tried before a drunken court. En route to Boone County, under guard, he made his escape and went to Quincy, Illinois. Armed militia mobs, carrying out the governor's orders, expelled the Mormons from Missouri. Joseph Smith and other leaders appealed to President Van Buren and Congress for redress from Missouri persecutions. The Saints settled in Nauvoo. The Prophet administered to the sick along the river bank. Wards headed by bishops were first created in Nauvoo.

1840   First immigrants arrived from England. The Prophet preached in Philadelphia and Washington before returning to Nauvoo. The *Millennial Star*, monthly periodical, was started in England. Joseph Smith, Sr., died.

1841   The Prophet was elected a member of the city council. The Saints were commanded to build a temple at Nauvoo. Joseph Smith was elected lieutenant general of the Nauvoo Legion. Work began on the Nauvoo Temple, April 6. The Prophet was arrested in Illinois on a fugitive warrant issued by Governor Boggs of Missouri, but Judge Stephen A. Douglas of Quincy ruled the writ ineffective and released the prisoner. The Nauvoo Temple baptismal font was dedicated and the first baptisms were performed there, November. The Prophet announced plans for an immigration agency to be established for Church immigrants from England.

1842   The Relief Society was organized, March 17. The Book of Abraham was published. The Prophet wrote the Wentworth letter (of which the Articles of Faith formed the conclusion). Introduced endowment ceremonies in private office above his store, May 4. Was elected mayor of Nauvoo, May 19. Prophesied on August 6 that the Saints would move to the Rocky Mountains. Was arrested as accessory in attempt on Governor Boggs's life by extradition proceedings, but later released. Went into hiding. Submitted to voluntary arrest in December; was taken to Springfield, Illinois, for trial and later released.

1843   June: was arrested without due process of law at Dixon and later discharged by Nauvoo municipal court. Wrote down revelation for eternal marriage and plurality of wives, July 12. Conspiracy arose against the Prophet by some Church members.

1844   The Prophet Joseph became a presidential candidate on an independent ticket. Instructed the Twelve to organize an exploring expedition to locate a site for the Saints in California or Oregon. Organized the Council of Fifty, a secret political body that directed the westward migration of the Saints and served as a "shadow government" in Utah during the nineteenth century. Prepared a memorial to Congress asking for a law protecting United States citizens emigrating to the unorganized territories known as California and Oregon, and offered volunteers to serve in such a protective force. At general conference in April, delivered the King Follett address, a revelation of eternal truths concerning glories of immortality. Charles Francis Adams and Josiah Quincy visited, May 15. Two indictments were sworn out against the Prophet for polygamy and for false swearing. He spoke out against the apostates and recounted his many trials and persecutions. Went to Carthage with several friends to meet the indictments head on. Was told of a conspiracy against his life. Returned home when he got bail. Was arrested for the destruction of the *Expositor*, tried before municipal court in Nauvoo, and acquitted. Proclaimed martial law in Nauvoo, ordering out the legion and police force. Delivered his last public oration in uniform to about 4,000 of the Nauvoo Legion. Asked Governor Ford to come to Nauvoo. Sent a letter to Governor Ford containing all affidavits showing the Saints' side of the conflict. Received a letter from Governor Ford stating that Joseph had committed one illegality after another. Was invited to Carthage under guarantee of safety. Left Nauvoo with Hyrum Smith and Willard Richards; they crossed the Mississippi River, intending to journey to the West, but returned to Nauvoo, June 23. In custody of Ford's posse, the Prophet stated, "I am going like a lamb to the slaughter." Saw Emma and his family for the last time, June 24.

In Carthage, Joseph and Hyrum were arrested for treason. Were arraigned before Justice R. F. Smith on charge of riot and bound over to circuit court for trial. Imprisoned at Carthage, Illinois, on false commitment, June 25. Asked for a change of venue to Quincy. Sent several messages to Ford, June 26. Ford visited the Prophet in prison and promised protection. The Prophet was taken again to the courthouse for a justice's examination; decided the court would be postponed until next day, and he was returned to jail. A military council, including Ford, decided to march troops to Nauvoo the next day, to return the following day. Joseph's trial was to be further postponed until June 29. Few men were left to guard the jail, June 26.

John Taylor, Willard Richards, Hyrum, and Joseph were guarded in jail by small detachment of Carthage Greys, June 27. Ford left for Nauvoo with remnants of the militia; the rest were disbanded. At five P.M. a mob of about 150 with painted faces and disguises rushed the jail. Joseph and Hyrum were killed by gunfire about 5:15 P.M. John Taylor was wounded in the attack; Willard Richards escaped injury.

The First Presidency and Council of the Twelve
During Joseph Smith's Administration

First Counselor	President	Second Counselor
*Sidney Rigdon 1833-44	**Joseph Smith First Elder: 1830-32 President: 1832-44	*Frederick G. Williams 1833-37
		**Hyrum Smith 1837-41
		*William Law 1841-44
	Assistant President	
	**Oliver Cowdery 1834-37	
	**Hyrum Smith 1841-44	

Additional Counselors		Assistant Counselors
*John Cook Bennett 1841-42		**Oliver Cowdery 1837-38
Amasa M. Lyman (1842) 1843-44		*Joseph Smith, Sr. 1837-40
		**Hyrum Smith Sept.-Nov. 1837
		*John Smith 1837-44

---

*Never ordained an apostle.
**An apostle but not a member of the Council of the Twelve.
Note: Joseph Smith and Oliver Cowdery were ordained apostles in 1829 by Peter, James, and John. See D&C 20:2, 27:12; also see Durham and Heath, *Succession in the Church*, pp. 2-3 and 12-29.

Excommunicated

1838—Oliver Cowdery   1842—John Cook Bennett
   (rebaptized 1848)   1844—Sidney Rigdon
1839—Frederick G. Williams   1844—William Law
   (restored to fellowship,
   1840)

Council of the Twelve (all ordained in 1835)

Thomas B. Marsh   Parley P. Pratt
David W. Patten   Luke S. Johnson
Brigham Young   William B. Smith
Heber C. Kimball   Orson Pratt
Orson Hyde   John F. Boynton
William E. M'Lellin   Lyman E. Johnson

Excommunicated

1837—John F. Boynton
1838—William E. M'Lellin
1838—Luke S. Johnson (rebaptized 1846)
1838—Lyman E. Johnson
1839—Thomas B. Marsh (rebaptized 1857)
1839—Orson Hyde (disfellowshipped
         in May; restored in June)
1842—Orson Pratt (rebaptized
         in 1843)

Died

1838—David W. Patten

Added

John E. Page (1838)   Willard Richards (1840)
John Taylor (1838)   Lyman Wight (1841)
Wilford Woodruff (1839)   Amasa M. Lyman (1842)
George A. Smith (1839)

Note: Dates in parentheses indicate date ordained member of the Council of the Twelve.

Council of the Twelve—1844

Brigham Young (1835)   John E. Page (1838)
Heber C. Kimball (1835)   John Taylor (1838)
Orson Hyde (1835)   Wilford Woodruff (1839)
Parley P. Pratt (1835)   George A. Smith (1839)
William B. Smith (1835)   Willard Richards (1840)
Orson Pratt (1835)   Lyman Wight (1841)

First Apostolic Presidency—June 27, 1844, to Dec. 27, 1847 (3½ years)

BRIGHAM YOUNG
Second President of the Church

Born: June 1, 1801, Whitingham, Vermont
Died: August 29, 1877, of ruptured appendix infection,
    Salt Lake City, Utah (age 76)
President of the Church: December 27, 1847, to August 29,
    1877 (30 years; age 46-76)
Ancestry: English
Education: Self-educated, School of the Prophets,
    apprenticeship
Occupation: Glazier, carpenter
Missions: 1832-33: Canada; 1836, 1843: Eastern States;
    1839-41: Britain
Apostle: Ordained February 14, 1835 (served 12 years; age
    34-46)
President of the Council of the Twelve: April 14, 1840, to
    December 27, 1847
General Authority: 42½ years
Church callings prior to presidency: Apostle, missionary
Selective works of teachings: *Discourses of Brigham Young*
Physical characteristics: Five feet ten inches tall, 185-200
    pounds, reddish to gray hair, wore a beard in later
    years, strong jaw, rugged and stocky physique
Family: Son of John and Abigail Howe Young. Following
    is a list of his wives: Miriam Works, Mary Ann
    Angell, Lucy Ann Decker, Harriet E. C. Cook,
    Augusta Adams, Clara Decker, Olive Grey Frost,
    Louisa Beaman, Clarissa Ross, Emily Partridge,
    Emeline Free, Margaret Maria Allen, Susan Snively,
    Margaret Pierce, Ellen Rockwood, Maria Lawrence,
    Martha Bowker, Zina D. Huntington, Naomah K. J.
    Carter, Mary Jane Bigelow, Lucy Bigelow, Eliza R.
    Snow, Eliza Burgess, Harriet Barney, Harriet Amelia
    Folsom, Mary Van Cott, Ann Eliza Webb. Had total
    of 57 children.

Profile of Brigham Young

"Brigham Young lived to become immortal in history as an American Moses, by leading his people through the wilderness into an unpromised land!" author George Bernard Shaw once said. (Bryant S. Hinckley, *The Faith of Our Pioneer Fathers*, p. 19.)

Perhaps no single figure in American history is associated more with western colonization than Brigham Young. Under his direction, thousands of immigrants transformed barren deserts into beautiful cities.

The story of the arduous trek westward is well known. The trying situations of the first settlers—crop failures, severe weather, lack of proper housing, clothing, and food—are repeated often as examples of great courage and faith.

And "Brother Brigham" has been lauded for the courage and wisdom he continually gave the Saints to bolster them up and remind them of their part in a divine plan. However, he has also been criticized because of his demands on the Saints. He was accused of usurping power and seeking for his own gain. Four years before his death, in a letter to the editor of the New York *Herald*, he wrote: "My whole life is devoted to the Almighty's service, and while I regret that my mission is not better understood by the world, the time will come when I will be understood, and I leave to futurity the judgment of my labors and their result as they shall become manifest." (Preston Nibley, *The Presidents of the Church*, 1974, p. 63.)

Today, as the world looks back, it recognizes in Brigham Young a dynamic, brilliant leader who, through inspired concern and love, helped his people overcome the most adverse conditions. He led them to prosper not only materially but also spiritually. His unyielding firmness was a strength to the Saints. His ability to organize, his strong will, and his uncompromising nature saw them through many trials. The results of his labors have truly earned him universal respect and admiration.

An article written about the secular leadership of Brigham Young stated:

Contemporary observers whom we have a right to respect—persons of education and experience and standing who traveled to Utah to observe him—emphasized three characteristics: his self-confidence, his sincerity, and his good common sense. Fitz Hugh Ludlow, a nationally known writer and artistic critic, found that Brigham Young had "absolute certainty of himself and his own opinions." Governor Young, he wrote, was convinced that he was doing God's work, and that if he and other mortals did all they could to establish the kingdom, God would see to the rest. This helps us to understand the governor's firmness, his calmness, and his unshakeable optimism in the face of seemingly impossible circumstances. (Leonard J. Arrington and Ronald K. Esplin, "Building a Commonwealth: The Secular Leadership of Brigham Young," *Utah Historical Quarterly*, Summer 1977, pp. 219-20.)

Like many of the other Church presidents, Brigham Young learned early in life to work hard and to acknowledge God as the source of spiritual strength. He was born June 1, 1801, in Whitingham, Vermont, the ninth child of John and Abigail Young. His family, settlers in Massachusetts, were very poor. His father was a strict disciplinarian and taught Brigham to obey Christian principles. Brigham recalled, "I was brought up so strict, so firm in the faith of the Christian religion by my parents, that if I had said 'Devil,' I believed I had sworn very wickedly." (JD 6:290.)

As a young boy Brigham learned respect for religion and a love for the scriptures. At age fourteen, after his mother died, he became an apprentice to a furniture maker and house painter. His hours of hard work were often followed by quiet times of introspection and Bible-reading. It was probably because of this background that

*Early photograph of Brigham Young from
an 1850 daguerrotype*

young Brigham was so serious about an "Indian Bible" that he read about in a newspaper article. By that time Brigham's family had moved to New York, where news of the day concerned a young man named Joseph who had purportedly seen an angel.

When Brigham's brother and his married sister each received a copy of the Book of Mormon from a missionary, Samuel Smith, Brigham immediately read it with great interest. He described his reactions to it: "I weighed the matter for a year and a half. I looked at it on all sides. . . . I reasoned on [it] month after month, until I came to a certain knowledge of its truth." (*Utah Genealogical and Historical Magazine,* July 1920, p. 110.)

He had not been carried away by a charismatic speaker or pushed prematurely into baptism by his own longings for certainty. Instead, his love for the truth led him into the search, and it just as surely led him to join the Church. Speaking as president, he summed up in a brief epigram what could have been his motto: "Truth is obeyed when it is loved." (JD 7:55.) Pragmatic and practical, he did not let matters of political expediency or popularity make decisions for him. When he knew the truth, he obeyed it by living it.

At the same time, he placed no unnatural restrictions on the truth, and chided some of the more doctrinaire and rigid Saints by reminding them: "Our doctrine and practice is, and I have made it mine through life—is to receive truth no matter where it comes from." (*Discourses of Brigham Young,* p. 11.) To those who tried to limit the gospel itself, he said: "Our religion is simply the truth. It is all said in this one expression—it embraces all truth, wherever found, in all the works of God and man that are visible or invisible to mortal eye." (*Discourses of Brigham Young,* p. 2.)

Within a few weeks following his baptism, Brigham had converted his wife, Miriam, as well as his brothers, sisters, and father. Several months after the baptism, Miriam gave birth to their second daughter; soon thereafter she contracted tuberculosis and died. Brigham then devoted himself completely to church service, giving away all his possessions and serving mission after mission. His close friends Heber and Vilate Kimball helped him care for his two daughters.

Shortly after Miriam's death, Brigham Young journeyed to Ohio to meet the Prophet Joseph Smith. He recorded this significant meeting:

. . . we found the Prophet, and two or three of his brothers, chopping and hauling wood. Here my joy was full at the privilege of shaking the hand of the Prophet of God, and receiving the sure testimony, by the Spirit of prophecy, that he was all that any man could believe him to be, as a true Prophet. . . .

In the evening a few of the brethren came in, and we conversed together upon the things of the kingdom. He called upon me to pray; in my prayer I spoke in tongues. As soon as we arose from our knees the brethren flocked around him, and asked his opinion concerning the gift of tongues that was upon me. He told them it was the pure Adamic language. Some said to him they expected he would condemn the gift brother Brigham had, but he said, "No, it is of God, and the time will come when brother Brigham Young will preside over this

Church." The latter part of this conversation was in my absence. (MS 25:439.)

Thus began a relationship between Brigham Young and Joseph Smith that was characterized by the strongest loyalties and admirations. Brigham often said he would gladly give his life for Joseph, and even at his death, he uttered the words, "Joseph, Joseph, Joseph!" Witnesses said it appeared Joseph Smith had come to take him to the spirit world. (*Comprehensive History of the Church* [CHC] 5:509.)

In the fall of 1837 the Church at Kirtland was rocked with apostasy from all sides; even leading men of the Church, including some of the Council of the Twelve, declared Joseph Smith to be a fallen prophet. At a meeting held on one occasion in the upper room of the Kirtland Temple for the purpose of appointing David Whitmer as president of the Church, Brigham Young arose and said "in a plain and forcible manner . . . that Joseph was a Prophet, and I knew it, and that they might rail and slander him as much as they pleased, they could not destroy the appointment of the Prophet of God, they could only destroy their own authority, cut the thread that bound them to the Prophet and to God, and sink themselves to hell." (MS 25:487.)

To the objective eye, there were times when obedience to the Prophet seemed beyond what one man could reasonably ask of another. But it was never more than Brigham Young, a faithful disciple of the Lord, was willing to give when instruction came through the Lord's mouthpiece, Joseph Smith. One particularly trying time was in 1839. The Saints had just survived the winter exodus from Missouri to settle on a bend of the Mississippi River in Illinois, where they contended with hunger, disease, poverty, and a shortage of materials in their efforts to build again a city of refuge. At this time, Brigham Young and his fellow apostles were called to leave their destitute families to preach the gospel in Great Britain. Almost to a man, they were ill; sickness plagued

Presumed to be the earliest photograph the Church has of Brigham Young. Authenticity is not fully established

their families as well. Brigham reported: "My health was so poor I was unable to go thirty rods [160 yards] . . . without assistance. . . . I left my wife sick, with a babe only ten days old, and all my children sick and unable to wait upon each other." (MS 25:646.)

But as president of the mission, he never let worry or loneliness sap his efforts. In twelve months and sixteen days, the missionaries in Great Britain baptized between seven and eight thousand converts, printed 5,000 copies of the Book of Mormon, published the Church's first periodical in England, the *Millennial Star,* and printed 3,000 hymnbooks and 50,000 tracts. Brigham also supervised the emigration of a thousand converts under the auspices of a Church-organized shipping agency.

Joseph Smith had relied greatly upon Brigham Young even before this time. During the dark days of persecution and apostasy in Kirtland, Brigham Young's firm leadership became a strength to the Saints. He was also a powerful leader in Missouri, directing the evacuation of the Saints while Joseph and Hyrum were in Liberty Jail. When the Prophet was murdered in 1844 several men stepped forward to lead the Church, causing confusion about whom they should follow. But at a special meeting Brigham Young led most of the Saints to accept the Twelve as rightful successors to Joseph Smith. He recorded in his diary on August 8, 1844: "I arose and spoke to the people, my heart was swollen with compassion toward them and by the power of the Holy Ghost, even the spirit of the prophets, I was enabled to comfort the hearts of the Saints."

As he arose to speak, he assumed the mantle of the prophet—the voice and physical features of the late Prophet—thus convincing those present that he was chosen by God to be their next leader. The following are two of the many testimonies of those who were there:

"If I had not seen him with my own eyes, there is no one that could have convinced me that it was not Joseph Smith, and any one can testify to this who was acquainted with these two men." (Wilford Woodruff, cited in B. H. Roberts, CHC 2:418.)

George Q. Cannon, who later became an apostle, testified: "Who that was present on that occasion can ever forget the impression it made upon them? If Joseph had risen from the dead, and again spoken in their hearing, the effect could not have been more startling than it was to many present at that meeting; it was the voice of Joseph himself; and not only was it the voice of Joseph which was heard, but it seemed in the eyes of the people as though it was the very person of Joseph which stood before them. A more wonderful and miraculous event than was wrought that day in the presence of that congregation we never heard of. The Lord gave his people a testimony that left no room for doubt, as to who was the man he had chosen to lead them." (Edward W. Tullidge, *Life of Brigham Young,* p. 115.)

Brigham Young became president of the Church at age forty-six. His thirty-year administration was the longest in Church history. He came into Church leadership with great missionary experiences, unwavering dedication to the kingdom of God, and a testimony so intense that, he said, "I wanted to thunder and roar out the Gospel to the nations. It burned in my bones like fire pent up . . . nothing would satisfy me but to cry abroad in the world, what the Lord was doing in the latter days." (JD 1:313.)

As president, first of the Twelve and then of the Church, he directed the colonization of the Great Basin and brought thousands of converts to settle in more than 350 villages, towns, and cities.

In 1847, when President Young led the first pioneer company of 143 men, three women, and two children to the Salt Lake Valley, he recognized the land as the future home of the Saints from having seen it in vision. Wilford Woodruff left this record of their arrival in the valley: "President Young expressed his entire satisfaction at the appearance of the valley as a resting place for the Saints

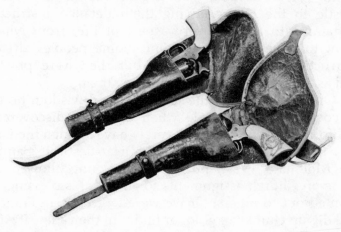

Pistols owned by Brigham Young

and felt amply repaid for his journey. While lying upon his bed, in my carriage, gazing upon the scene before us, many things of the future, concerning the valley, were shown to him in vision." (Anderson, *Life of Brigham Young,* p. 83.)

Two years after the Saints settled in the valley, Brigham Young established the provisional State of Deseret. It became a territory in 1850, with President Young appointed as the first governor. He served as governor of the Territory of Utah for eight years.

Under his direction, the Saints built roads, canals, businesses, schools, and cultural institutions. They also worked an experimental farm on the outskirts of Salt Lake City to determine which crops would best accommodate themselves to the Utah climate. President Young's work in irrigation set patterns for years to come.

An outstanding city planner, Brigham Young directed the laying out of Salt Lake City in ten-acre blocks, and also supervised the building of extensive telegraph lines through the area.

Under his direction temple sites were dedicated in Salt Lake City, St. George, Logan, and Manti. He lived to see the St. George Temple completed. He also supervised the building of the Salt Lake Tabernacle.

In 1847, President Young sent out his first general epistle to the Saints, giving them detailed instructions pertaining to almost every aspect of life, from what to plant to how to use their time. Some people felt these instructions were highhanded, but they were practical, and as a rule the people tried to obey them.

One example was the judgment and wisdom he used in counseling the people when gold was discovered in California. To some it must surely have seemed the Lord's way to insure the survival of the near-destitute Saints in the Mountain West, but Brigham Young allowed only those on Church assignments to go with his blessing, and pointed out to others: "If we were to go to San Francisco and dig up chunks of gold, or find it in the valley, it would ruin us. The true use of gold is for paving streets, covering houses and making culinary dishes and when the Saints shall have preached the gospel, raised grain and built up cities enough, the Lord will open up a way for a supply of gold to the perfect satisfaction of his people." After this touch of humor, he added more seriously, "Until that time, let them not be over anxious, for the treasures of the earth are in the Lord's storehouse and he will open the doors thereof when and where he pleases." (Clarissa Young Spencer and Mabel Harmer, *Brigham Young at Home*, p. 252.)

President Young felt there was no separation of the spiritual and the material welfare of his people. His policy was to encourage domestic manufacture. In 1856 the Deseret Agricultural and Manufacturing Society was organized, and in 1869 Zion's Cooperative Mercantile Institution was established. These organizations were to encourage cooperative production and trade. He also encouraged the members to try many new industries, such as the manufacturing of paper, iron, silk, chinaware, pottery, and beet sugar, and the production of woolen products, cotton and cotton goods, and leather and leather goods. All this was part of his effort to make Utah self-sustaining and to create economic and social order.

His inspired leadership, backed up with a minute attention to every detail, made the Mormon experiment in the desert effective. In the early 1850s he began extensive tours throughout the territory giving "practical advice on building houses, growing cotton and planting trees. . . . The overall purpose of these visits," sums up Gordon Irving of the Church Historical Department, "can best be seen as pastoral, since they gave Brigham a chance to provide encouragement and guidance to his people. Also inherent was the desire to achieve social control by fostering patterns of life and behavior compatible with the president's vision of the kingdom of God." (*Utah Historical Quarterly*, Summer 1977, p. 237.)

C. R. Savage, a photographer who accompanied President Young on these visits, testified to the president's passion for details. He carried "rawhide to mend the wagons, marbles for the children and tobacco for the Indians." (*Church News,* May 26, 1979, p. 5.)

In Salt Lake, his business acumen showed itself even in so small a detail as having his study near his bedroom, apparently "so it would be convenient for work at any hour of the day or night." (*Utah Historical Quarterly,* Summer 1977, p. 225.)

In a typical afternoon, he visited with several commercial and manufacturing officials, counseled with a bishop about the design of a windmill, discussed improvements in the sugar factory, and talked with someone about slate and flagstone samples for paving. Additionally, he received a report on a tunnel project, conferred on a related canal project, met with Levi Stewart, who wanted to buy one of his businesses, and in the evening worked on legal matters as governor "drawing up release, pardon and remission[s] until after 9 P.M." (*Utah Historical Quarterly,* Summer 1977, p. 227.)

He was a self-educated man, with only eleven days of formal education—although he did attend the School of the Prophets. He read widely. He wrote with difficulty, but the language of his sermons, which were extemporaneous, was vivid, clear, and appropriate to his audience.

Wilford Woodruff once commented on President Young's speaking ability, which, for sheer endurance, was astonishing. On one of his tours through the territory, from May 3 to September 29, 1865, he "delivered 62 addresses which occupied 24 hours and 22 minutes." His talks averaged 24 minutes apiece. These public meetings were in addition to his " 'personal contact with key men and women throughout the territory by letter, traveling to them, or meeting them in his office; . . . providing detailed instructions and advice; . . . receiving regular oral and written reports; and . . . providing encouragement for projects both large and small.' " (*Utah Historical Quarterly,* Summer 1977, p. 222-23.)

In private interviews, however, it was his silence as much as his speaking that gave him such wisdom. "At the beginning of an interview, he would often sit back for the first three minutes while his guest talked and in that short period of time 'he always knew exactly the sort of man he was dealing with, and the nature—greedy, benign or sinister—of his business. . . . Brigham Young used to say that no man, if allowed to speak, could possibly avoid revealing his true character.' " (*Church News*, May 26, 1979, p. 5.) The combination of all these factors gives weight to Herbert E. Bolton's conclusions, after comparing Brigham Young to Calvert, Oglethorp, and Stephen F. Austen: " 'It is doubtful if any of these men so completely molded his people and their institutions as Brigham Young molded the Mormons.' " (*Church News*, May 26, 1979, p. 5.)

He advanced the cause of education, founding the Deseret University (1850), now the University of Utah; the Brigham Young Academy (1875), now Brigham Young University; and the Brigham Young College in Logan, Utah (closed in the early twentieth century when there was no longer a need for it). He also encouraged the establishment of elementary schools. He constantly counseled the members to involve themselves in every field of learning.

Persecutions did not cease although the Saints had moved into the desert. Gentiles came to the territory, and many of them sent false reports to Washington stating that Brigham Young and Church members were in rebellion against the government. President Young became a bold denouncer of the false propaganda circulated against the Saints and the Church.

President James Buchanan failed to personally investigate the false reports. He replaced Brigham Young with a Gentile governor and sent troops to Utah. President Young saw the Church through the crisis of the Utah War in 1857-58. He and the government officials arrived at peaceful agreements and the "war" was bloodless—no engagements were fought. Even though Brigham Young was no longer governor, he remained the most powerful man in Utah until his death.

President Young emphasized cultural arts among the Saints. A great believer in recreation, he encouraged

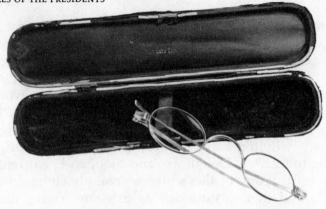

Eyeglasses belonging to Brigham Young

theater, music, picnics, dancing, and other forms of wholesome entertainment, commenting:

"Recreation and diversion are as necessary to our well-being as the more serious pursuits of life. There is not a man in the world but what, if kept at any one branch of business or study, will become like a machine. Our pursuits should be so diversified as to develop every trait of character and diversity of talent." (*Discourses of Brigham Young*, p. 238.)

In expressing his approval of music and dancing, he said: "I want it distinctly understood, that fiddling and dancing are no part of our worship. The question may be asked, What are they for, then? I answer, that my body may keep pace with my mind. My mind labors like a man logging, all the time; and this is the reason why I am fond of these pastimes—they give me a privilege to throw everything off, and shake myself, that my body may exercise and my mind rest. What for? To get strength, and be renewed and quickened, and enlivened and animated, so that my mind may not wear out. (JD 1:30-31.)

Although Brigham Young appeared to be serious-minded and firm, he also loved a good time. He was jovial and fun-loving, and his sense of humor endeared him to the Saints.

To an embittered woman who had written to him asking that her name be removed from the records of the

Church he dictated the following: "Madam . . . I have this day examined the records of baptism for the remission of sins in the Church . . . and not being able to find [your name] recorded therein, I was saved the necessity of erasing your name therefrom. You may therefore consider that your sins have not been remitted you and you can enjoy the benefits thereof." (Letter of Brigham Young to Elizabeth Green, Dec. 28, 1951.) To a woman who called upon him to complain that her husband had told her to go to hell, he replied, simply, "Sister, don't go, don't go!" (*Utah Historical Quarterly*, Summer 1977, p. 223-24.)

The characteristic that made the members honor and respect "Brother Brigham" was the love that showed in his interest for each one of them. On the plains, at a stopping place named Hickory Grove, he was out in the rain all day arranging wagons, helping with the tents, chopping wood, and doing what he could so all were comfortable. Later, in Utah, he enjoyed meeting every wagon train or handcart company he could, and he would not leave until every person had a place to stay and a job assignment by which he could be secure for the present.

Leah D. Widtsoe, granddaughter of Brigham Young, recalled a conversation with her mother, Susa Young Gates, concerning the manner of discipline her grandfather used with his large family: "[The children] said that they had memories of being disciplined by their father as they needed it, but he never did it in front of anybody else. He never gave them the humiliation of correcting or punishing them before the other children or before the family or strangers. He took them aside, then or later, and in his kind, fatherly way told them what he felt they had coming to them in the way of correction or discipline. . . . One of his practices was: 'No child should ever be punished while the parent is angry.' " (IE, June 1961, p. 449.)

Although he was the subject of scorn and ridicule because he lived in polygamy, these unkindnesses had no effect upon Brigham Young or his home. Clarissa Young Spencer, one of his children, wrote that "our home was as peaceful and serene as any home could be. . . . I believe that a finer group of women never lived together than my father's wives. They cooperated with one another to a remarkable degree, and to each one of us children the 'aunts' were almost as dear as our own mothers." (Spencer and Harmer, *Brigham Young at Home,* p. 58.)

Brigham Young was a natural leader at home, in the territory, and especially in church affairs, inaugurating changes directly affecting the operation of the Church on the local level. He released members of the Council of the Twelve from presiding over local positions. He reorganized stakes and defined the duties of the apostles, high priests, seventies, elders, and those of the lesser priesthood. He expanded the role of the bishop. He made it Church policy that all bishops were to be ordained both as high priests and as bishops and were to have two counselors who were high priests. The ward became an important structure, and the Aaronic Priesthood was given to great numbers of youth and at an earlier age.

President Young also did much to promote the welfare of Indians. He often gave them gifts, clothes, blankets, rifles, and oxen. At a meeting with several Indian chiefs, he said: "I love the Indian like a father and I want to be friends with all of them. I will give them plenty of clothing and good food if they will be friends with the white man and not fight and kill any more." (Spencer and Harmer, *Brigham Young at Home,* p. 124.)

One of the greatest tributes paid Brigham Young by an Indian was by Chief Peteetneet, brother of the famous Chief Walker, who had caused so much trouble for the settlers: "What the other white men say go in one ear and out the other, but what Brigham says goes to the heart and stays there." (Spencer and Harmer, *Brigham Young at Home,* pp. 127-128.)

The labors of Brigham Young have been recognized worldwide and many honors came to him, both before and after his death. The largest private university in the United States, Brigham Young University, is named after him. Brigham City in northern Utah also bears his name.

Brigham Young in 1844, during his residence in Nauvoo

During World War II, the United States government honored him by naming one of the liberty ships in the U.S. Navy after him. And in 1940, Twentieth Century-Fox made a movie of his life entitled *Brigham Young,* which is still shown occasionally on television. In Whitingham, Vermont, Brigham Young's hometown, President George Albert Smith dedicated a monument in President Young's honor. In June 1950 a statue of Brigham Young was dedicated in Washington, D.C., in the rotunda of the capitol. Vice-President Alben Barkley praised him, saying: "He was a true pioneer and promoted the right of free worship. He was an advocate of justice and democracy—of the kind of democracy we must preserve." (IE, Aug. 1950, p. 630.)

Even more important than the monuments that honor him is his testimony, a compelling beacon of truth:

My testimony is the positive. I know that there are such cities as London, Paris, and New York—from my own experience or from that of others; I know that the sun shines, I know that I exist and have a being, and I testify that there is a God, and that Jesus Christ lives, and that he is the Savior of the world. Have you been to heaven and learned to the contrary? I know that Joseph Smith was a Prophet of God, and that he had many revelations. Who can disprove this testimony? Any one may dispute it, but there is no one in the world who can disprove it. I have had many revelations; I have seen and heard for myself, and know these things are true, and nobody on earth can disprove them. The eye, the ear, the hand, all the senses may be deceived, but the Spirit of God cannot be deceived; and when inspired with that Spirit, the whole man is filled with knowledge, he can see with a spiritual eye, and he knows that which is beyond the power of man to controvert. What I know concerning God, concerning the earth, concerning government, I have received from the heavens, not alone through my natural ability, and I give God the glory and the praise. Men talk about what has been accomplished under my direction, and attribute it to my wisdom and ability; but it is all by the power of God, and by intelligence received from him. (JD 16:46.)

Important Dates and Events
in Lifetime of Brigham Young

Church Membership, 1844: 35,000 (est.) 1877: 155,000 (est.)
1877   Stakes: 20   Missions: 12   Temples:1
       Number of General Authorities: 26
       Missionaries Called in 1877: 211

1801	Brigham Young was born in Whitingham, Windham County, Vermont, June 1.
1815	His mother died. Brigham began to earn his own way in life, eventually becoming a carpenter.
1822	Joined the Methodist Church, September.
1824	Married Miriam Works in Aurelius, New York, October 8.
1829	Moved to Mendon, New York, where his father and most of his brothers and sisters lived.
1830	Samuel H. Smith, as a missionary, sold a copy of the Book of Mormon to Phineas Young, brother to Brigham; first Phineas and then Brigham read it.
1832	Brigham was baptized into the Church by Eleazar Miller, who ordained him an elder, April 14. He converted all his brothers and sisters, his father, and his wife. Brigham's wife, Miriam, died of tuberculosis, September. Brigham arrived at Kirtland with his brother Joseph and Heber C. Kimball; they met with the Prophet Joseph Smith.
1832-33	Served a mission with his brother to Canada and later led many converts to Kirtland.
1833	Moved his family to Kirtland.
1834	Joined the march of Zion's Camp. Traveled to Missouri and back with Zion's Camp.
1834-35	Worked on Kirtland Temple, supervising carpentry work.
1835	Was ordained an apostle by Oliver Cowdery, David Whitmer, and Martin Harris, February 14 (age 33); he was a member of original Council of the Twelve. Served a mission to Eastern States with the Twelve. Attended Hebrew School in Kirtland.
1836	Helped complete the Kirtland Temple; attended the dedica-

	tion. Served a mission to the eastern states and New England.
1837	Served a business mission to the eastern states with Willard Richards, March. Served a mission to New York and Massachusetts, June. Fled to Missouri due to persecution, December.
1838	Became senior member of the Council of the Twelve; directed the Church while Joseph Smith was in prison; led the exodus from Missouri.
1839	Moved his family to Quincy, Illinois, February; then to Montrose, Iowa, May.
1839-41	Served a mission to Great Britain.
1840	Was sustained as president of Council of the Twelve, April 14 (age 38).
1843	Served a short mission to the eastern states to collect funds for the Nauvoo House and the Nauvoo Temple.
1844	Martyrdom of the Prophet Joseph Smith, June. Brigham Young spoke to the Saints on August 8 and was transfigured before them; the Saints accepted him as their leader. Became leader of the Church as president of the Council of the Twelve (age 43). Apostolic presidency lasted 3 ½ years.
1845	Directed the Saints' preparations to leave Nauvoo.
1846	Directed the exodus of the Saints from Nauvoo, February. The Nauvoo Temple was dedicated by Orson Hyde, May 1. The Mormon Battalion was organized, July 16. The Nauvoo Temple was captured by a mob, September.
1847	Received a revelation giving instructions for the westward exodus of the Saints, January 14. The first pioneers left Winter Quarters April 5, arrived in the Salt Lake Valley July 24. Mormons began irrigation of land in Utah. President Young selected the site for the Salt Lake Temple, July 28. He returned to Winter Quarters, August, and was sustained as president of Church at general conference on the Missouri River, December 27, with Heber C. Kimball and Willard Richards as counselors (age 46).
1847-69	85,000 pioneers made trek to Utah.
1848	President Young left Winter Quarters for Salt Lake Valley with 1,229 persons, May. Seagulls saved crops from destruction by crickets, June.
1849	The Church organized the provisional State of Deseret, with Brigham Young elected as governor. Gold rush to California made Utah a national highway to gold fields, established a number of non-Mormon merchants in Salt Lake City.
1850	Was appointed governor of Utah Territory by President

Millard Fillmore. Was also chosen as president of the Perpetual Emigrating Fund Company.

1851   Visited settlements in Davis, Weber, and Utah counties. Located settlements in Parowan. Located the territorial capital at Fillmore.

1852   Took an exploring trip to southern Utah; visited Indian tribes.

1853   Laid the cornerstone for the Salt Lake Temple.

1854   Traveled to southern settlements. Signed a peace treaty with the Ute Indian chief.

1855   Ordained his son, John W. Young, an apostle.

1856   Organized relief efforts to assist handcart pioneers stranded on plains.

1857   President Buchanan removed Brigham Young from the governorship and ordered troops to Utah to suppress an alleged rebellion of Mormons, resulting in the Utah War. President Young declared martial law in Utah (age 56), and prohibited U.S. troops from entering the territory.

1857-58 The Utah War.

1858-61 The U.S. Army passed through Salt Lake City en route to Cedar Valley.

1858   President Young directed the abandonment of northern Utah communities in face of the approaching army. Moved his family to Provo, Utah.

1859   Was interviewed by Horace Greeley, editor of the New York *Tribune.*

1860s   Took part in the construction of the Union Pacific Railroad from Omaha, Nebraska, to Ogden, Utah.

1861   Visited southern Utah settlements. Instructed the Saints that he did not wish them mixed up with the secession movement. Sent the first telegram over the newly completed overland telegraph.

1862   Visited southern Utah settlements. Dedicated the Salt Lake Theater.

1863   Was arrested on charges of bigamy under the anti-bigamy law of 1862; placed under bond. Visited southern Utah settlements.

1864   Ordained his sons Joseph and Brigham, Jr., as apostles, February 4. Visited southern Utah settlements.

1864-65 Visited settlements of the Saints north and south of Salt Lake City.

1866   *Juvenile Instructor,* official organ of the Sunday School, was established.

1867   The Salt Lake Tabernacle was completed, with the first general conference held there October 6. The Deseret Telegraph Company was established from Salt Lake City to St. George, with Brigham Young as president. The School of the Prophets was organized. The union of local Sunday Schools was organized. Relief Societies were organized Churchwide.

1868   Zions Cooperative Mercantile Institution was established, with Brigham Young as president.

1869   The Utah Central Railroad was organized, with Brigham Young as president. The "Young Ladies Cooperative Retrenchment Association" (later YWMIA) was organized, November.

1870   President Young drove the last spike of the Utah Central Railroad. Visited settlements in southern Utah and Arizona.

1871   Visited settlements in northern Utah and Idaho. Was arrested on charge of unlawful cohabitation and confined to home. Was admitted to bail. Dedicated the St. George Temple site, November 9.

1872   Appeared in Third District Court. Case continued for several months. Was released from custody on writ of habeas corpus, April 25.

1873   Called five additional counselors to assist in the First Presidency. Was named president of Zion's Savings Bank and Trust. Organized the United Order in southern Utah settlements.

1874   Organized the United Order in Salt Lake City wards. Experienced ill health. Traveled to St. George, Utah.

1875   Organized Young Men's Mutual Improvement Association. Organized Brigham Young Academy (now University), Provo, Utah; Brigham Young College, Logan, Utah. Visited with President Ulysses S. Grant in Salt Lake City.

1876   Called his son John W. Young to serve as first counselor in the First Presidency.

1876-77   Set all priesthood quorums in order and commenced more complete organization of stakes.

1877   Attended general conference in St. George. Presided over the St. George Temple dedication. Dedicated a temple site at Manti, Utah. Gave his last public discourse at Brigham City, Utah, August 19. Died of infection from a ruptured appendix, Salt Lake City, August 29, at age 76.

The First Presidency and Council of the Twelve During Brigham Young's Administration

First Counselor	President	Second Counselor
Heber C. Kimball (1835)	Brigham Young (1835)	Willard Richards (1840)
1847-68	1847-77	1847-54
George A. Smith (1839)		*Jedediah M. Grant
1868-75		1854-56
*John W. Young		*Daniel H. Wells
1876-77		1857-77

Additional Counselors	Assistant Counselors (1874-77)
Joseph F. Smith (1867)	*John W. Young
1866-77	1874-76
Lorenzo Snow (1849)	Lorenzo Snow (1849)
1873-74	1874-77
Brigham Young, Jr. (1868)	George Q. Cannon (1860)
1873-74	1874-77
Albert Carrington (1870)	Brigham Young, Jr. (1868)
1873-74	1874-77
George Q. Cannon (1860)	Albert Carrington (1870)
1873-74	1874-77
*John W. Young	
1873-74	

Note: Dates in parentheses indicate date ordained member of the Council of the Twelve.
*An apostle but not a member of the Council of the Twelve.

Council of the Twelve—October 1848

Orson Hyde (1835)
Parley P. Pratt (1835)
Orson Pratt (1835)
John Taylor (1838)
Wilford Woodruff (1839)

George A. Smith (1839)
Lyman Wight (1841)
Amasa M. Lyman (1842)
Ezra T. Benson (1846)

Excommunicated

1845—William B. Smith
1846—John E. Page
1848—Lyman Wight

Died

1854—Willard Richards
1857—Parley P. Pratt
1869—Ezra T. Benson
1875—George A. Smith

1870—Amasa M. Lyman (deprived of apostleship in 1867)

Added

Charles C. Rich (1849)
Lorenzo Snow (1849)
Erastus Snow (1849)
Franklin D. Richards (1849)

George Q. Cannon (1860)
Joseph F. Smith (1867)
Brigham Young, Jr. (1868)
Albert Carrington (1870)

October 1877

John Taylor (1838)
Wilford Woodruff (1839)
Orson Hyde (1839)**
Orson Pratt (1843)**
Charles C. Rich (1849)
Lorenzo Snow (1849)

Erastus Snow (1849)
Franklin D. Richards (1849)
George Q. Cannon (1860)
Joseph F. Smith (1867)
Brigham Young, Jr. (1868)
Albert Carrington (1870)

Second Apostolic Presidency—Aug. 29, 1877, to Oct. 10, 1880

(3 years)

**In 1875 Brigham Young took him from his original position in the quorum and placed him in the order he would have been in when he was restored to fellowship. See Durham and Heath, *Succession in the Church*, pp. 73-76.

JOHN TAYLOR
Third President of the Church

Born: November 1, 1808, Milnthorpe, England
Died: July 25, 1887, probably of kidney failure, Kaysville,
    Utah (age 78)
President of the Church: October 10, 1880, to July 25, 1887
    (6 years, 9 months; age 71-78)
Ancestry: Scottish, Welsh, French
Education: English private schools, School of the Prophets,
    self-educated
Occupation: Farmer, woodturner, Methodist preacher
Missions: 1839-41: Britain; 1849-52: France, Germany;
    1853-54: Deseret; 1855-57: Eastern States
Apostle: Ordained December 19, 1838 (served 41 years;
    age 30-71)
President of the Council of the Twelve: October 6, 1877,
    to October 10, 1880
General Authority: 49 years
Church callings prior to presidency: In charge of Church
    in Canada, apostle, missionary, mission president
Selective works of teachings: *The Gospel
    Kingdom* and *The Mediation and Atonement*
Physical characteristics: Five feet eleven inches tall, 180
    pounds, gray eyes, white hair, beard
Family: Son of John and Agnes Taylor. Married: Leonora
    Cannon, Elizabeth Kaighin, Jane Ballantyne, Mary
    Ann Oakley, Sophia Whitaker, Harriet Whitaker,
    Margaret Young. Had total of 35 children.

Profile of John Taylor

June 27, 1844, was a dark time for the Church. The Prophet Joseph Smith and his brother Hyrum were in Carthage Jail, along with some of the Prophet's most valiant friends. Among them was an English convert, John Taylor, who had left his thriving Illinois farm to be at Joseph's side in the bleak prison cell. Even when offered liberty, John Taylor had loyally refused, choosing to stay by the Prophet's side.

On that hot afternoon, Joseph asked Brother Taylor to sing one of his favorite hymns, "A Poor Wayfaring Man of Grief." He obliged, but later described the song as sounding plaintive and pathetic, "very much in accordance with our feelings at the time for our spirits were all depressed, dull and gloomy and surcharged with indefinite ominous forebodings." (HC 7:101.)

Moments after the last strains of melody ended, a mob broke through the doors of Carthage Jail; a fusillade of shots killed Hyrum and Joseph, severely wounding John Taylor with four bullets.

Wilford Woodruff several years later recorded a revelation he had received in 1880 concerning this terrible incident: "I the Lord have raised up unto you my servant John Taylor to preside over you and to be a lawgiver unto my Church. He has mingled his blood with that of the martyred prophets. Nevertheless, while I have taken my servants Joseph and Hyrum Smith unto myself I have preserved my servant John Taylor for a wise purpose in me." (*Journal of Wilford Woodruff*, 1880, p. 8.)

As one examines the situation of the Church in those

early days, it is clear to see the purpose in the Lord's sparing John Taylor's life. Amid bitter persecutions, he emerged as a pillar of strength, intellect, and wisdom to provide sure footings for a struggling church.

John Taylor was born in Milnthorpe, Westmoreland, England, on November 1, 1808, one of ten children. He is the only Church president who was not a native-born American. As a young boy, he worked on his father's farm until he was apprenticed to a barrel maker at age fourteen. After one year he decided to be a woodturner, and he became a skilled workman. Years later he built one of the first sawmills in Utah and worked it himself.

His parents were members of the Church of England; John was baptized into that church as an infant. He grew up with a deep reverence for God, studying the scriptures carefully. When he heard the Methodist doctrine taught, it seemed to be more spiritual, less ritualized than the Church of England. At the age of sixteen he joined the Methodist church.

As a young man John Taylor felt he had a special destiny when he saw in a vision an angel blowing a trumpet and proclaiming some important heavenly message. Accompanying this experience was a strong impression that he should go to America to preach the gospel.

In 1832 he immigrated to Canada, where he joined a Methodist Bible-study group. There he met and married Leonora Cannon, and together they studied religion.

According to John, this study group "met together for the purpose of searching the Scriptures; and we found that certain doctrines were taught by Jesus and the Apostles, which neither the Methodists, Baptists, Presbyterians, Episcopalians, nor any of the religious sects taught; and we concluded that if the Bible was true, the doctrines of modern Christendom were not true; or if they were true, the Bible was false. . . . In addition . . . we prayed and fasted before God; and the substance of our prayers was, that if he had a people upon the earth anywhere, and ministers who were authorized to preach the Gospel, that

87

he would send us one. This was the condition we were in." (JD 23:30.) Their prayers were soon answered.

In 1836, they heard of Mormonism for the first time through a three-week series of lectures presented by Elder Parley P. Pratt. The Taylors copied eight of Elder Pratt's sermons to compare them with their own Bible. Finding that these sermons answered their questions and illuminated the scriptures, John and Leonora joined the Church along with others in their study group.

Almost immediately after his conversion, John Taylor was placed in charge of Church affairs in Canada. Joseph Smith himself ordained John Taylor a high priest during a visit to Toronto. Then one year after his conversion, upon request of the Prophet, the Taylors moved to Missouri where John was called to be an apostle in a revelation given on July 8, 1838. (D&C 118.)

From the beginning of his service to the end of his life, John Taylor received unceasing harassment and threats from both governmental and private groups. But he met each event of persecution with unusual strength and courage.

One example occurred as he was speaking at a public meeting in Columbus, Ohio. The crowd was hostile; some had come with the intent of tarring and feathering him. Though he knew of their evil intentions, he defied such threats by his bold appearance and his courageous discourse. He told his listeners that Canada, the country from which he had recently emigrated, was still under the control of a monarch. He praised the efforts of their American forefathers who gave their lives for freedom. He continued fearlessly: ". . . I have been informed that you purpose to tar and feather me, for my religious opinions. Is this the boon you have inherited from your fathers? Is this the blessing they purchased with their dearest heart's blood—this your liberty? If so, you now have a victim, and we will have an offering to the goddess of liberty."

Then the courageous young missionary threw open his vest and stated: "Gentlemen come on with your tar and feathers, your victim is ready; and ye shades of venerable

John Taylor in 1853

patriots, gaze upon the deeds of your degenerate sons! Come on, gentlemen! Come on, I say, I am ready!" (B. H. Roberts, *Life of John Taylor*, pp. 54-55.) No one stepped forward.

John Taylor was a notable missionary. When he received his first mission call to England in 1839, he thrilled to the opportunity to teach his own people: "The thought of going forth at the command of the God of Israel to revisit my native land, to unfold the principles of eternal truth and make known the things that God had revealed for the salvation of the world, overcame every other feeling." (Ibid., p. 68.)

It was hard for him to leave his family at a time when anti-Mormon sentiment ran high. He lacked money and was in poor health, but the Lord blessed and protected his family in his absence, and helped him complete a very successful mission.

Reporting to the British Saints at the end of his mission, he said: "I feel to rejoice before God that He has blessed my humble endeavors to promote His cause and Kingdom and for all the blessings I have received from this island; for although I have traveled 5,000 miles without purse or scrip, besides traveling so far in this country on railroads, coaches, steamboats, wagons, on horseback, and almost every way, and been amongst strangers and in strange lands, I have never for once been at a loss for either money, clothes, friends or a home, from that day until now." (Preston Nibley, *The Presidents of the Church*, p. 74.)

John Taylor was active in civic affairs. In Nauvoo, he served on the Nauvoo City Council, as a member of the board of regents for Nauvoo University, and as judge-advocate and colonel in the Nauvoo Legion. He was associate editor of the *Times and Seasons*, the primary newspaper of the Church; and the editor and owner of another paper, the *Nauvoo Neighbor*.

Because of his journalistic pursuits, he became known as "Defender of the Faith" and also as the "Champion of Liberty." He continually defended the position of Joseph Smith, and campaigned with editorial vigor for the Prophet's nomination as president of the United States.

When mobs began destroying Elder Taylor's newspapers by burning them at local post offices, he would carry them thirty or forty miles from Nauvoo before mailing them. Once he arranged for the papers to be carried as far as St. Louis, two hundred miles from Nauvoo, to insure their reaching their destinations safely.

Later in his life, when the Saints were in Utah, he continued his involvement in civic affairs. Between 1857 and 1877 he served as a member of the Utah territorial legislature, was elected speaker of the house for five successive sessions, and was elected probate judge of Utah County. He was active in his efforts to secure admission of the State of Deseret into the Union. His interest in education flowered when he was elected in 1877 to the office of territorial superintendent of district schools.

This watch may have saved John Taylor's life in Carthage Jail

Throughout his life, John Taylor was an energetic advocate of the truth, a cause to which he unstintingly devoted his keen intellect and writing ability. His book *Mediation and Atonement* made a vital contribution to clarifying the contemporary Mormon understanding of the nature and mission of Christ. His speeches in defiance of U.S. laws against polygamy were headlined nationally for their 'stirring defense of freedom of religion. So were his series of letters, one series of five, another of six, blasting the

*John Taylor's dignity and impressive bearing are evident
in this photograph*

government and upholding the law of God. His *Reply to
Colfax*, the report of a lengthy debate between himself and
Vice-president Schuyler Colfax of the United States, de-
fended the Saints' view on plural marriage.

He published *The Mormon* in New York, the first
Mormon paper designed for gentile readership. He actively encouraged Hubert Howe Bancroft, a nonmember

historian, and helped him obtain essential information for his fine historical work, *The History of Utah.*

Even when he was in exile at the end of his life to avoid being prosecuted for polygamy, President Taylor issued a constant stream of epistles for conferences and other occasions to keep in touch with his people. He encouraged intellectual freedom and wrote numerous articles, pamphlets, and poems on gospel topics. Several of his poems have been set to music, and at least three of them are currently found in our hymnbook: "Go Ye Messengers of Glory," "Oh Give Me Back My Prophet Dear," and "The Seer, Joseph, The Seer." He also directed the translation of the Book of Mormon into French and German.

Following the death of Brigham Young in 1877, the Council of the Twelve became the presiding quorum of the Church, with John Taylor leading the Church as quorum president until the First Presidency was formally reorganized in 1880, three years later. Again, persecution plagued the Church; hundreds of families were disrupted as husbands and fathers were sent to prison. Many wards and stakes lost their leaders. The Saints were deprived of the right to vote.

John Taylor was sustained as president of the Church on October 10, 1880, with George Q. Cannon and Joseph F. Smith as counselors. At the solemn assembly, President Taylor set the precedent of having the quorums of the priesthood separately sustain the new First Presidency as well as the president.

John Taylor had been president of the Church for only two years when the United States passed the Edmunds Law, which, among other things, made it unlawful to live with more than one wife. As the crusade against plural marriage became more bitter, he counseled some Saints to move to Mexico to avoid prosecution. Nothing more could be done, so to prevent any further trouble he went into exile for about two and a half years until his death in Kaysville, Utah, on July 25, 1887, at age seventy-eight.

Although his seven years as Church president were

made difficult by the bitterness and hostility of anti-Mormons, he rose above these trials to set an example of positive leadership and faith. In his last public address, President Taylor counseled the Saints:

It is for us to do what is right, to fear God, to observe His laws, and keep His commandments, and the Lord will manage all the rest. But no breaking of heads, no bloodshed, no rendering evil for evil. Let us try and cultivate the spirit of the Gospel, and adhere to the principles of truth. Let us honor our God, and be true to those eternal principles which God has given us to hold sacred. Keep them as sacredly as you would the apple of your eye. And while other men are seeking to trample the Constitution under foot, we will try to maintain it. (JD 26:156.)

His Christlike attitude showed forth clearly when he wrote a letter on November 1, 1886, his seventy-eighth birthday, to his wives, children, and friends:

As I am prevented from being with you on the present occasion, I desire to send to you my benediction and blessing. . . .

Some people suppose that persecutions and trials are afflictions; but sometimes, and generally, if we are doing the will of the Lord and keeping His commandments, they may be truly said to be blessings in disguise. . . .

Although for the time being, these things may be painful, yet if properly comprehended and realized, we should look at them in another view, and feel as Paul. . . .

The Prophet Joseph gave a special charge to me while living, as near as I can remember as follows: "Brother Taylor, never arise in the morning or retire at night, without dedicating yourself unto God and asking His blessings upon you through the day or night, as the case may be, and the Lord God will hear and answer your prayers; and don't let any circumstances prevent it." I had been in the habit of doing so, for years before this; but since that time I have not omitted, to my knowledge, the observance of this duty, morning or evening.

Some of you have written that you "would like to have a peep at me." I heartily reciprocate that feeling, and would like to have a "peep" at you on this occasion; but in my bodily absence my spirit and peace shall be with you. (Roberts, Life of John Taylor, pp. 391-99.)

John Taylor was a family man: a kind and noble father, a gentle and loving husband. He possessed superb self-control, which, with his sense of justice and honor, enabled him to be remarkably successful in the patriarchal order of marriage. Each of his seven wives, along with the children, shared equally in the blessings and material goods he was able to give them. He enjoyed family and social gatherings with his neighbors and friends. He was a good conversationalist and vocalist, and had an inexhaustible fund of humor.

Sensitive to the feelings of others, he once used music to soothe irritation. On one occasion while he was president of the Council of the Twelve, two old and faithful brethren went to him concerning a quarrel over some business affairs. They had agreed to accept whatever counsel Brother Taylor might give, and asked him if he would listen to their story. He said, "Brethren, before I hear your case, I would like very much to sing one of the songs of Zion for you." He then sang a hymn to the men. Seeing its effect, he told them that he wanted to sing one more. So the two brethren consented to hear a second hymn. After the second hymn, President Taylor remarked that he had heard there was luck in odd numbers, so with their consent he would sing still another hymn. Afterwards he said, "Now, brethren, I do not want to wear you out, but if you will forgive me and listen to one more hymn, I promise to stop singing and will hear your case." By the time he had finished with his fourth selection, the two brethren were melted to tears; they got up, shook hands and asked President Taylor to excuse them for having called upon him. His singing had reconciled their feelings toward each other! (IE, Sept. 1940, p. 522.)

President Taylor seldom spoke from a text, and his style was impressively deliberate. His voice was clear, strong and resonant, his gestures few but significant. The Saints remembered his commanding presence, his personal magnetism, and the vigor and power of his discourses.

Scrupulously honest, he once remarked, "I prefer a faded coat to a faded reputation," and his biographer noted: "President Taylor was a man who could not get down to grovel with the low-lived, the vicious, the ribald, nor any who indulged in the follies and vanities of mortal life." (Roberts, *Life of John Taylor*, p. 447.)

During his administration he continued the efforts begun by Brigham Young to put the priesthood in order. He asked bishoprics to hold weekly meetings, stake priesthood meetings, and regular quarterly conferences in every stake; and so that there would be no misunderstanding, he had conference dates published six months in advance. He received a revelation on October 13, 1882, that contained much valuable instruction pertaining to Church policy and purity of priesthood officers. (Ibid., pp. 349-51.)

He organized the Primary Association and completed the organization of the other auxiliaries. He opened missions in the Northwest United States, Mexico, Pakistan, Turkey, and the Indian Territory. The Manti and Logan temples and the Assembly Hall on Temple Square were built during his administration.

In 1880 he declared a jubilee year throughout all the Church because he wanted the Saints to have greater love and unity among themselves. It had been fifty years since the Church was organized. He urged members to practice the old Hebrew custom of forgiving debts. The Church forgave many of the debts owed by partakers of the Perpetual Emigration Fund, and wealthy individual members were asked by President Taylor to forgive their debtors. Many of the worthy poor were blessed by this unselfish act.

John Taylor has been described as one of the most capable men who has ever led the Church. At his funeral, Elder Lorenzo Snow, who later became president of the Church, said of him: "The Latter-day Saints feel that they have lost a friend; that we have lost a mighty counselor; that we have lost one of the greatest men that have stood upon the earth since the days of the Son of God—a man whose virtue, whose integrity, whose resolution to pursue the path of righteousness is known, and well known." (Roberts, *Life of John Taylor*, p. 443.)

Brigham H. Roberts, his biographer, called him a

A rare formal portrait of President Taylor

martyr to the principles of loyalty and integrity. He wrote:

> Today he occupies the place of a double martyr. President John Taylor has been killed by the cruelties of officials who have, in this Territory, misrepresented the Government of the United States. There is no room for doubt that if he had been permitted to enjoy the comforts of his home, the ministrations of his family, the exercise to which he had been accustomed, but of which he was deprived, he might have lived for many years yet. His blood stains the clothes of the men, who with insensate hate have offered rewards for his arrest and have hounded him to the grave. History will yet call their deeds by their right names; but One greater than the combined voices of all historians will yet pronounce their dreadful sentence. (*Life of John Taylor*, p. 414.)

President John Taylor lived, worked, and died the embodiment of his favorite motto: "The Kingdom of God or Nothing." His personal testimony acknowledged his total faith in God and his personal desire to learn the will of God and then do it wholeheartedly:

We are engaged in a great work, and laying the foundation thereof—a work that has been spoken of by all the holy prophets since the world was; namely, the dispensation of the fullness of times, wherein God will gather together all things in one, whether they be things in the earth, or things in the heavens; and for this purpose God revealed Himself, as also the Lord Jesus Christ, unto His servant the Prophet Joseph Smith, when the Father pointed to the Son and said: "This is my beloved Son, in whom I am well pleased, hear ye Him." He further restored the everlasting gospel; together with the Aaronic and Melchizedek Priesthoods; both of which are everlasting as God is; and in the interest of humanity sent forth His gospel to the nations of the earth. I am happy to say that I have been a bearer of this gospel to several nations, and have been the means of bringing many to the knowledge of the truth. . . .

I believe in God, in Jesus Christ, and in the exaltation of the human family, and consequently have acted and do act in accordance with that belief. . . .

I do not believe in a religion that cannot have all my affections, but I believe in a religion that I can live for, or die for.

I would rather trust in the living God than in any other power on earth. I learned [while on missions] that I could go to God and He always relieved me. He always supplied my wants. I always had plenty to eat, drink and wear, and could ride on steam-boats or railroads, or anywhere I thought proper: God always opened my way, and so He will that of every man who will put his trust in Him.

I would rather have God for my friend than all other influences and powers outside. (Roberts, *Life of John Taylor*, pp. 394, 422-23.)

Important Dates and Events
in Lifetime of John Taylor

Church Membership, 1877: 155,000 (est.) 1887: 192,000 (est.)
1887   Stakes: 31   Missions: 12   Temples: 3
         Number of General Authorities: 28
         Missionaries Called in 1887: 282

1808	John Taylor was born in Milnthorpe, Westmoreland County, England, November 1.
1822	Went to work as a cooper, later as a woodturner.
1824	Joined the Methodist Church (age 16).
1825	Received an impression that he would preach the gospel in America.
1827-32	Became a Methodist preacher.
1830	Family moved to Canada; John stayed in England to settle family affairs.
1832	Emigrated from England (age 24).
1833	Married Leonora Cannon.
1836	Was baptized, along with his wife, by Parley P. Pratt. Was placed in charge of the Church in Canada.
1837	Visited with Joseph Smith in Canada; was ordained a high priest. Received word from Joseph to join the Saints in Missouri.
1838	Arrived in Far West, Missouri, after spending some time working in order to secure funds for the journey. Later fled from Missouri to Illinois. Was ordained as an apostle by Brigham Young and Heber C. Kimball at Far West, December 19.
1839-41	Served a mission to England.
1841	Was appointed with Elias Higbee as a member of a committee to petition Congress for redress of wrongs in Missouri.
1842	Became judge-advocate of the Nauvoo Legion, a member of the Nauvoo city council, and regent of the University of Nauvoo.
1842-46	Acted as editor of *Times and Seasons*.

1843-45 Acted as editor of *Nauvoo Neighbor*.

1844 Was in Carthage Jail with the Prophet and Hyrum Smith and was seriously wounded, June 27 (age 36).

1846 Assisted in organizing the Mormon Battalion at Winter Quarters.

1846-47 Served a second mission to England.

1847 Led a company of Saints from Winter Quarters to Salt Lake City.

1849 Was chosen associate judge of the Supreme Court, the provisional State of Deseret.

1849-52 Served a mission to France and Germany. While in France he became acquainted with process of sugar manufacturing; under his direction machinery was purchased and shipped to Utah. Had the *Book of Mormon* published in French and German; also published the papers *Étoile du Deseret* and *Zion's Panier*.

1851 Published the book *The Government of God*.

1854 Was elected a member of the territorial legislature, but resigned to fill a mission in New York.

1855-57 Presided over the Eastern States Mission; published *The Mormon*.

1857-76 Was elected a member of the Utah territorial legislature.

1868-70 Served as a probate judge of Utah County.

1869 Participated in a nationally publicized written debate over plural marriage with Schuyler Colfax, vice-president of the U.S.

1877 Was elected territorial superintendent of district schools in Utah; became president of the Council of the Twelve, October 6 (age 69). Apostolic presidency lasted 3 years.

1878 Primary Association was organized, August 25.

1880 John Taylor was sustained as president of the Church, with George Q. Cannon and Joseph F. Smith as counselors (age 72). Precedent was set of quorums sustaining the new First Presidency. The Pearl of Great Price was formally accepted as scripture. Jubilee year (50th anniversary) of the Church. The Church struck off one-half of the indebtedness held by the Perpetual Emigration Fund Company, against accounts of individuals classed as worthy poor.

1882 President Taylor published his book *Mediation and Atonement of Our Lord and Savior Jesus Christ*. Anti-Mormon legislation was passed by Congress (Edmunds Law), making punishable the contracting of plural marriage and polygamous living; many Church members were apprehended and forced to serve terms in prison. President Taylor issued a statement at general conference in April concerning persecutions because of plural marriage; he told people to obey the law, but that they should be granted their rights as citizens. Church members 21 years of age and older were required to take an oath testifying they were not violating the law of the United States prohibiting bigamy or polygamy. Most communities practicing the United Order abandoned the project. Deseret Hospital was dedicated.

1884   President Taylor dedicated the Logan Temple, May 17. A mob attacked and killed a number of Saints in Tennessee. Rudger Clawson was the first person to be tried under the Edmunds Law; he was found guilty and fined and imprisoned. Many Church leaders went into exile because of persecution. President Taylor ordained his son, John Whittaker Taylor, as an apostle.

1885   Millard Academy was opened at Fillmore, Utah. Mormon colonies began spreading to Mexico and Canada. President Taylor made his last public appearance before withdrawing to voluntary exile in view of laws against plural marriage. Visited the Saints in Mexico.

1887   Congress passed the Edmunds-Tucker Law, dissolving the corporation of The Church of Jesus Christ of Latter-day Saints and turning its properties over to the Federal Government. Members appealed through the courts but lost, March. Escheatment proceedings were conducted by the Federal Government; the U.S. marshal took charge of real and personal property of the Church, July 30. John Taylor died of kidney failure at Kaysville, Utah, July 25, age 78.

The First Presidency and Council of the Twelve
During John Taylor's Administration

First Counselor	President	Second Counselor
George Q. Cannon	John Taylor	Joseph F. Smith
(1860)	(1838)	(1867)
1880-87	1880-87	1880-87

Council of the Twelve—October 1880

Wilford Woodruff (1839) Brigham Young, Jr. (1868)
Orson Pratt (1843) Albert Carrington (1870)
Charles C. Rich (1849) Moses Thatcher (1879)
Lorenzo Snow (1849) Francis M. Lyman (1880)
Erastus Snow (1849) John Henry Smith (1880)
Franklin D. Richards (1849)

Died

1878—Orson Hyde
1881—Orson Pratt
1883—Charles C. Rich

Added

George Teasdale (1882)
Heber J. Grant (1882)
John W. Taylor (1884)

Excommunicated

1885—Albert Carrington (baptized
again prior to death in 1889)

Note: Dates in parentheses indicate date ordained member of the Council of the Twelve.
Orson Hyde and Orson Pratt (reference to seniority in the Council of the Twelve—see Durham and Heath, *Succession in the Church,* pp. 73-76.)

July to October 1887

Wilford Woodruff (1839)   Moses Thatcher (1879)
Lorenzo Snow (1849)   Francis M. Lyman (1880)
Erastus Snow (1849)   John Henry Smith (1880)
Franklin D. Richards (1849)   George Teasdale (1882)
Brigham Young, Jr. (1868)   Heber J. Grant (1882)
                                 John W. Taylor (1884)

Third Apostolic Presidency—July 25, 1887, to April 7, 1889 (2 years)

WILFORD WOODRUFF
Fourth President of the Church

Born: March 1, 1807, Farmington, Connecticut
Died: September 2, 1898, of bladder infection, San
    Francisco, California (age 91)
President of the Church: April 7, 1889, to September 2,
    1898 (9 ½ years; age 82-91)
Ancestry: English
Education: Private schools, School of the Prophets,
    self-educated
Occupation: Miller, farmer
Missions: 1834-38: Southern States; 1837-38: Fox Islands;
    1839-41: Britain; 1844-46: Europe; 1848-50: Eastern
    States
Apostle: Ordained April 26, 1839 (served 50 years; age 32-
    82)
President of the Council of the Twelve: October 10, 1880,
    to April 7, 1889
General Authority: 59 years
Church callings prior to presidency: Missionary, apostle,
    assistant and Church historian, temple president,
    president of YMMIA, general Church recorder
Selective works of teachings: *Discourses of Wilford Woodruff*
Physical characteristics: Five feet eight inches tall, 170
    pounds, stocky build, blue eyes, beard
Family: Son of Aphek and Beulah Woodruff. Married:
    Phoebe Whittemore Carter, Mary Ann Jackson,
    Emma Smith, Sarah Brown, Sarah Delight Stocking.
    Had total of 33 children.

Profile of Wilford Woodruff

"In the passing of President Woodruff," said George Q. Cannon, who was closely associated with Wilford Woodruff for years in the Council of the Twelve and the First Presidency, "a man has gone from our midst whose character was probably as angelic as that of any person who has ever lived upon this earth." Humble-hearted, President Woodruff never deliberately injured another human being, "nor was he too proud, even in his Apostolic calling, to toil as other men toiled," President Cannon continued. "He was of a sweet disposition and possessed a character so lovely as to draw unto him friends in every walk of life. . . . He was gentle as a woman and his purity was like unto that of the angels themselves." President Cannon concluded this catalogue of virtues simply: "He was a heavenly being. It was heaven to be in his company." (Preston Nibley, *The Presidents of the Church*, pp. 134-35.)

All these virtues of Wilford Woodruff were grounded in and grew from one compelling master trait, less a characteristic than a spiritual gift: his faith. In the days of Joseph Smith he was called "Wilford the Faithful." The title was a tribute to his loyalty and self-sacrificing dedication, but even those traits came because he was literally filled with faith. He understood as few men could that "God moves in a mysterious way/His wonders to perform"; hence, the miracles that follow the believers accompanied him throughout his life. This is not to say that he rested his faith upon them: They merely confirmed what he believed with all his heart.

Wilford Woodruff was born in Farmington, Connecticut, on March 1, 1807, the son of Aphek and Beulah Woodruff. His mother died when he was only fifteen months old, but his stepmother was a concerned and loving woman. When Wilford looked back over his own life, he saw that the special providences of God had operated even during his childhood to spare his life. At the age of three he fell in a cauldron of scalding water; later he tumbled from a beam in the barn, landing on his face. Other falls broke both arms. A fall from a carriage broke a leg; he once fell fifteen feet from a tree and landed flat on his back, but escaped permanent injury. A runaway horse threw him in another incident, breaking one of his legs in two places and dislocating both ankles. Another runaway animal made the wagon in which he was riding turn over. A rabid dog bit him. An ox kicked him in the stomach. A bull gored him. But for the intervention of passersby, he would have drowned in thirty feet of water or, another time, might have frozen to death. And this was all before he was twenty years old!

His young manhood seemed no safer. Twice he fell from the top of a mill wheel, narrowly escaping being crushed. Twice he was dragged behind a runaway horse. Someone accidentally snapped the trigger of a gun aimed at his chest, but it misfired. A falling tree pinned him against a standing tree, breaking his breastbone and three ribs and badly bruising his left thigh, hip, and arm.

Looking back, he could see that he had been preserved for the great work he would do—to testify as an apostle of Jesus Christ and to lead the Church through what may have been its time of greatest outward peril and its most wrenching inner turmoil: the polygamy persecutions and the Manifesto.

Even without that foreknowledge, however, these experiences were good training in withstanding pain and privation and rising above circumstances. His boyhood also brought him the pleasures of fishing (he was perhaps the first man to fly-fish for trout in the streams of the Rocky Mountains), the value of work (he worked with his father in the Farmington grist mills), the importance of writing (he kept one of the most valuable journals in the Church), and a love of reading.

It is probably no accident that Wilford's favorite book was the Bible. During his teen years and early twenties, he

Wilford Woodruff around 1853

sought the Lord with increasing intensity. A very devout man in his neighborhood, Robert Mason, recognized the boy's love for truth, and they established such a close relationship that the old man shared with Wilford a vision he had received in 1800 revealing that he would live to see the restoration of the gospel but would not partake of its blessings in this life. "Wilford," the venerable patriarch prophesied, "I shall never partake of this fruit in the flesh, but you will and you will become a conspicuous actor in the new kingdom." (Matthias F. Cowley, *Wilford Woodruff*, p. 17.)

Wilford redoubled his efforts to search for the restored church. From the Bible he knew that it must contain apostles, and he wondered why no church had apostles in that day, little dreaming that he himself would one day be ordained to that office. In 1832, two years after his talk with Father Mason, he saw a sarcastic editorial about Mormonism. Even through the mockery, something reached twenty-five-year-old Wilford and he longed to meet these people who apparently claimed the ancient gifts of the spirit.

However, there was a living to earn. He and his brother Azmon moved to Richland, New York, in 1833. A few days after Christmas, he met some Mormon missionaries and invited them to his home.

During the opening prayer by Elder Zera Pulsipher, Wilford writes, "the spirit of the Lord rested upon me and bore witness that he was a servant of God." The same spirit "rested mightily" on Elder Pulsipher while he preached, "and he bore a strong testimony of the divine authenticity of the Book of Mormon, and of the mission of the Prophet Joseph Smith. I believed all that he said."

At the conclusion of the meeting, the missionaries invited responses—"for or against what they had heard"—from the audience. "Almost instantly," says Wilford, "I found myself on my feet. The spirit of the Lord urged me to bear testimony to the truth of the message delivered by these elders. I exhorted my neighbors and friends not to oppose these men; for they were the true servants of God. They had preached to us that night the pure gospel of Jesus Christ." What might have been a debate evolved into a testimony meeting as Wilford's brother, then several others, rose to bear similar testimony.

On December 31, 1833, only two days later, Wilford Woodruff was baptized. "The snow was about three feet deep," he wrote, "the day was cold, and that water was mixed with ice and snow, yet I did not feel the cold." (Cowley, *Wilford Woodruff*, pp. 33, 35.)

A few months later he felt a strong desire to go on a mission but felt that it would be improper for him to ask for such a blessing. So he went into the snowy woods, knelt, and pleaded with the Lord that he might be called on a mission. He was just walking out of the trees when Elias Higbee, one of the missionaries who had baptized him, approached him and said, "Brother Wilford, the spirit of the Lord tells me that you should be ordained to go and preach the gospel."

That mission, in 1834, was the beginning of a life of missionary work. A later Church president, Heber J. Grant, said of Wilford Woodruff, "I believe that no other man who ever walked the face of the earth was a greater converter of souls to the gospel of Jesus Christ." (*Gospel Standards*, p. 20.)

From the beginning of his ministry in 1834 until the

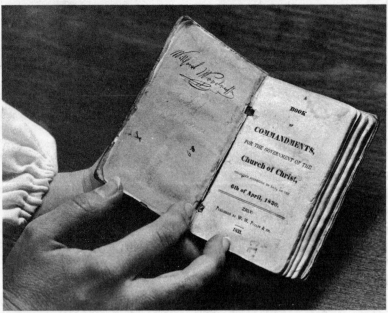

Wilford Woodruff signed this copy of the Book of Commandments

close of 1895 Wilford himself calculated that as a missionary he had traveled 172,369 miles, held 7,655 meetings, preached 3,526 discourses, organized 51 branches of the Church and 77 "preaching places" in England, Scotland, and Wales, and in 23 states and 5 territories of the United States, and had baptized 2,000 people. (Cowley, *Wilford Woodruff*, p. vi.)

He came back from one of those missions in 1837. The Church was in Kirtland by then, and there he met and married a young convert, Phoebe Carter, on April 13, 1837. Within one month he was called on another mission to the Fox Islands, off the coast of Maine. Obediently he left his bride and devoted himself to missionary work, converting several hundred people. The Church, meanwhile, moved on to Missouri, and Joseph Smith called Wilford to be an apostle. He terminated his mission, returned to Kirtland for Phoebe, and set off for Far West to be ordained. On the way, Phoebe became so ill that she seemed dead. Quickly Wilford anointed her with oil, blessed her, and commanded her spirit to reenter her body. The results were miraculous, and she was able to continue the journey three days later.

Wilford Woodruff was thirty-two when he was ordained an apostle by Brigham Young in Far West on April 26, 1839, a calling he was to fill for fifty years. On the same day he was called on another mission to England with the rest of the Twelve. This mission, his third and most famous, was a turning point in the history of the Church. Acting under inspiration, Elder Woodruff left the industrial area of Preston for a rural area south of Herefordshire, where he was led to the home of John and Jane Benbow, prosperous farmers. He soon learned that an organization known as the United Brethren had broken away from the Methodist church and had been praying for the Lord to send messengers with the gospel's fulness to them. They welcomed Wilford Woodruff as such a messenger.

From this group alone, he baptized forty-five preachers and six hundred members of the group. One of the po-

111

The Wilford Woodruff home in Salt Lake City

licemen sent to arrest him waited till the end of the sermon and asked for baptism instead. Two local officials sent by the Church of England to observe the proceedings also requested baptism. In 1840 alone he brought eighteen hundred people into the Church.

His missionary labors were interrupted by the martyrdom of Joseph and Hyrum Smith; from then on he was closely associated with building Zion in the West. He traveled with the advance company to the Salt Lake Valley; it was from his carriage that Brigham Young, suffering with fever, first saw the valley and confirmed that it was the chosen destination of the Saints.

Obedient to the Prophet's teachings, he entered the divinely revealed order of marriage and, in addition to Phoebe, married four other wives; the five women bore him seventeen sons and sixteen daughters. His family life was loving, kindly, and simple. One biographer records, "In his home he found relaxation and rest from the strenuous life he led. His children loved him." A deeply obedient person himself, he raised children who valued the same principle because he had taught them by example, while at the same time honoring their free agency by giving them every opportunity "to reason and persuade." They eagerly shared their thoughts and feelings with him, for he was "free, easy and approachable. His discipline never carried with it any severity." And he taught them to work. Their family life, "devoid of every

Four generations of the Woodruff family

show of ostentation," taught the children to be industrious, learning "their duties by doing them." (Cowley, *Wilford Woodruff*, p. 651.) He never shirked an honorable

113

task and never asked any man to do a job he was not willing to do himself.

One friend, John A. Woolf, praised him: "I never knew a harder worker than Wilford Woodruff," and added: "I have seen him feed a threshing machine with bundles from a stack, when three ordinary men complained of the task. He was never particular where he worked, usually he got in the most disagreeable place about a thresher in order to favor those with whom he worked. When he might have chosen his place, he went to the chaff-pen where the smut and dirt were almost unbearable." (Cowley, *Wilford Woodruff*, p. 644.)

He did much of his own farm work until he was well beyond the age of seventy-five; at ninety, he seemed embarrassed when a grandchild finished hoeing a garden row ahead of him. "Well," he commented, almost in surprise, "it is the first time in my life that one of my children has ever outdone me in hoeing." (Andrew Jenson, *LDS Biographical Encyclopedia* 1:26.)

Despite his accident-ridden youth, President Woodruff had good health and an industrious character. He simply "loved to work" and considered it "a blessing, a privilege, an opportunity," said Joseph M. Tanner, a close friend and educator. "To sweat, was a divine command as much so as to pray; and in his life he exemplified in the highest degree that simple Christian life that makes for the physical, mental, and moral well-being of man. He believed sincerely in the moral supremacy of manual toil. He loved it and enjoyed it." (Cowley, *Wilford Woodruff*, p. 645.)

A further blessing was his outlook. "By nature," commented Joseph Tanner, "he was an unsuspicious man and that made his life free from the jealousies, envies, and misgivings so destructive of human happiness. That nature made him an optimist. He went about life not only looking for the good, but with ability to see it." (Ibid., pp. 647-48.)

His life blessed the Church in many ways. He acted as a member of the senate of the provisional State of Deseret and served several terms in the territorial legislature. He offered dedicatory prayers for the Nauvoo Temple before the Saints were forced to abandon it. He had the great joy of dedicating the Manti Temple and the even more satisfying culmination of forty years' labor by the Saints, the Salt Lake Temple. A meticulous and intelligent farmer, he was noted for his thoughtful application of horticultural and irrigation principles, and became president of the Salt Lake City Horticulture Society. In 1856 he became assistant Church historian; in 1883 he was made Church historian. He was deeply involved in genealogy, and it was to him that the revelation came clarifying that sealings should be done within family lines, not by "adoptions" into the families of righteous men. He helped found the Utah Genealogical Society and served as president of the St. George Temple.

Deeply spiritual, he told the gathered Saints before leaving St. George in 1877 that on two successive nights, all the signers of the Declaration of Independence appeared to him requesting that the temple ordinances be performed for them. With the assistance of another brother, Wilford Woodruff was baptized for these men and "fifty other eminent men . . . including John Wesley, Columbus, and others; I then baptized him for every President of the United States, except three." (JD 19:229.)

Another equally well-known example of President Woodruff's sensitivity to the Spirit occurred in 1848 when he was traveling with his wife and children to Indiana. They camped for the night and had been in bed only a few minutes when the Spirit told him to move his carriage. Obediently, he got up, explaining what he was doing to Phoebe, who, naturally, wanted to know why. "I don't know," he replied, but moved the carriage about ninety feet away. He returned to bed and the same spirit told him to move his horses. He untied them from the oak tree where they had been tethered and put them in a hickory grove. He had been back in bed about thirty minutes when a whirlwind swept down upon them, snapped off the oak tree two feet from the ground, swept it over four fences, and deposited it on the site of Wilford's wagon. (MS 53:643.)

On another occasion, in 1850, he was assigned to collect the Saints in the East and take them west to Salt Lake Valley. At Pittsburgh he arranged for passage on a steamboat the next day, then had the distinct prompting that he should not board the steamer nor allow any member of his company to do so. Five miles downriver the steamer caught on fire, and three hundred of its passengers either died in the fire or were drowned. (MS 53:643.)

Without doubt, one of the greatest contributions of President Woodruff's intensely active life was his personal journal, a record so important that it formed the basis for much of the early Church history. In 1857, the year after he became assistant Church historian, he wrote: "Some of the most glorious gospel sermons truths and revelations that were given from God to this people through the mouth of the Prophets . . . could not be found upon the earth on record only in my journals." He felt sincerely, despite his whirlwind schedule, that "I have never spent any of my time more profitably for the benefit of mankind than in my journal writing." (*Deseret News Weekly*, Nov. 7, 1896.)

His commitment to journal keeping grew out of his faithfulness. When the Prophet Joseph organized the Council of the Twelve, he advised them to keep a record of their lives, and Elder Woodruff had been so diligent that he later commented, a little ruefully, "Many times . . . the Quorum of the Twelve and others considered me rather enthusiastic upon this subject." But he acknowledged, with profound respect, "I have had this spirit and calling upon me since I first entered this Church." Even before the charge from Joseph Smith, he had begun his journal, recording the "first sermon I heard" and making daily entries since then. His record is especially valuable in shedding light on the teachings of the Prophet, for "whenever I heard Joseph Smith preach, teach, or prophesy, I always felt it my duty to write it; I felt uneasy and could not eat, drink, or sleep until I did write; and my mind has been so exercised upon this subject that when I heard Joseph Smith teach and had no pencil or paper, I would go home and sit down and write the whole sermon, almost word for word and sentence by sentence as it was delivered, and when I had written it it was taken from me, I remembered it no more." He concludes with simple power, "This was the gift of God to me." (Cowley, *Wilford Woodruff*, pp. 476-77.)

He would need all of his faith and faithfulness during the time of crisis approaching over the issue of polygamy. Increasingly stiff antipolygamy laws—and unrelenting enforcement of those laws—were already taking their toll in the 1870s before Brigham Young's death. The situation grew worse during John Taylor's administration. Soon nearly all of the leaders of the Church were either in prison or in hiding.

President Woodruff, officially in hiding himself since the early days of 1879, risked his freedom by appearing in public for short periods of time to reassure the people and to transact official Church business. During his enforced absences from Salt Lake City, he did much missionary work in the southwest part of Utah, but by January of 1885 he was living constantly on the underground. In November Phoebe died and President Woodruff, back in Salt Lake for the funeral, had to watch the procession pass below the windows of the Church Historian's Office—the same spot where he was to stand two years later to watch the funeral procession of President John Taylor.

On July 25, 1887, Wilford Woodruff, then president of the Council of the Twelve, became head of the Church. By then federal laws had not only made plural marriage illegal, but also prohibited those who practiced it from voting or holding public office. The Church was disincorporated, tithing funds had been seized, and Church properties were in receivership.

On April 7, 1889, at the age of eighty-two, Wilford Woodruff was sustained as president of the Church. On September 24, 1890, he issued the Manifesto announcing

President Woodruff's courage and determination are evident in this photograph

that the practice of plural marriage was now suspended. About two weeks later, on October 6, 1890, he told the general conference: "I want to say to all Israel that the step which I have taken in issuing this Manifesto has not been done without earnest prayer before the Lord." Movingly, he continued, "I am about to go into the spirit world, like other men of my age. I expect to meet the . . . Father of my spirit; I expect to meet . . . Joseph Smith, Brigham Young, and John Taylor . . . and for me to have taken a stand in anything which is not pleasing in the sight of God, or before the heavens, I would rather have gone out and been shot." To that deeply reassuring message, so badly needed by the Saints, he added this prophetic principle: "I say to

Israel, the Lord will never permit me nor any other man who stands as the President of this Church, to lead you astray. . . . If I were to attempt that, the Lord would remove me out of my place." (Cowley, *Wilford Woodruff*, pp. 570-72.)

Despite the heartaches of many Latter-day Saints in relinquishing a divine principle that they had defended so staunchly, they sustained President Woodruff in his actions. Four years later, President Grover Cleveland restored all political and civil rights to those who had been disfranchised by antipolygamy legislation. Two years after that, in 1896, Utah's repeated attempts at statehood were successful and she was admitted to the Union, a source of personal joy to President Woodruff.

In another two years, on September 2, 1898, President Woodruff himself died of a bladder infection in San Francisco, where he had gone to rest from a recurring condition of insomnia that was alleviated at sea level.

It is perhaps fitting that this intensely spiritual man presided over the Church at the moment of its greatest political challenge. The joy with which Utah became a state was matched by the joy with which the Salt Lake Temple was dedicated on April 6, 1893. And by shifting fast day from Thursday, where it had been since pioneer times, to Sunday, President Woodruff emphasized its spiritual nature, a very real step toward heightening awareness of spiritual things in the Church.

From President Woodruff also came one of the most powerful appeals for personal righteousness and spirituality that members have ever heard. Speaking at Weber Stake conference in 1896, he related a dream in which he, Brigham Young, and Heber C. Kimball were driving together to a conference. When they arrived, President Woodruff asked President Young if he would preach to the congregation, and he heard Brother Brigham answer, "No, I have finished my testimony in the flesh[.] I shall not talk to this people any more. But [said he] I have come to see you; I have come to watch over you, and to see what the people are doing. Then [said he] I want you to teach the people—and I want you to follow this counsel your-self—that they must labor and so live as to obtain the Holy Spirit, for without this you cannot build up the kingdom . . . And, said he, Brother Joseph taught me this principle.' " (JD 21:318.)

Continuing that line of prophetic counsel, President Woodruff reiterated, "Every man and woman in this Church should labor to get that Spirit." He shared several experiences from his missionary journeys of being led by the Spirit, and concluded his remarks by insisting again, in tones that ring true to us today: "I want you to get the same Spirit. All the Elders of Israel, whether abroad or at home, need that Spirit. . . . This is the Spirit that we must have to carry out the purposes of God on the earth. We need that more than any other gift. . . . We are in the midst of enemies, in the midst of darkness and tempta-tion, and we need to be guided by the Spirit of God. We should pray to the Lord until we get the Comforter." Then he added, possibly with the deeply humble knowledge of personal experience, "This is what is promised to us when we are baptized. It is the spirit of light, of truth, and of revelation." (*Deseret Weekly*, Nov. 7, 1896, p. 643.)

The year before he died, Wilford Woodruff bore this powerful testimony, which was recorded on tape for posterity:

I bear my testimony that Joseph Smith was a true prophet of God, ordained of God to lay the foundation of his church and kingdom in the last dispensation and fulness of times. I bear my testimony that in the early spring of 1844 in Nauvoo, the Prophet Joseph Smith called the Twelve Apostles together, and he delivered unto them the ordi-nances of the Church and kingdom of God; and all of the keys and powers that God had bestowed upon him, he sealed upon our heads. He told us we must round up our shoulders and bear off this kingdom or we would be damned. I am the only man now living in the flesh who heard that testimony from his mouth, and I know it is true by the power of God manifest through him. At that meeting he began to speak about three hours upon the subject of the kingdom. His face was as clear as amber, and he was covered with a power that I had never seen in the flesh before. In all his testimony to us, the power of God was visibly manifest in the Prophet Joseph Smith.

This is my testimony, spoken by myself into a talking machine on this the nineteenth day of March, 1897, in the ninety-first year of my age. (Transcribed in *New Era*, Jan. 1972, p. 66.)

Important Dates and Events
in Lifetime of Wilford Woodruff

Church Membership 1887: 192,000 (est.)   1898: 228,032
1898   Stakes: 40   Missions: 20   Temples: 4
        Number of General Authorities: 26
        Missionaries Called in 1898: 843

1807   Wilford Woodruff was born in Farmington, Hartford County, Connecticut, March 1.

1821   Began work, learning trade of miller.

1830   Was informed by Robert Mason of the restoration of the gospel.

1832   Read of Mormonism in a newspaper article.

1833   Was baptized in icy waters by Zera Pulsipher, December 31.

1834   Arrived in Kirtland; met Joseph Smith and made his home with him. Participated in the march of Zion's Camp (age 26).

1834-36 Served a mission to the Southern States.

1837   Married Phoebe Whittemore Carter. Received a patriarchal blessing from Joseph Smith, Sr., April 15.

1837-38 Served a mission to the Eastern States and Fox Islands.

1839   Was ordained an apostle by Brigham Young at Far West, Missouri, April 26 (age 32).

1839-41 Served a mission to Great Britain.

1840   Arrived in Ledbury, Herefordshire, on March 4, and baptized about 600 persons in the next 38 days.

1841   Secured the copyright to the Book of Mormon (with Heber C. Kimball) at Stationer's Hall, London, in the name of Joseph Smith, Jr., February 8. Was appointed a member of the Nauvoo City Council, October 5. Viewed the Urim and Thummim at Joseph Smith's home in Nauvoo, December 26.

1842   Became business manager of *Times and Seasons*, January. Hauled stone for the Nauvoo Temple, January.

1843   Served a mission to the Eastern States to solicit money for building the Nauvoo Temple.

1844   Served a mission to the Eastern States.

1844-46   Presided over the European Mission.

1846   Aided in the Saints' exodus westward.

1847   Entered Salt Lake Valley with Brigham Young.

1848-50   Presided over the Church in the Eastern States.

1850   Left New York with a company for the West, April 9.

1851   Was appointed to the territorial legislature; served one term in the lower house and twenty sessions in the upper house.

1856   Was appointed assistant Church historian.

1858-77   Served as president of Deseret Agricultural and Manufacturing Society (which position later became president of Utah State Fair Board).

1867   Participated in the reestablishment of the School of the Prophets in Salt Lake City.

1871   Pioneered in Rich County, Utah.

1877   Was appointed president of the St. George Temple, January 1. Was baptized for the signers of the Declaration of Independence, St. George Temple, August 21.

1879   Did missionary work among the Indians while in hiding because of plural marriage persecutions.

1880   Received a revelation concerning the duties of the apostles and elders of Israel, which was submitted to the Twelve on April 4 and accepted by that body as the word of God. Was sustained as president of the Council of the Twelve, October 6. Wrote a prefatory prayer confirming his revelation of January 26, 1880, which had received the approval of President John Taylor. Was sustained as superintendent of the YMMIA.

1881   Became president of the YMMIA.

1883   Was sustained as Church historian and general Church recorder.

1884   Attended the dedication of the Logan Temple.

1885-87   Went into self-imposed exile (Edmunds Act) with headquarters in St. George.

1887   Became leader of the Church as president of the Council of the Twelve (age 80). Apostolic presidency lasted two years.

1888   Dedicated the Manti Temple in private services, May 17. The Church Board of Education was organized to establish and direct work of Church schools.

1889   Wilford Woodruff was sustained as president of the Church, April 7 (age 82), with George Q. Cannon and Joseph F. Smith as counselors in the First Presidency.

1890   The Manifesto was issued, discontinuing the practice of plural marriage, September 24.

1893   President Woodruff dedicated the Salt Lake Temple, April 6 (age 86). U. S. President Benjamin Harrison issued amnesty to all polygamists who had entered into that relationship before November 1, 1890.

1894   The Genealogical Society was established, November 13. President Grover Cleveland, by proclamation, restored all political and civil rights to those who had been disfranchised by antipolygamy legislation.

1896   Fast day was changed from Thursday to the first Sunday of the month, December 6. Congress passed a resolution restoring the escheated property of the Church. Utah became a state.

1897   President Woodruff dedicated the Brigham Young Monument. Ordained his son, Abraham Owen Woodruff, an apostle.

1898   Delivered his last public address at a July 24 celebration at Pioneer square. Departed for the Pacific Coast, hoping to benefit his health, in July. Died of bladder infection in San Francisco, September 2 (age 91).

The First Presidency and Council of the Twelve During Wilford Woodruff's Administration

First Counselor	President	Second Counselor
George Q. Cannon	Wilford Woodruff	Joseph F. Smith
(1860)	(1839)	(1867)
1889-98	1889-98	1889-98

Council of the Twelve—April to October 1889

Lorenzo Snow (1849)
Franklin D. Richards (1849)
Brigham Young, Jr. (1868)
Moses Thatcher (1879)
Francis M. Lyman (1880)
John Henry Smith (1880)

George Teasdale (1882)
Heber J. Grant (1882)
John W. Taylor (1884)
Marriner W. Merrill (1889)
Anthon H. Lund (1889)
Abraham H. Cannon (1889)

Died

1888—Erastus Snow
1896—Abraham H. Cannon

Added

Matthias F. Cowley (1897)
Abraham O. Woodruff (1897)

Dropped from the Council

1896—Moses Thatcher

September 1898

Lorenzo Snow (1849)
Franklin D. Richards (1849)
Brigham Young, Jr. (1868)

Heber J. Grant (1882)
John W. Taylor (1884)
Marriner W. Merrill (1889)

Note: Dates in parentheses indicate date ordained member of the Council of the Twelve.

Francis M. Lyman (1880)   Anthon H. Lund (1889)
John Henry Smith (1880)   Matthias F. Cowley (1897)
George Teasdale (1882)   Abraham O. Woodruff (1897)

Fourth Apostolic Presidency—Sept. 2 to Sept. 13, 1898 (11 days)

128

LORENZO SNOW
Fifth President of the Church

Born: April 3, 1814, Mantua, Ohio
Died: October 10, 1901, of bronchitis, Salt Lake City, Utah
(age 87)
President of the Church: September 13, 1898, to October
10, 1901 (3 years; age 84-87)
Ancestry: English
Education: Private schools, Oberlin College, School of the
Prophets, self-educated
Occupation: Educator
Missions: 1837: Ohio; 1838-39: Southern States; 1840-43:
Britain; 1849-52: Europe; 1864: Hawaii; 1872-73: Holy
Land; 1885: Lamanites
Apostle: Ordained February 12, 1849 (served 49 ½ years;
age 34-84)
President of the Council of the Twelve: April 7, 1889, to
September 13, 1898
General Authority: 52 years
Church callings prior to presidency: Missionary, apostle,
counselor and assistant to the First Presidency,
temple president
Selective works of teachings: *Biography and Family Records of
Lorenzo Snow*
Physical characteristics: Five feet six inches tall, 125-130
pounds, slender build, gray eyes, full beard, white
hair
Family: Son of Oliver and Rosetta Pettibone Snow.
Married: Charlotte Squires, Mary Adaline Goddard,
Sarah Ann Prichard, Eleanor Houtz, Harriet Amelia
Squires, Caroline Horton, Mary Elizabeth Houtz,
Phoebe Amelia Woodruff, Sarah Minnie Jensen. Had
total of 40 children.

Profile of Lorenzo Snow

In the early fall of 1898 Lorenzo Snow, senior apostle and president of the Salt Lake Temple, was going about his duties when word came of President Wilford Woodruff's impending death.

The eighty-five-year-old President Snow immediately dressed himself in temple clothes and knelt at an altar to pour out his heart to the Lord. He pleaded that President Woodruff might not die before him, for he felt unable to bear the responsibilities of president at his advanced age.

A short time after, word came of President Woodruff's death. President Snow again prayed fervently, this time with these words: "I have not sought this responsibility, but if it be Thy will, I now present myself before Thee for thy guidance and instruction." (Thomas C. Romney, *The Life of Lorenzo Snow*, p. 421.)

The Lord did show President Snow what to do as president of the Church, and then gave him physical and spiritual strength to do it. President Snow told his fellow General Authorities: "I do not want this administration to be known as Lorenzo Snow's administration, but as God's, in and through Lorenzo Snow."

For the next three years the Lord used Lorenzo Snow to accomplish great works. One of the most important was his reemphasis on the law of tithing, which helped save the Church from financial ruin and laid the foundation for its present strength and growth.

Although the smallest president in stature, at five feet six inches tall, Lorenzo Snow was mighty in faith and ability. He literally fulfilled his patriarchal blessing, which said, "There shall not be a mightier man on earth than thou."

Lorenzo Snow was born in Mantua, Ohio, on April 3, 1814, to Oliver and Rosetta Pettibone Snow, the oldest son in a large family that read the Bible daily and learned respect and tolerance for the religious beliefs of others. As a young boy, Lorenzo loved books. When his farm chores were completed he would take a book and go off to read undisturbed. He read widely and became acquainted with history, geography, and literature.

From his boyhood he also had ambitions and talents toward a military career; however, his sister Eliza encouraged him to enroll instead at Oberlin College to pursue a formal education. At Oberlin he became disillusioned with organized religion and did not change his mind until early in 1836, when he visited his sister in Kirtland and met Joseph Smith.

Lorenzo was baptized on June 23, 1836, at age twenty-two, the youngest convert who later became president, excluding Joseph Smith. Two weeks later, he still yearned for a "fullness of the Spirit" that he had not yet felt, so he retreated to a field and sought the Lord in prayer. He recorded:

I had no sooner opened my lips in an effort to pray, than I heard a sound, just above my head, like the rustling of silken robes, and immediately the Spirit of God descended upon me, completely enveloping my whole person, filling me, from the crown of my head to the soles of my feet, and O, the joy and happiness I felt! No language can describe the almost instantaneous transition from a dense cloud of mental and spiritual darkness into a refulgence of light and knowledge, as it was at that time imparted to my understanding. I then received a perfect knowledge that God lives, that Jesus Christ is the Son of God, and of the restoration of the holy Priesthood, and the fulness of the Gospel. It was a complete baptism—a tangible immersion in the heavenly principle or element, the Holy Ghost. (Eliza R. Snow Smith, *Biography and Family Record of Lorenzo Snow*, p. 8.)

This experience provided the foundation for Lorenzo's lifetime devotion to the Lord. He had always had a desire to serve mankind, but this experience gave him the direction he had prayed for. Within a few months he left on his

Lorenzo Snow in 1853

first mission, his tremendous determination, courage, and faith standing him in good stead. His first missions were "walking missions" without food or money. During one of these he was forced to walk hundreds of miles with little food or shelter. By the time he reached Kirtland, even his friends did not recognize him because he was so thin and sick.

He was ordained an apostle on February 12, 1849, by Heber C. Kimball. The call came as a great surprise to him. He was informed that this appointment had come as a result of his faithfulness and devotion, and that he would now be called upon to assume greater responsibilities in the Church.

Over the years Lorenzo served seven missions. His missionary zeal proved a great asset to the Church as he was called to open the Italian Mission, and also to help solve problems in Hawaii, where an apostate was misleading the Saints. His missions were always filled with experiences of faith and miracles that opened the way for his preaching and softened the hearts of nonmembers. In Italy he restored a dying boy to health, an experience that led to several baptisms. In Hawaii he was involved in a miraculous healing himself. A small boat carrying the missionaries from the ship to the mainland overturned, and when Elder Snow's body was found, he was stiff and lifeless. But he was miraculously restored to life and health after his companions administered to him.

Between these numerous missions, he moved his family to Salt Lake City, but no sooner had he settled in than another mission call came—this time to Brigham City to strengthen the economic situation of the Saints. His

"O My Father" was written by Lorenzo Snow's sister Eliza R. Snow on this small lap desk

outstanding talents in leadership and industry resulted in his organizing cooperative businesses, a forerunner of the United Order. He and his family spent forty years in Brigham City and strengthened that community in many ways.

Few men have been more highly endowed with a spiritual nature than was Lorenzo Snow. In March 1891 while he was speaking in the Brigham City Tabernacle, he was handed a note stating that a young girl, Ella Jensen, had just died, and asking that he arrange the funeral program. He left immediately, taking with him the stake president, Roger Clawson; they arrived at the Jensen home more than two hours after the girl's death. Her father, Jacob, remembered what happened:

> After standing at Ella's bedside for a minute or two, President Snow asked if we had any consecrated oil in the house. I was greatly surprised, but told him yes and got it for him. . . . During the administration . . . he said: "Dear Ella, I command you, in the name of the Lord Jesus Christ, to come back and live, your mission is not ended." . . . After President Snow had finished the blessing, he turned to my wife and me and said; "Now do not mourn or grieve any more. It will be all right. Brother Clawson and I are busy and must go . . . but you just be patient and wait, and do not mourn." An hour went by and friends, hearing the news of Ella's death, came to offer condolences. . . . We were sitting there watching by her bedside, . . . when all at once she opened her eyes. She looked about the room, saw us sitting there, but she looked for someone else, and the first thing she said was: "Where is he? Where is he?" We asked, "Who? Where is who?" "Why, Brother Snow," she replied. "He called me back." (IE, Sept. 1929, pp. 881-86.)

Ella then gave a thrilling account of her experience in the three hours after her death. She lived to become the mother of eight children.

In slightly more than two years following the restoration to life of Ella Jensen, the power of the Lord was again made manifest through Lorenzo Snow in the healing of Andrew May, whose body had been pierced with a hay fork. The doctor examined him and said: "There is no use doing anything for a dead man; all he needs is a wooden

Lorenzo Snow as an apostle

overcoat [a coffin]. . . . I cannot do anything for him."
(Romney, *The Life of Lorenzo Snow,* p. 395.) Andrew was
administered to and was still alive the next morning when
Elder Snow called. The apostle gave him a blessing and
told him he would not die, but he would live as long as life
was desirable to him, and if he would be faithful to the
gospel he would hold responsible positions in the Church
and would fill a mission. This promise came true, for
Andrew May filled a mission to the Eastern States. He
later served as a bishop for seventeen years.

Lorenzo Snow was a natural leader. Wherever he went
men and women rallied about him, confident in his
counsel. He served as captain of the Nauvoo Legion under

Brigham Young. And later, when he was imprisoned for polygamy, he organized a school for the men in prison and served as their teacher. He believed time was valuable, and he couldn't bear to see it wasted. He served as general president of both the YMMIA and the Deseret Sunday School Union.

President Snow served as a counselor to Brigham Young, and then as president of the Council of the Twelve for nine years before becoming president of the Church on September 13, 1898, at age eighty-four. During his administration he struggled to free the Church from financial difficulties. He declared: "Before I die I hope to see the Church cleared of debt and in a commanding position financially." (IE, June 1919, p. 651.) Because of the depression of the 1890s and problems caused by anti-polygamy legislation, the Church was in financial difficulty and tithing revenues had declined. In answer to his pleas for guidance, he was called by revelation to go to St. George, for southern Utah had been suffering from drought for the last eighteen months. There he conducted a conference with the Saints on May 17, 1899, and as he was speaking, the Lord revealed to him the purpose of his visit. He told the Saints:

"The Lord requires me to say something to you. . . . The time has now come for every Latter-day Saint, who calculates to be prepared for the future and to hold his feet strong upon a proper foundation, to do the will of the Lord and pay his tithing in full. That is the word of the Lord to you, and it will be the word of the Lord to every settlement throughout the land of Zion. . . . The time has come when every man should stand up and pay his tithing in full." (James R. Clark, *Messages of the First Presidency* 3:312.)

The faithful Saints of St. George paid their tithing, the drought was broken, and a tithing reform began throughout the entire Church, greatly improving the Church's financial standing.

Although President Snow soberly faced the great

burdens placed upon him, he always radiated the inner peace that came with his faith and dependence on the Lord. And his sense of humor delighted the Saints. On the way to the conference in St. George, he and his party set off by carriage to preach at as many settlements as possible. President Snow's buggy led the procession, with Joseph F. Smith's carriage second in line. As they rode along, President Smith drove up even with President Snow and said, "Perhaps it would be as well to go a trifle faster over these good roads, President Snow." "Very well," was the answer, "just follow us." Thomas Romney, his biographer, recorded:

President Snow gave his teamster a knowing nudge and in another minute both teams were on a forty-mile gait, over sage brush and ditches, and those behind saw only a cloud of dust, with now and then a glimpse of something resembling a buggy top. On and on the horses dashed, and the excitement of the occupants increased with every leap. It was invigorating. The horses had traveled neck and neck for two miles or more. The eyes of the aged leader flashed like diamonds as he rose in his seat and watched the progress of the race. "Go on, go on!" he shouted, "never mind the ruts. We'll get beat. Go!" and the driver did so. President Smith's team was slightly outclassed, and the other managed to maintain the lead. Clumps of sage brush and five-foot washouts were as pebbles to these venerable leaders, now thoroughly enshrouded in their boyhood days. Up in the air and down, touching only the high places here and there, the contest lasted for fifteen miles, and President Snow loves to relate how his team came out victorious, though the honors are disputed by President Smith. (*The Life of Lorenzo Snow*, pp. 428-29.)

During President Snow's administration, he continued the emphasis on missionary work and spoke of sending the gospel to all nations. He sent missionaries to Japan and opened a mission in Mexico. He stressed that Zion should be built in foreign lands, and discouraged Saints from immigrating to Utah. As part of this new missionary effort, he assigned the Council of the Twelve to travel throughout the world testifying of Christ.

Although President Snow was a skilled businessman, promoter, and manager of various enterprises, he devoted most of his efforts to serving both the Church and the

Lorenzo Snow was a scholar and deep thinker

community. He served for thirty years in the territorial legislature and for ten years was president of the upper house.

A great champion of education, he was the first of the Church presidents to have some college education, and he served as a member of the General Church Board of Education. Snow College, located in Ephraim, Utah, was named in his honor. As a teacher, it was reported, "he gained a high reputation in managing wild country boys and bringing them up to a high degree of excellence in their studies." (MS 63:676.)

Many non-Mormons recognized President Snow's greatness. So distinguished did this good man become and so impressive was his character and personality that a lec-

Lorenzo Snow served for over fifty years as a General Authority

turer and writer, the Reverend Prentis from South Carolina, said of him:

I had expected to find intellect, intellectuality, benevolence, dignity, composure and strength depicted upon the face of the President of the Church of Jesus Christ of Latter-day Saints; but when I was introduced to Pres. Lorenzo Snow for a second I was startled to see the holiest face but one I had ever been privileged to look upon. His face was a poem of peace, his presence a benediction of peace. In the tranquil depths of his eyes were the "home of silent prayer" and the abode of spiritual strength. As he talked of the more sure word of prophecy and the certainty of the hope which was his, and the abiding faith which had conquered the trials and difficulties of a tragic life . . . I watched the play of emotions and studied with fascinated attention, the subtle shades of expression which spoke so plainly the workings of his soul. (Romney, *The Life of Lorenzo Snow*, pp. 2-3.)

One of President Snow's greatest contributions to the Church and to the world in general was his understanding of man's divine potential. His lifelong precept was: "The destiny of man is to be like his Father—a God in eternity." Early in his ministry he received a direct, personal revelation that God himself was once as we are now and is an exalted man, that he sits enthroned in heaven, and that men have to learn how to be gods. Later, in a conversation with the Prophet Joseph Smith, Elder Snow related his revelation and was pleased to have the Prophet say, "Brother Snow, that is true gospel doctrine, and it is a revelation from God to you." President Snow summarized the concept in one of the best-known couplets in the Church: "As man is God once was; / As God is, man may be." (Romney, *The Life of Lorenzo Snow*, pp. 34-35.)

In 1898, just prior to becoming president of the Church, Lorenzo Snow had a glorious manifestation, which he related to his granddaughter, Allie Young Pond, of seeing the Savior in the Salt Lake Temple. He showed her the place where it had happened and said:

"It was right here that the Lord Jesus Christ appeared to me at the time of the death of President Woodruff. He instructed me to . . . reorganize the First Presidency of the Church at once and not wait as had been done after the death of the previous presidents, and that I was to succeed President Woodruff. . . . He stood right here, about three feet above the floor. It looked as though He stood on a plate of solid gold." She recalled: "Grandpa told me what a glorious personage the Savior is and described His hands, feet, countenance, and beautiful, white robes, all of which were of such a glory of whiteness and brightness that he could hardly gaze upon Him. Then Grandpa came another step nearer me and put his right hand on my head and said: 'Now, granddaughter, I want you to remember that this is the testimony of your grandfather, that he told you with his own lips that he actually saw the Savior here in the Temple and talked with Him face to face." (Leroi C. Snow, Church News, April 2, 1938, p. 6.)

Three years after this experience, on October 10, 1901, Lorenzo Snow died of bronchitis in Salt Lake City. He was eighty-seven years old. He had been a soldier, politician, educator, businessman, missionary, temple worker, apostle, and prophet—truly "a mighty man on earth."

A formal portrait of Lorenzo Snow

Lorenzo Snow's testimony of the divine calling of the Prophet Joseph Smith and of the great importance of priesthood power in our lives has lost none of its impact in the years that have since elapsed. Speaking to a congregation of the Saints at general conference in 1880, when he was an apostle, he said:

I will close . . . by bearing my testimony to the knowledge of God that I have received in relation to this work. It is true. I received a knowledge of the truth of this work by a physical administration of the blessings of God. And when receiving the baptism of the Holy Ghost I knew I was immersed in a divine principle that filled my whole system with inexpressible joy; and from that day to the present has blessing crowned my labors. And when baptizing people and administering the ordinances of this holy priesthood, God has confirmed those administrations by imparting the Holy Ghost, giving a knowledge to the individuals to whom I administered, convincing them that the authority was delegated from heaven. And every Elder

141

who has gone forth to preach this everlasting Gospel, and acted in the spirit of his calling, can bear the same testimony, that through their administrations in these holy ordinances the glory and power of God has been made manifest in a convincing manner upon the heads of those to whom they have administered.

This is our testimony; this was the testimony fifty years ago of a certain individual who stood forth and claimed that God had authorized him to baptize people for the remission of sins, and lay hands upon them for the reception of the Holy Ghost, which should impart unto them a knowledge from the eternal worlds that he had this authority. This person was Joseph Smith; and he conferred this authority, which was given unto him by holy angels, upon others who were sent forth to bear testimony to the world that those who would receive those holy ordinances, should receive the testimony from the Almighty that they were thus authorized to so administer. And this is our testimony; and this is my testimony before this people and before the world.

And may God bless us; may he pour out his Spirit upon the Latter-day Saints. And may we be faithful in all of our labors, having the motto indelibly stamped upon our hearts, "The Kingdom of God or nothing." (CR, April 8, 1880, pp. 81-82.)

Important Dates and Events
in Lifetime of Lorenzo Snow

Church Membership, 1898: 228,032   1901: 278,645
1901   Stakes: 50   Missions: 21   Temples: 4
        Number of General Authorities: 26
        Missionaries Called in 1900: 1500

1814   Lorenzo Snow was born in Mantua, Ohio, April 3.
1831   Lorenzo's mother and sister Leonora joined the Church. Lorenzo heard the Prophet Joseph Smith speak at Hiram, Ohio.
1835   Lorenzo's military career ended and he was awarded a lieutenant's commission; entered Oberlin College. Eliza R. Snow, Lorenzo's sister, joined the Church.
1836   Lorenzo was baptized on June 23 by John Boynton of the Council of the Twelve. Attended the School of the Prophets in Kirtland (age 22).
1837   Served a mission in Ohio.
1838-39 Moved to Far West; served a mission to southern Missouri, Illinois, Kentucky, and Ohio.
1840-43 Served a mission to Great Britain.
1843   Taught school at Lima, Illinois. Led a company of 250 Saints to Nauvoo.
1844   Learned of the martyrdom of Joseph Smith while on an electioneering mission for the Prophet in Ohio.
1845-46 Became superintendent of Nauvoo grammar schools.
1846-48 Crossed the plains. Presided over Mt. Pisgah, grain settlement in Ohio. Became very ill and almost died.
1848   Arrived in Salt Lake Valley.
1849   Was ordained an apostle on February 12 by Heber C. Kimball (age 34). Helped organize the Perpetual Emigration Fund.
1849-52 Served a mission to Europe (Italy, England, Switzerland, Malta).
1850   Organized the Church in Italy; sent elders to Malta and to Bombay, India.

143

1852	Organized the Polysophical Society, an organization for mutual development in many fields of thought.
1853	Was called to preside over the colonization of Brigham City.
1854	Participated in the organization of the Philosophical Society, later called Universal Scientific Society.
1864	Served a short-term mission to Hawaii. Was saved from drowning in Hawaii.
1864-66	Labored among the Saints, especially in Brigham City.
1865	Organized the Brigham City Cooperative Association.
1872-73	Became president of the Utah Territorial Legislative Council. Toured Europe and Asia Minor and participated in the dedication of Palestine for the gathering of the Jews.
1873	Was sustained as counselor to President Brigham Young.
1874	Was sustained as assistant counselor.
1885	Served a short-term mission to Indian Israel in the northwestern United States.
1886-87	Served an eleven-month prison term on a plural marriage charge.
1888	Dedicated the Manti Temple.
1889	Became president of the Council of the Twelve (age 75).
1893	Became president of the Salt Lake Temple (age 79).
1897	*Improvement Era* began publication, sponsored by the YMMIA.
1898	Lorenzo Snow saw the Savior in the Salt Lake Temple. He was sustained as president of the Church on September 13 (age 84), with George Q. Cannon and Joseph F. Smith as counselors. Church bonds were issued because of financial difficulties ensuing from disincorporation of the Church.
1899	Was called by revelation to St. George, Utah, where he told the Saints to obey the law of tithing, May 17. At a solemn assembly in the Salt Lake Temple, held on July 2, a resolution was adopted by 623 leaders who pledged to observe the law of tithing and to teach the Saints to do the same.
1901	Lorenzo Snow died of bronchitis in Salt Lake City, October 10 (age 87).

The First Presidency and Council of the Twelve During Lorenzo Snow's Administration

First Counselor	President	Second Counselor
George Q. Cannon (1860) 1898-1901	Lorenzo Snow (1849) 1898-1901	Joseph F. Smith (1867) 1898-1901
Joseph F. Smith* (1867) 1901		Rudger B. Clawson* (1898) 1901

Council of the Twelve—October 1898

Franklin D. Richards (1849)
Brigham Young, Jr. (1868)
Francis M. Lyman (1880)
John Henry Smith (1880)
George Teasdale (1882)
Heber J. Grant (1882)

John W. Taylor (1884)
Marriner W. Merrill (1889)
Anthon H. Lund (1889)
Matthias F. Cowley (1897)
Abraham O. Woodruff (1897)
Rudger Clawson (1898)

Died

1899—Franklin D. Richards

Added

Reed Smoot (1900)

April 1900

Brigham Young, Jr. (1868)
Francis M. Lyman (1880)

Marriner W. Merrill (1889)
Anthon H. Lund (1889)

---

*At the death of George Q. Cannon, Joseph F. Smith was sustained as first counselor on October 6, 1901, with Rudger Clawson as second counselor. They were sustained but not set apart because this First Presidency was dissolved four days later by the death of President Snow.

Note: Dates in parentheses indicate date ordained a member of the Council of the Twelve.

John Henry Smith (1880)   Matthias F. Cowley (1897)
George Teasdale (1882)   Abraham O. Woodruff (1897)
Heber J. Grant (1882)   Rudger Clawson (1898)
John W. Taylor (1884)   Reed Smoot (1900)

Fifth Apostolic Presidency—Oct. 10 to Oct. 17, 1901 (7 days)

148

JOSEPH F. SMITH
Sixth President of the Church

Born: November 13, 1838, Far West, Missouri

Died: November 19, 1918, of bronchopneumonia, Salt Lake City, Utah (age 80)

President of the Church: October 17, 1901, to November 19, 1918 (17 years; age 62-80)

Ancestry: English, Scottish

Education: Ward schools, self-educated

Occupation: Farmer

Missions: 1854-57: Hawaii; 1860-63: Britain; 1864: Hawaii; 1874-75, 1877: Europe; 1885-87: Hawaii

Apostle: Ordained July 1, 1866 (served 35 years; age 27-62)

President of the Council of the Twelve: No record

General Authority: 52 years

Church callings prior to presidency: Missionary, high councilor, historian, apostle, member of the First Presidency, mission president

Selective works of teachings: *Gospel Doctrine*

Physical characteristics: Five feet eleven inches tall, 185-195 pounds, full beard, gray hair, brown eyes, wore glasses

Family: Son of Hyrum and Mary Fielding Smith. Married: Levira Annett Clark Smith, Julina Lambson, Sarah Ellen Richards, Edna Lambson, Alice Ann Kimball, Mary Taylor Schwartz. Had total of 48 children (3 adopted).

Profile of Joseph F. Smith

Only the Lord could have known that it was the right time for a future prophet to be born. To anyone else in Far West, Missouri, on November 13, 1838, it was a dreadful time. The baby's father, Hyrum Smith, had been imprisoned for two weeks with the Prophet Joseph, and would remain in prison for months. His mother, Mary Fielding Smith, was ill with worry and with physical deprivation that had made her pregnancy more difficult. Outside the door the Reverend Bogart, a fiery preacher and self-appointed mob leader, exhorted the violent members of his group. Mary was alone except for Hyrum's five children by his first marriage, her sister Mercy Rachel Fielding Thompson (who was consumed with worry about her own husband, who had been forced to flee for his life), and her newborn son, Joseph Fielding, named for their beloved brother.

The mobbers burst through the door, forced the women and children into a corner of the room, and began to rummage through the house, ostensibly in search of weapons, breaking open a trunk, throwing the bedding around, and, in the process, burying the infant Joseph under the bedding. By the time the ruffians left and he was rescued, he was blue from lack of oxygen but still breathing. Seventy-eight years of storm and hardship had begun.

Despite his perilous beginnings, Joseph F. Smith did not become hardened, defensive, or embittered. Elder Edward H. Anderson, assistant Church historian and a personal friend, described him as "a reflex of the best character of the Mormon people—inured to hardships, patient in trial, God-fearing, self-sacrificing, full of love for the human race, powerful in moral, mental and physical strength." He commented on the man's "imposing physical appearance," and on the "intense earnestness" of his public speaking. "He touches the hearts of the people with the simple eloquence of one who is himself convinced of the truths presented." (Cited in Andrew Jenson, *Latter-day Saint Biographical Encyclopedia* 1:73-74.)

His ability to withstand hardship began in infancy. His family was driven out of Missouri before he could do more than toddle. His father was murdered when he was six. At the age of eight, he drove an ox team over two hundred miles from Nauvoo to Winter Quarters. At the age of nine, in Iowa, he was guarding a herd of cattle when suddenly a band of Indians rode up. Showing more courage than caution, Joseph stuck with the herd, but was helpless as two of the Indians swooped down, one on each side, took him by the arms, and lifted him from his saddle and dropped him to the ground. Just then they saw men working in the fields and, alarmed, rode away. (Joseph Fielding Smith, *Life of Joseph F. Smith*, pp. 135-37.)

Joseph helped his family prepare for the trek west and drove his own team of oxen over a thousand miles to Salt Lake City. Tenderhearted, he suffered with his patient animals, and when they lowed from fatigue and thirst he threw his arms about their necks and wept. As a ten-year-old in the Salt Lake Valley he was again responsible for the family herd, and never lost an animal placed in his care. In addition to that responsibility, he plowed, chopped down trees in the canyons, planted, and harvested.

The family was in dire need of his assistance. Mary Fielding Smith and her little brood of children lived in their covered wagons for two winters until she was able to build a modest home in the Mill Creek area. She taught Joseph, by example, that the tithing office would receive their best loads of potatoes, since she believed unwaveringly that she would be blessed by that sacrifice. And Joseph remembers: "We never lacked so much as many others did. . . . We were never without corn-meal and milk or butter, to my knowledge." (CR, April 1900, p. 48-49.)

But the unremitting hardship of Mary Fielding Smith's life since she had joined the Church in Canada told heavily on her, and she died in 1852, when Joseph was

Joseph F. Smith at age 19

only thirteen. The life he had led during all the tribulations had made him a man at that tender age. For the next two years he lived with his brother John, and then, only fifteen, he was called to fulfill a mission in the Sandwich Islands, now known as the Hawaiian Islands.

It was an agonizing experience for him. He remembered being "almost naked and entirely friendless," except for the affection extended by the Hawaiians themselves. "I felt as if I was so debased in my condition of poverty, lack of intelligence and knowledge, just a boy, that I hardly dared look a white man in the face." Suffering from this crisis in self-esteem, he received a powerful kind of help. He dreamed he saw himself entering heaven, being greeted by his beloved mother and father, President Brigham Young, and the Prophet Joseph Smith. To him, it was not just a dream but "a reality. There never could be anything more real to me. I felt the hand of Joseph Smith, I felt the warmth of his stomach, when I put my hand against him. I saw the smile upon his face. . . . I know that that was a reality, to show me my duty, to teach me something, to impress upon me something that I cannot forget." The effect of this manifestation was life-changing: "When I awoke that morning I was a man, although only a boy. There was not anything in the world that I feared. I could meet any man or woman or child and look them in the face, feeling in my soul I was a man every whit." He summarized simply: "That vision, that manifestation and witness that I enjoyed at that time has made me what I am, if I am anything that is good." (Smith, *Life of Joseph F. Smith*, pp. 445-47.)

That new maturity, that unflinching confidence lasted during the rest of his three-year mission. He learned Hawaiian in only one hundred days; he resisted illness, fatigue, and the loss of his possessions by flood and fire. As an elder he preached, healed the sick, cast out devils, and presided over numerous branches of the Church. On his way home from the mission, between California and Salt Lake City, he and his companions encountered a group of Mormon-haters at their evening camp, and the leader of the group swore he would kill anyone who was a Mormon. Leveling his gun at Joseph, he demanded, "Are you a Mormon?" Without hesitation, Joseph affirmed, "Yes, siree; dyed in the wool; true blue, through and through." Disarmed by such boldness, the Mormon-hater shook hands with young Joseph, praised him for his courage, and led his men away. (Smith, *Life of Joseph F. Smith*, p. 189.)

Back in Salt Lake City, the nineteen-year-old Joseph was ordained a seventy, then at age twenty was made a high priest and a stake high councilor. It was 1857, and Johnston's Army was on its way to Utah to repress the so-called rebellion of the Saints. Joseph joined the militia to harass their supply lines and delay their progress, then took part in an Indian mission. At age twenty-one he married Levira Smith. At age twenty-two he was called on a mission to Great Britain, and within five months of his return home received another call—this time to return to Hawaii, where he served as an assistant to two apostles, Elders Ezra T. Benson and Lorenzo Snow.

When he returned from Hawaii, he became the recorder and officiator in the Endowment House and worked in the Church Historian's Office. In that capacity he often served as secretary for the Council of the Twelve, attending many meetings and recording the discussions.

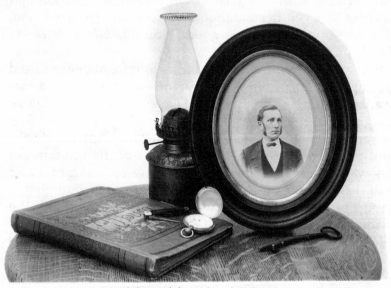

Memorabilia of Joseph F. Smith

On July 1, 1866, he was attending such a meeting when, after the closing prayer, Brigham Young said to the assembled group, "Hold on, shall I do as I feel led?" then answered his own question: " 'I always feel well to do as the Spirit constrains me. It is my mind to ordain Brother Joseph F. Smith to the Apostleship, and to be one of my counselors.' " (Smith, *Life of Joseph F. Smith*, p. 227.)

The procedure was unusual. Not only was Joseph only twenty-eight years old, but there was no vacancy in the quorum. The ordination thus was not announced publicly until April 8, 1867, when he was sustained as a member of the Council of the Twelve to replace Amasa M. Lyman.

His tutelage under Brigham Young was the beginning of careful training for the Church presidency. He served for seven consecutive terms in the territorial legislature's House of Representatives and for two years in the Senate. He also served as a member of the Salt Lake City Council. He became thoroughly acquainted with the doctrines and history of the Church, and worked as a traveling missionary in various parts of the territory.

He also was able to spend concentrated time with his growing family. The husband of five wives and the father of forty-eight children, he had a near-ideal home life. His biographers give us some insights into that loving household: "To the astonishment of the unbelieving world, the wives loved each other dearly. In times of sickness they tenderly waited upon and nursed each other. When death invaded one of the homes and a child was taken, all wept and mourned together with sincere grief. . . . Two of the wives were skilled and licensed practitioners in obstetrics, and brought many babies into the world. They waited upon . . . the other wives, and when babies came all rejoiced equally with the mother.

"The children recognized each other as brothers and sisters, full-fledged not as half, as they would be considered in the world. They defended each and stood by each other no matter which branch of the family was theirs. . . .

"Joseph F. Smith loved his wives and children with a

155

holy love that is seldom seen, never surpassed. Like Job of old, he prayed for them night and day and asked the Lord to keep them pure and undefiled in the path of righteousness." (Joseph Fielding Smith, Jr., and John J Stewart, *Life of Joseph Fielding Smith*, pp. 46-47.)

Joseph himself paid a high tribute to his wives: "Truer wives have never lived, nor more loving mothers, nor better women, according to their knowledge. Not only would they die for me but they live for me and my happiness, and they have been not only faithful to me but to my children and to God! Oh! how I have been, am, and will be, blessed in them in time and eternity!" (Smith, *Life of Joseph F. Smith*, p. 451.)

Ten of his children died, and this father, whom his namesake son called "the most tenderhearted man I ever knew," shared some of his touching feelings of grief as he remembered a little daughter:

"I look down the garden walk, peer around the house, look here and there for a glimpse of a little golden, sunny head and rosy cheeks, but no, alas, no pattering little footsteps. No beaming little black eyes sparkling with love for papa; no sweet little enquiring voice . . . no soft little dimpled hands clasping me around the neck . . . but a vacant little chair. Her little toys concealed, her clothes put by, and only the one desolate thought forcing its crushing leaden weight upon my heart—she is not here, she is gone!" (Smith, *Life of Joseph F. Smith*, p. 456.)

Yet his was not simply a sentimental fondness. He loved his children as eternal children of his Heavenly Father, and diligently taught them his own great faith and scriptural knowledge. His son, Joseph Fielding Smith, recalled: "Among my fondest memories are the hours I have spent by his side discussing principles of the gospel and receiving instruction as only he could give it. In this way the foundation for my own knowledge was laid in truth." (Smith and Stewart, *Life of Joseph Fielding Smith*, p. 40.)

Because of that deep and abiding faith, Joseph could look at his children, loving them as he did, and say: "There are a great many things which are far worse than

Joseph F. Smith as a young man

death. With my present feelings and views and the understanding that I have of life and death I would far rather follow every child I have to the grave in their innocence and purity, than to see them grow up to man and womanhood and degrade themselves by the pernicious practices of the world, forget the Gospel, forget God and the plan of life and salvation, and turn away from the only hope of eternal reward and exaltation in the world to come." (JD 24:76.)

In 1874, at age 36, Joseph was called as president of the European Mission. He used his three-year service to become closely acquainted with the Saints in Scandinavia, Germany, Switzerland, and France. When he returned to the United States in 1877, he visited Church historical sites in Independence, Kirtland, Palmyra, and Manchester, and took special pains to call on David Whitmer, the last survivor of the three witnesses to the Book of Mormon.

In 1880, President John Taylor chose Joseph as one of his counselors. The First Presidency at that time had to combat foes who were more determined than ever, and Joseph's duty—at President Taylor's express request—was to go into hiding. He probably knew more about the records of the Church, including the vital records in the Endowment House, than any living being, and his arrest could have severely damaged the Church. Obediently he went into exile, enduring the separation from his family and the death of another child.

That exile lasted seven years. He visited the Saints in Mexico, the Southwest, Hawaii, Canada, and the East, using the name of Jason Mack, his grandmother's oldest brother. Elder Charles Penrose, who accompanied him, was known as Charles Williams.

Joseph returned to Utah on March 8, 1889, but remained in hiding, meeting secretly with his family to bless them and teach them the gospel. At last, on September 7, 1891, he received official word that he had been granted amnesty by the president of the United States. At general conference on Sunday, October 4, 1891, the members of the First Presidency were seated together on the stand for the first time in seven and a half years. By then Wilford Woodruff was president—and again Joseph was a counselor. Seven years later, Lorenzo Snow would succeed to the presidency, and for the fourth time Joseph would serve as a counselor. It was a seasoned man who was sustained by the members of the Church as its sixth president on November 19, 1901, (age sixty-three), at a special conference.

The polygamy crisis was over but, like his immediate predecessors, President Smith had to cope with the financial chaos and the negative public sentiment left in its wake.

Part of the battle took place on the national scene. Reed Smoot, an apostle and an elected senator, was denied his seat in Congress on the grounds that he was a polygamist and he also believed in polygamy. During the Senate hearings, which began in January 1904 and lasted for the next thirty months, it became apparent that the Church itself was on trial. President Smith responded by issuing an official statement on April 5, 1904, upholding the provisions of the 1890 Manifesto and ordering the excommunication of people who contracted new plural marriages. He ordered the Manifesto itself to be added to the Doctrine and Covenants, satisfying critics who pointed out that LDS scriptures contained the revelation authorizing plural marriage but no revelation terminating it. Along with other Church leaders, President Smith himself was called to testify—and he took advantage of the opportunity to make influential contacts and to meet newsmen so sincerely and candidly that they were disarmed. It was the beginning of a new public image for the Church.

At the same time, opposition at home was hostile. Between 1905 and 1911, an anti-Mormon political party in Utah, using a Salt Lake City newspaper, "almost daily cartooned" him in "a spirit of wicked and malicious vilification. . . . The people of the nation and even beyond the borders of the United States, reached the conclusion that the President of the Church, Joseph F. Smith, was the lowest and most despicable character in all the world. Missionaries . . . were persecuted and insulted in all parts of the earth." (Smith, *Life of Joseph F. Smith*, p. 350.) Yet Joseph Fielding Smith, whom Elder John A. Widtsoe once called "the Fighting Apostle" for his "relentless watchfulness" (*Gospel Doctrine*, p. 511), refused absolutely to respond to these attacks, by even so much as a letter to the editor. At the height of the attacks, he explained his position to the Saints in conference:

"I feel in my heart to forgive all men. . . . I bear no malice toward any of the children of my Father. But there are enemies to the work of the Lord, as there were enemies to the Son of God. There are those who speak only evil of the Latter-day Saints. There are those . . . who will shut their eyes to every . . . good thing connected with

159

Joseph F. Smith as an apostle

this latter-day work, and will pour out floods of falsehood and misrepresentation against the people of God. I forgive them for this. I leave them in the hand of the just Judge." (CR, Oct. 1907, p. 5.)

This kindliness would reemerge during World War I when hate was so tempting. Even though he had six of his own sons serving in the armed forces by the time the Armistice was signed, he counseled soldiers to remember that they were "ministers of life and not death," that they were "fighting to defend liberty and not to destroy their enemies."

Another part of his project to improve the image of the

Church was to welcome visitors. Even before the Smoot hearings, in 1902, the Church established a bureau of information on Temple Square, the first of many information centers. President Smith's interest in history led to the use of Church history sites as tourist information centers.

He coped with the financial chaos left by the polygamy persecutions by continuing to stress President Snow's emphasis on paying an honest tithe. He used the funds to retire the bonded indebtedness of the Church and, by April conference 1907, he was able to tell the Saints: "Today the Church of Jesus Christ of Latter-day Saints owes not a dollar that it cannot pay at once. At last we are in a position to pay as we go. We do not have to borrow any more, and we won't have to if the Latter-day Saints continue to live their religion and observe the law of tithing. It is the law of revenue of the church." (CHC 6:421.)

The prosperity of the Church showed up in a variety of ways. Many stakes and wards built new chapels and tabernacles. The LDS Hospital came into being. Administrative machinery was housed in the Bishop's Building and the Church Administration Building. The first man to visit Europe as president of the Church, President Smith told the Saints that they should build up the Church in their own lands, and he took immediate steps to see that they would have the blessings of the temple. He dedicated ground for temples in Cardston, Alberta, Canada, in 1913 and in Laie, Hawaii, in 1915, promising the Saints that someday a temple would be built in New Zealand.

In 1914, he prophetically warned the Saints that "there are at least three dangers that threaten the Church within, and the authorities need to awaken to the fact that the people should be warned unceasingly against them. As I see these, they are flattery of prominent men in the world, false educational ideas, and sexual impurity." (*Gospel Doctrine*, pp. 312-13.) He took steps to counter these dangers—none of them apparent at the time—by enlarging the Church school system, by encouraging the seminary system, then only two years old, and by issuing an official announcement in 1915 urging the Saints to begin holding family home evening, "at which time fathers and mothers may gather their boys and girls about them in the home and teach them the word of the Lord." Two important magazines, the *Children's Friend* and the *Relief Society Magazine,* began publication, strengthening the women and children of the Church for the next sixty years.

In addition to these administrative and public-relations advances, he provided the Church with the inspiring example of a man who lived close to the Spirit. Charles W. Nibley recalled traveling with him by train on their way back from the East:

> Just east of Green River, I saw him go out to the end of the car on the platform, and immediately return and hesitate a moment, and then sit down in the seat just ahead of me. He had just taken his seat when something went wrong with the train. A broken rail had been the means of ditching the engine and had thrown most of the cars off the track. In the sleeper we were shaken up pretty badly, but our car remained on the track.
>
> The President immediately said to me that he had gone on the platform when he heard a voice saying, "Go in and sit down." He came in, and I noticed him stand a moment, and he seemed to hesitate, but he sat down. He said further that as he came in and stood in the aisle he thought, "Oh, pshaw, perhaps it is only my imagination;" when he heard the voice again, "Sit down," and he immediately took his seat, and the result was as I have stated. He, no doubt, would have been very seriously injured had he remained on the platform of that car, as the cars were all jammed up together pretty badly. He said, "I have heard that voice a good many times in my life, and I have always profited by obeying it." (IE, Jan. 1919, p. 197.)

Just six weeks before his death, President Smith received the magnificent manifestation known as the "Vision of the Redemption of the Dead," which was canonized at the April 1976 general conference. While pondering the scriptures related to the atonement, he was shown the mission of Jesus in organizing the missionary forces of the righteous dead to go among the spirits in prison. President Smith also saw that many who had accepted the gospel since leaving the earth were waiting for the ordinances of the gospel to be performed for them by proxy in the temples. He had his son Joseph Fielding Smith record the vision, then submitted it to the other General Authorities, who unanimously accepted it. It was published in the December 1917 issue of the *Improvement Era* and is now section 138 of the Doctrine and Covenants.

Joseph F. Smith during his presidency

But the end was near. His beloved son Hyrum Mack Smith, an apostle, died suddenly in January 1918 as a result of complications from appendicitis. President Smith, who also was ailing, was shocked and grieved by his son's death. Ten months later, on November 19, 1918, he passed quietly away of bronchopneumonia. Because of the nationwide influenza epidemic, public gatherings were forbidden, but at a graveside service the next president of the Church, Heber J. Grant, exclaimed, "I loved Joseph F.

Smith as I never loved any other man that I have ever known." He singled out President Smith's faith for special praise: "No man that ever lived had a more powerful testimony of the living God and of our Redeemer than Joseph F. Smith. From my earliest childhood days he has thrilled my very being with the testimony that he has borne to all those with whom he has come in contact." (Nibley, *Presidents of the Church,* pp. 208-9.)

Following is President Smith's testimony:

I desire to bear my testimony to you; for I have received an assurance which has taken possession of my whole being. It has sunk deep into my heart; it fills every fiber of my soul; so that I feel to say before this people, and would be pleased to have the privilege of saying it before the whole world, that God has revealed unto me that Jesus is the Christ, the Son of the living God, the Redeemer of the world; that Joseph Smith is, was, and always will be a prophet of God, ordained and chosen to stand at the head of the dispensation of the fulness of times, the keys of which were given to him, and he will hold them until the winding up scene—keys which will unlock the door into the kingdom of God to every man who is worthy to enter and which will close that door against every soul that will not obey the law of God. I know, as I live, that this is true, and I bear my testimony to its truth. If it were the last word I should ever say on earth, I would glory before God my Father that I possess this knowledge in my soul, which I declare unto you as I would the simplest truths of heaven. I know that this is the kingdom of God, and that God is at the helm. He presides over his people. He presides over the president of this Church, and has done so from the Prophet Joseph down to the Prophet Lorenzo, and he will continue to preside over the leaders of this Church until the winding-up scene. He will not suffer it to be given to another people, nor to be left to men. He will hold the reins in his own hands; for he has stretched out his arm to do this work, and he will do it, and have the honor of it. At the same time God will honor and magnify his servants in the sight of the people. He will sustain them in righteousness. He will lift them on high, exalt them into his presence, and they will partake of his glory forever and ever. . . .

It is by his power that [the Church] has grown and continued, and has become what it is, and it will continue to grow and spread, until it shall fill the earth with the glory of God, and with the knowledge of the Father and of the Son, whom to know is life eternal. This is my testimony to you, my brethren and sisters, and I bear witness of it in the name of the Lord Jesus Christ. Amen. (*Gospel Doctrine,* pp. 501-2, 506.)

Important Dates and Events
in Lifetime of Joseph F. Smith

Church Membership, 1901: 278,645   1918: 495,962
1918   Stakes: 75   Missions: 22   Temples: 4
       Number of General Authorities: 26
       Missionaries Called in 1918: 245

1838	Joseph F. Smith was born in Far West, Missouri, November 13.
1844	His father, Hyrum Smith, was martyred.
1846-48	Drove an ox-team across the plains from Nauvoo to Salt Lake Valley (age 8-10).
1848-52	Worked as a herd boy.
1852	Became an orphan at the death of his mother, Mary Fielding Smith.
1854-57	Served a mission to Hawaii (age 15).
1857	Served in the Echo Canyon campaign of the Utah War.
1859	Was called to Salt Lake Stake high council (age 21). Married Levira Annett Clark Smith.
1860-63	Served a mission to Great Britain.
1864	Was employed in Church Historian's Office. Served a special mission to Hawaii.
1865-74	Served as a member of the territorial House of Representatives.
1866	Was ordained an apostle by Brigham Young, July 1, at Salt Lake City (age 27), and named as a counselor in First Presidency.
1867	Was sustained as a member of the Council of the Twelve. Went to Provo to help build up the city and Utah County; served one term on the Provo City Council.
1874-75	Served as president of the European Mission.
1876	Presided over settlements in Davis County, Utah.
1877	Served a second term as president of the European Mission.
1878	Served a short-term mission to the eastern United States.
1880	Was named second counselor to John Taylor in the First Presidency (age 42).

1880-84 Served in the upper branch of the Utah legislature.

1884-91 Went into voluntary exile because of polygamy persecution; served among the Saints in the southwest United States, Mexico, Hawaii, Canada, eastern United States.

1889 Was named second counselor to Wilford Woodruff in the First Presidency.

1893 Served in the constitutional convention for Utah.

1898 Was named second counselor to President Lorenzo Snow in the First Presidency.

1901 Was sustained as president of the Church, November 10, at a special conference (age 63); with John R. Winder and Anthon H. Lund as counselors. Ordained his son Hyrum Mack Smith as an apostle, October 24.

1902 Established the Church Bureau of Information in Salt Lake City to help tell the truth about the Church. Enhanced the Church patriarch's role by asking him to speak at general conference and by adding his name to the list of General Authorities customarily sustained as "prophets, seers, and revelators." The *Children's Friend* was established by the Primary.

1903 Authorized the purchase of Church historic sites.

1904 Issued an official statement reaffirming the Church's position forbidding plural marriages. Testified at the Reed Smoot hearings. Reed Smoot, a member of the Council of the Twelve, was elected to the United States Senate.

1905 Dedicated the Joseph Smith Monument at Sharon, Vermont, birthplace of the Prophet.

1905-12 Came under personal attack and abuse from the enemies of the Church. Did not defend himself, but rather showed forth love and concern.

1906 Toured the missions in Europe—the first president to visit Europe while serving as president. The Church was cleared entirely of debt. President Smith foretold the time when all church programs would be carried on by the priesthood.

1909 Visited the Hawaiian Islands. First Presidency issued statement on doctrine of the origin of man.

1910 Ordained his son Joseph Fielding Smith as an apostle, April 7. Visited Europe.

1912 The Church's seminary program began.

1913 President Smith dedicated the site for a temple in Cardston, Alberta, Canada. First Presidency issued warning about false revelation.

1913-18 Persecution of the Church throughout the United States subsided; a period of prosperity and toleration began. The LDS Hospital in Salt Lake City, Bishop's Building, Church

Administration Building, and many meetinghouses and tabernacles were erected.

1915   President Smith dedicated the site for a temple in Laie, Oahu, Hawaii. The *Relief Society Magazine* began publication. The First Presidency stressed holding a home evening.

1916   Visited the Hawaiian Islands. The First Presidency issued a "doctrinal exposition" on the Father and the Son.

1917   Visited the Hawaiian Islands. Made his last public trip to visit the Saints; journeyed to Southern Utah.

1918   Received a vision concerning the salvation of the dead and the visit of the Savior to the world of spirits after His crucifixion; this vision was subsequently published, after first being submitted to the First Presidency and the other General Authorities. (It was canonized in April 1976.) Joseph F. Smith died of bronchopneumonia in Salt Lake City, November 19, at age 80; no public funeral was held because of a nationwide influenza epidemic.

The First Presidency and Council of the Twelve During Joseph F. Smith's Administration

First Counselor	President	Second Counselor
*John R. Winder 1901-10	Joseph F. Smith (1867) 1901-18	Anthon H. Lund (1889) 1901-10
Anthon H. Lund (1889) 1910-18		John Henry Smith (1880) 1910-11
		Charles W. Penrose (1904) 1911-18

Council of the Twelve—November 1901

Brigham Young, Jr. (1868)   Marriner W. Merrill (1889)
Francis M. Lyman (1880)   Matthias F. Cowley (1889)
John Henry Smith (1880)   Abraham O. Woodruff (1897)
George Teasdale (1882)   Rudger Clawson (1898)
Heber J. Grant (1882)   Reed Smoot (1900)
John W. Taylor (1884)   Hyrum Mack Smith (1901)

Died   **Added**

1903—Brigham Young, Jr.   George Albert Smith (1903)
1904—Abraham O. Woodruff   Charles W. Penrose (1904)
1906—Marriner W. Merrill   George F. Richards (1906)
1907—George Teasdale   Orson F. Whitney (1906)
1916—Francis M. Lyman   David O. McKay (1906)

---

*Never ordained an apostle.
Note: Dates in parentheses indicate date ordained a member of the Council of the Twelve.

1918—Hyrum Mack Smith   Anthony W. Ivins (1907)
Joseph Fielding Smith (1910)
James E. Talmage (1911)
Stephen L Richards (1917)
Richard R. Lyman (1918)

Excommunicated

1911—John W. Taylor

Resigned from the Council

1905—Matthias F. Cowley

October 1918

Heber J. Grant (1882)   David O. McKay (1906)
Rudger Clawson (1898)   Anthony W. Ivins (1907)
Reed Smoot (1900)   Joseph Fielding Smith (1910)
George Albert Smith (1903)   James E. Talmage (1911)
George F. Richards (1906)   Stephen L Richards (1917)
Orson F. Whitney (1906)   Richard R. Lyman (1918)

Sixth Apostolic Presidency—Nov. 19 to Nov. 23, 1918 (4 days)

HEBER J. GRANT
Seventh President of the Church

Born: November 22, 1856, Salt Lake City, Utah

Died: May 14, 1945, of heart failure, Salt Lake City, Utah (age 88)

President of the Church: November 23, 1918, to May 14, 1945 (26½ years; age 62-88)

Ancestry: English, Scottish, Dutch

Education: Ward school, self-educated

Occupation: Businessman

Missions: 1901-1903: Japan; 1904-1906: Europe

Apostle: Ordained October 16, 1882 (served 36 years; age 25-62)

President of the Council of the Twelve: November 23, 1916, to November 23, 1918

General Authority: 63 years

Church callings prior to presidency: Secretary of general YMMIA, ward MIA superintendent, stake president, apostle, mission president

Selective works of teachings: *Gospel Standards*

Physical characteristics: Six feet tall, 175-180 pounds, slender build, gray eyes, dark to gray hair, wore glasses

Family: Son of Jedediah and Rachel Ivins Grant. Married: Lucy Stringham, Hulda Augusta Winters, Emily J. Harris Wells. Had total of 12 children.

Profile of Heber J. Grant

In the mid-1800s, Heber C. Kimball held a small boy in his arms and prophesied in the name of the Lord Jesus Christ that he would become an "apostle of the Lord." (*Church News,* Sept. 3, 1938, p. 7.) At a Relief Society meeting, Eliza R. Snow reportedly watched the same child play on the floor, and spoke in tongues a similar prophecy. (*Instructor,* Mar. 1970, p. 111.) The boy's own mother told her son that if he would "behave himself," he would be an apostle someday. (Bryant S. Hinckley, *Faith of Our Pioneer Fathers,* p. 71.)

These prophecies concerning the mission of Heber J. Grant came to pass. Just one month before Heber's twenty-sixth birthday in October 1882 he received a call from President John Taylor to be an apostle. He was the youngest man ordained a member of the Council of the Twelve who later became president. The young man, doubting his worthiness, questioned the Lord concerning his call. In February 1883 he had a marvelous vision in which it was manifested to him that his call had indeed originated in heaven, that the Prophet Joseph Smith and his deceased father had desired his appointment, and that he was worthy because of his clean living. It remained for him to make a success or failure of that calling. From that time on, he received great joy in testifying of the gospel. At age sixty-two, he would be called to preside over the Church. (Heber J. Grant, *Gospel Standards,* pp. 195-96.)

Heber J. Grant epitomized the principle of developing God-given talents. His favorite motto was from Ralph Waldo Emerson: "That which we persist in doing becomes easier for us to do, not that the nature of the thing itself has changed, but that our power to do is increased."

Those words motivated him continually throughout his life to overcome, to strive harder, and to achieve. Although he had his share of handicaps and difficulties, he applied a strong will and an unwavering faith in God to turn his weaknesses to strengths.

Heber was born on November 22, 1856, in Salt Lake City, a son of Jedediah Morgan and Rachel Ivins Grant. Nine days after his birth, his father, counselor to President Brigham Young, died of pneumonia. Thus, as a child Heber had to work hard and assume responsibilities beyond his years. Often he would forgo boyhood activities to help his widowed mother with household chores. Although his mother raised him by herself, he did have ten half-brothers and -sisters. His father had married six other wives, but they did not all live together.

Young Heber, like most boys his age, wanted to be a good baseball player. But because he never had time to develop running and throwing skills, he was assigned to play on a school team with boys younger than himself. When his school friends teased and taunted him, he became even more determined to measure up. With money he made by polishing boots, he bought his own baseball, and day after day, he practiced by throwing the ball against a barn. Often his arm ached so much he could hardly sleep, but he accomplished his goal and played on a baseball team that won the championship in Utah, California, Colorado, and Wyoming. (*Gospel Standards*, pp. 342-43.)

This example of determination surfaced again when Heber was teased for his poor handwriting. Vowing to be a good penman, he spent many hours practicing until he finally earned first prize in a writing contest, and later he was hired to teach handwriting at the University of Deseret. (Bryant S. Hinckley, *Highlights in the Life of a Great Leader*, pp. 40-41.)

Later, President Grant had a great desire to sing the beloved hymns of the Church. As a young boy he had taken singing lessons, but had been unable to carry a tune. His music instructor had told him he could sing, but added, "I would like to be at least forty miles away when you are doing it!"

But President Grant set a goal and sang "O My Father" hundreds of times before he learned to sing it well. He recounted that once, on a trip to Arizona with J. Golden Kimball and other brethren, he asked if they had any objections if he sang one hundred hymns that day. They thought it was a joke and said they would be delighted. So he began to sing. President Grant wrote later: "We were on the way back from Holbrook to St. Johns, a distance of about 60 miles. After I had sung about 40 hymns, they assured me that if I sang the remaining 60, they would have nervous prostration. I paid no attention to their appeal, but held them to their bargain and sang the full 100!" (*Gospel Standards,* pp. 351, 354.)

One of his very favorite hymns was "Let Each Man Learn to Know Himself." Its chief message is condensed at the end of the last stanza: "So first improve yourself today and then improve your friends tomorrow." He sang this hymn from one end of the Church to the other. (Francis M. Gibbons, *Heber J. Grant: Man of Steel, Prophet of God,* p. 42.)

President Grant's determination came in part from his mother. He often said she was "all to me." She set an example of courage, love, and honor that he acknowledged and followed. He said that one of the reasons he was president of the Church was because he followed the advice and counsel and the burning testimony of God that came to him from his mother. She taught him he would be a success if he would always do what was right.

One of the things Heber did faithfully was to write in his journal, although it was difficult for him. " 'I sometimes feel almost like stopping the writing of a journal,' he wrote on January 9, 1884, 'as my grammar is so poor also my spelling that I dislike to leave any such a record as I have to make under the circumstances; but I am of the opinion that it is almost a matter of duty that I keep a

Heber J. Grant as a young man

journal and this is the main reason that I am willing to do so.' " As his father had died when he was just a baby, Heber had never known this great man. He lamented, " 'I would be willing to pay any reasonable amount of money for a record of father's life; but he never recorded any of his acts and there is today nothing worthy of mention on record regarding him.' " (Gibbons, *Heber J. Grant,* p. viii.)

Success came to him not only in church affairs and missionary effort, but in community service and business affairs also, and he unhesitatingly put the Lord first.

As a young man, Heber attended a meeting and heard an appeal for donations. After the meeting he handed his bishop $50. The

175

bishop returned $45 to him and said that $5 was his fair share. Heber J. Grant gave the bishop the entire $50 and said, "Bishop Woolley, didn't you preach here today that the Lord would reward fourfold? My mother is a widow and she needs two hundred dollars." He said: "My boy, do you believe that if I take this other forty-five dollars you will get your two hundred dollars quicker?" I said: "Certainly." Well, he took it. As Heber walked from the meeting, he got an idea. He wired a man he didn't know and completed a business transaction. Heber J. Grant's profit was $218.50. The next day he went to his bishop and said: "Bishop, I have made two hundred eighteen dollars and fifty cents, after paying that fifty dollars donation the other day, and so I owe twenty-one dollars and eighty-five cents in tithing. I will have to dig up the difference between twenty-one dollars eighty-five cents and eighteen dollars fifty cents. The Lord did not quite give me the tithing in addition to his 'four to one' income." (*New Era*, Jan. 1972, pp. 46-47.)

This beautifully crafted desk was used by President Grant for many years

His willingness to sacrifice was one of the reasons he could stick with good resolutions. He said: "I assert with confidence that the law of success, here and hereafter, is to have a humble and a prayerful heart, and to work, *work*, WORK." (*Gospel Standards*, p. 182.)

When Heber was called as a stake president at age twenty-four, he felt inadequate because of his poor speaking ability. He described one of his first speeches as "a complete fizzle" because he had not relied on the Spirit. He repented before the Lord with tears of humility and promised the Lord that he would never again speak without a total dependence on divine guidance. He kept that promise and came to be in great demand as a speaker, often getting standing ovations at non-Church gatherings. (*BYU Quarterly*, Nov. 1934, pp. 24-26.)

Heber engaged in a number of ventures at various times, including banking, a woolen mill, lumber, sugar and refining factories, insurance, ranching, cattle raising, vinegar manufacturing, the newspaper business, a brokerage, soapmaking, bee culture, merchandising, and an implement business.

Heber M. Wells, a boyhood associate and later the first governor of Utah, said of him: "He has probably been instrumental in establishing and furthering the cause of more successful intermountain industries than any other man of his time. His personal credit, his unquestioned integrity, his supersalesmanship brought capital to the aid of the Church, the community, and private enterprises. In times of panic and in times of plenty Heber J. Grant has been able to raise a few dollars or millions where other men have failed to raise any amount." (Hinckley, *Life of a Great Leader*, p. 51.)

In fact, one of his greatest assets was his keen business sense, which manifested itself early in his life. As a boy, he became an expert marble player and then hired other boys to do his chores, paying them with marbles. (Ibid., p. 43.)

"Young Heber J. Grant quickly displayed his talents in a remarkable fashion. At the age of fifteen, he joined the

Heber J. Grant as president of the Japan Mission (1901-1903)

insurance firm of H. R. Mann and Company as an office
boy and policy clerk. After business hours he marketed
fire insurance. By nineteen, he had bought out his em-
ployers and organized his own successful agency. During
his early twenties he broadened out into other business
activities." (Ronald W. Walker, *Ensign*, July 1979, p. 49.)

When he was a young man, he declined an appointment to the Naval Academy and made up his mind to be a
businessman. He pursued his goal through good times and
bad, through successes and reversals. Many of the great
financiers of the country were his personal friends and
trusted him in money matters. Even after he was deeply
involved in Church affairs, he retained these friendships.

Preston Nibley noted that "perhaps the most outstanding contribution President Grant made to the Church during the years of his presidency was his ability to meet and mingle with the prominent and influential people of the nation; to break down opposition; to remove prejudice and to make and win friends for the Latter-day Saints. He was a great and outstanding missionary." (*Presidents of the Church*, p. 253.)

Many people called President Grant a financial genius. But he had little interest in accumulating money for its own sake. Speaking in a conference in 1893, he stated: "So far as our property is concerned it is of no actual value to us, only as we are ready and willing to use it for the advancement of God's kingdom." (Ibid., p. 232.)

In terms of the Church, his expertise had great value. He saved two Church banks during the disastrous, prolonged panic of 1891-1893, making a trip to New York City in 1891 to borrow on $100,000 worth of ZCMI notes owned by one of the banks. The New York Stock Exchange was then lending money at one-half of 1 percent a day—182.5 percent a year—but he was able to get 6 percent annual interest on the notes.

President Woodruff had given Heber J. Grant a special blessing that he would get all the money he needed, but directors of the Deseret National Bank laughed at the idea of his being able to cash ZCMI notes in the East at 6 percent per annum. He stopped off in Omaha and then in Chicago to try to cash some of the notes, but was turned down. When he arrived in New York he had not sold a single one of his notes, but from then on his fortunes changed, and he successfully borrowed $336,000 in all. (Hinckley, *Faith of Our Pioneer Fathers*, pp. 76-78.)

In his lifetime, President Grant gave away thousands of dollars. He paid off mortgages from the homes of widows, helped people find jobs, supported missionaries in the field, and saw that people who needed medical attention received it.

His daughter Lucy told of incidents that typified his great kindness and generosity:

A man who had served on a mission with him died leaving a family of five children; the baby was but four months old. Father took this woman into his office where she worked for fifteen years. . . . He took a fatherly interest in this family, assisting them all he could. . . .

One night I was reading the paper and came to the story of a sister who was a widow who had two sons on missions; he said that was quite a burden for her, and immediately got in touch with the family and sent money to help the boys. . . .

One of our neighbors lost her husband; Father was among the first to call, and he pressed $100 into her hand. This generous act was repeated scores of times when death entered the homes of those he knew. (Hinckley, *Life of a Great Leader*, pp. 204-5.)

At one time in his life, Heber J. Grant suffered severe financial reverses and, in his own words, was "$100,000 worse off than nothing." At that same time he was called to open a mission in Japan and was given a year to put his affairs in order prior to departing. He put himself in the hands of the Lord and prayed constantly for help in getting out of debt. Within the year's time, all of his creditors had been paid, and after he paid $4,600 in tithing, he had enough money to sustain himself in the mission field. (IE, Nov. 1936, p. 688.)

Heber J. Grant's keen business mind was guided by his integrity. During the depression of the 1930s he had to go to a specialist in Chicago for surgery. The doctor charged him $2,500, which was more than he could afford. He wrote the doctor and enclosed a statement of his finances, mentioning that his holdings had depreciated as a result of the Depression. The doctor responded kindly, reducing the bill to $1,500. The fee was promptly paid. But in 1936, when President Grant's financial condition improved, he sent the doctor a check for another thousand dollars. (Joseph Anderson, *Prophets I Have Known*, p. 29.)

This sense of fairness typified all his dealings and contributed to his great missionary skills. And never in the history of the Church was President Grant's missionary skill and financial expertise more needed than from 1918 to 1945, the years of his administration. Anti-Mormon sentiment over polygamy still existed, and two world wars, as well as the depression of the 1930s, brought physical and emotional strain to the Church.

Heber J. Grant was sustained as president of the Church on November 23, 1918, at age sixty-two, with Anthon H. Lund and Charles W. Penrose as counselors.

During his administration, the Church pulled into an era of prosperity and popularity. Because of the Church's rapid growth, Assistants to the Council of the Twelve were added to the General Authorities. New missions were opened, and three new temples were dedicated— Hawaii, Alberta, and Arizona.

At general conference in April 1936, President Grant announced the new welfare plan (security plan) to take care of the needs of the poor. It provided them with useful employment whereby they could earn their own living. He said: "The aim of the Church is to help the people to help themselves." (*Gospel Standards,* pp. 123-24.)

The institute of religion program was started to provide week-day religious education to young people on the college level. The Tabernacle Choir began weekly radio broadcasts. And President Grant became the first president to give gospel messages to the Church member- ship over the radio.

President Grant emphasized important themes: home industry, tithing and financial support of the Church, and the Word of Wisdom. Speaking of the Word of Wisdom, he counseled the Saints:

> I would like it known that if we as a people never used a particle of tea or coffee or of tobacco or of liquor, we would become one of the most wealthy people in the world. Why? Because we would have increased vigor of body, increased vigor of mind; we would grow spiritually; we would have a more direct line of communication with God, our Heavenly Father; we would be able to accomplish more—to say nothing about the fact that we do not produce these things that the Lord has told us to leave alone, and the money that is expended in breaking the Word of Wisdom goes away from our communities. (IE, Feb. 1941, p. 73.)

He also renewed emphasis on temple work and set the example for the entire Church. He hired research workers to take names from his records, and attended a weekly temple session with many of his family members; his daughter Lucy recalled that one night President Grant and his family performed thirteen hundred sealings.

In 1941, the secretary of the Genealogical Society, Archibald F. Bennett, remarked in a letter: "It is probable that no other family in the Church has accomplished so much in connected genealogical research and in the total of temple ordinances administered [as the Grant family]." (IE, Nov. 1941, p. 697.)

President Grant's love for the temple was evidenced throughout his life, even as a young man. When he was preparing for marriage, his friends tried to talk him into being married by the local bishop and then being sealed when the Salt Lake Temple was completed. But he ignored them, and made the long journey to St. George to be "married properly to start out with."

Heber J. Grant was devoted to his family and always put their needs before any business pursuits. His three wives were remarkable women. They were all well educated for that period, and they had all taught school. Each had descended from a pioneer family, and each had a strong testimony.

The children have happy home memories. There were picnics, drives through the city, ward parties, and various other family activities. Lucy Grant Cannon, one of President Grant's ten daughters, recalled: "In our home we seemed to observe an unwritten law that Church service came first and home duties second. . . . We early became aware that the best way to show our love and appreciation for our parents was to do our best to help in Church organizations. There was no way we could make them happier than to be faithful in Church duties." (IE, Nov. 1936, p. 681.)

Illness and death in President Grant's family burdened his life. He lost his only two sons, one as a baby and the other as a small boy. Then death took two of his three wives.

One daughter who lived away from home said: "Father was a prodigious letter writer, and had I answered his letters as promptly as he did mine, we would have been writing each other twice a week. . . . They all started the same: 'It is two [sometimes three] in the morning and I can't sleep, so I thought I would have a little visit with my beloved daughter.' Nobody will know how I missed those letters after he passed away." (As quoted in Leon R. Hartshorn, *New Era*, Jan. 1972, p. 46.)

Some of his most sacred experiences came in connection with his family, particularly on two occasions when the veil between mortality and the spirit world was "made thin."

When his second and only living son was about to die, President Grant dreamed he saw the boy's deceased mother coming to take her child and himself making a great effort to prevent the boy from leaving him. In his dream he met Brother Joseph E. Taylor, who counseled with him and helped him decide that he should accept the boy's dying. Then the dream ended. Soon afterwards the

Heber J. Grant with his wife Emily and their daughters

child worsened. President Grant hurried to his bedside, and as he sat in the room he felt the presence of his deceased wife, waiting to take her son away. Brother Grant said, "I sat by the deathbed of my little boy and saw him die, without shedding a tear." (IE, June 1940, p. 383.)

When his first wife, Lucy Stringham, was on her deathbed, President Grant tried to explain to his five little daughters and son that she would not recover, but the oldest girl could not understand why he could not heal her by an adminstration. President Grant prayed that the girl would not lose her faith in the power of the priesthood, but that the Lord's will would be done. Sister Grant died, and not one hour later President Grant heard his oldest daughter comforting her little brother with these words: "Do not weep, do not cry, Heber; since we went out of this room the voice of the Lord from heaven has said to me, 'In the death of your Mamma the will of the Lord shall be done.' " (IE, June 1940, p. 330.)

Heber J. Grant's life was filled with faith, courage, and love. He was as considerate and compassionate to strangers as he was to his own family, and was especially sensitive to nonmembers. Often while taking visitors on rides through the beautiful Salt Lake canyons he would stop along the way and conveniently disappear for a time so the nonmember guests could smoke if they desired.

Once as he spoke to a cigar-smoking friend, his sense of humor could not be contained. He wrote of the experience: "I remember upon one occasion a friend of mine, not in the Church, saying: 'How can you afford to spend hundreds of dollars every year in giving books away to your friends?' I said: 'Oh, I get a great deal of pleasure out of it, and in addition I sometimes give pleasure to four or five hundred others. Sometimes I give away in a year a thousand or two thousand pamphlets that cost only ten cents each, and it is my cigar money. I am sure it does not cost me any more than you spend to gratify your own appetite in smoking cigars.' He said, 'Well, you have knocked me out in the first round and with the first blow.' " (*Gospel Standards*, p. 248.)

Heber J. Grant as an apostle

His preoccupation with family, church, and business affairs, the volume of which constantly increased, did not alter President Grant's lifelong recreational habits. " 'Played volley ball from after lunch until about three p.m., having nearly an hour of pleasure,' he recorded on March 9, 1921, during the time he was wrestling with the selection of a new counselor and a new member of the Twelve. 'I play this game almost as a matter of duty to keep myself in proper trim physically; at the same time I thoroughly enjoy it.' " (Gibbons, *Heber J. Grant*, p. 179.)

Other forms of entertainment and relaxation that he enjoyed were attending sports events, reading, going to plays and movies, golfing, and going for automobile rides.

Heber J. Grant served for twenty-six and a half years as president of the Church, longer than any president except Brigham Young. He was a pioneer for the Church in many ways. His life was full of significant contributions to the Church in general and to individual members. Like the prophets before him, he gave all that he had, spiritually and physically, to build the kingdom of God.

In 1940 he suffered partial paralysis, and five years later he died of heart failure at age eighty-eight in Salt Lake City. His counselor, J. Reuben Clark, Jr., paid him this tribute:

> God fashioned him in heart and mind and body, in ability, in experience, and in wisdom, just as he has fashioned every man whom he has ever called to lead his people. . . . His was a simple faith. . . . He so lived his life that it had no dark place across which he must draw a curtain. . . . He had the "Pure and undefiled religion" of James; he "visited the fatherless and the widows in their affliction and kept himself unspotted from the world." He was loyal almost to a fault; he was generous beyond compare. . . . He was one of the great ones of the earth. (Hinckley, *Life of a Great Leader,* pp. 262-64.)

President Heber J. Grant's life was a reflection of his total devotion to Jesus Christ. During his life, he openly acknowledged that his successes were only the fruits of living the gospel. His own testimony bore evidence that following the Savior meant "eating of the fruits that are sweet, above all that is sweet":

> I bear witness to you today that I do not believe that any man on earth . . . has had sweeter joy, more perfect and exquisite happiness than I have had . . . in lifting up my voice, in bearing witness to those with whom I have come in contact that I know that God lives, that I know that Jesus is the Christ, the Savior of the world, the Redeemer of mankind; that I know that Joseph Smith was and is a prophet of the true and living God, that I have the abiding testimony in my heart that Brigham Young was a chosen instrument of the living God, that John Taylor, that Wilford Woodruff, that Lorenzo Snow were, and that to-day [1918] Joseph F. Smith is the representative of the living God, and the mouthpiece of God here upon the earth.
>
> I do not have the language at my command to express the gratitude to God for this knowledge that I possess; and time and time again my heart has been melted, my eyes have wept tears of gratitude for the knowledge that he lives and that this gospel called "Mormonism" is in very deed the plan of life and salvation, that it is the only true gospel upon the face of the earth, that it is in very deed the gospel of the Lord Jesus Christ. (CR, Oct. 1918, pp. 24-25.)

Important Dates and Events
in Lifetime of Heber J. Grant

Church Membership, 1918: 495,962   1945: 979, 454
1945   Stakes: 155   Missions: 38   Temples: 7
        Number of General Authorities: 31
        Missionaries Called in 1941: 1,257

1856   Heber J. Grant was born in Salt Lake City, November 22. His father died nine days later.
1860s   Played baseball on several championship teams.
1871   Was employed as a bank clerk and started a career in the business world.
1875   Worked as a bookkeeper and policy clerk for Wells Fargo and Company. Was called to the presidency of the First Ward YMMIA.
1877   Married Lucy Stringham.
1880   Was called as secretary to the general YMMIA presidency. Was called as president of Tooele Stake. Formed a syndicate and bought $350,000 worth of ZCMI stock.
1882   Was ordained an apostle (age 25) by George Q. Cannon, October 16.
1884   Married Augusta Winters and Emily Harris Wells. Traveled with a party to the Yaqui Indian nation in Sonora, Mexico, to find a settlement of refuge for those indicted for polygamy.
1886-95 Was engaged in establishing a life insurance company and other business enterprises, culminating in the Heber J. Grant Insurance Company in 1895.
1890   Became president of the State Bank of Utah (age 34).
1891-93 Saved two Church banks during a prolonged panic.
1896   Was considered as a candidate for governor of Utah but withdrew from nomination.
1897   Became a member of the general presidency of YMMIA and business manager of the *Improvement Era* (of which he was a founder).

1901-03	Organized and presided over the Japanese Mission (age 45-47).
1904-06	Served as president of the British and European missions.
1906	Had an interview with King Oscar of Sweden.
1907	Instructed the Saints in the Mormon colonies in Mexico in the task of establishing permanent communities.
1916	Was sustained as president of the Council of the Twelve (age 60).
1918	Was sustained as president of the Church, November 23 (age 62), with Anthon H. Lund and Charles W. Penrose as counselors. The Church entered new era of prosperity and popularity.
1919	Dedicated the Hawaii Temple, November 27.
1920	Selected a site for the Arizona Temple, along with Elders David O. McKay and George F. Richards, February 1.
1921	Established an unusual precedent by inviting a nonmember, an educator, to speak in April general conference.
1922	Was one of the main speakers as the Church began broadcasting on radio KZN (later KSL).
1923	Dedicated the Alberta Temple, July 27. Radio broadcasting began of general conference sessions.
1926	Intensified his campaign among the Saints to promote frugality and freedom from debt. The institute of religion program in colleges was instituted.
1927	Dedicated the Arizona Temple at Mesa, October 23.
1929	The Tabernacle Choir began broadcasting on radio, June 15.
1930	The Centennial of Church's organization was observed.
1932	President Grant visited the Saints in the East. Visited U.S. President Herbert Hoover at the White House. Had an operation in Chicago in October and was bedridden for two months.
1933	Citizens of Utah voted to repeal Prohibition, against President Grant's wishes.
1936	The Church Security Plan (later called welfare plan) was established.
1937	President Grant visited missions in Europe.
1940	President Grant's health was impaired because of partial paralysis, but his mind was clear and alert.
1941	Assistants to the Council of the Twelve as General Authorities were named, April 6.
1944	Spoke in general conference for the last time, October.
1945	Died of heart failure in Salt Lake City, May 14 (age 88).

The First Presidency and Council of the Twelve During Heber J. Grant's Administration

First Counselor	President	Second Counselor
Anthon H. Lund (1889) 1918-21	Heber J. Grant (1882) 1918-45	Charles W. Penrose (1904) 1918-21
Charles W. Penrose (1904) 1921-25		Anthony W. Ivins (1907) 1921-25
Anthony W. Ivins (1907) 1925-34		*Charles W. Nibley 1925-31
J. Reuben Clark, Jr. (1934) 1934-45		J. Reuben Clark, Jr. (1934) 1933-34**
		David O. McKay (1906) 1934-45

Council of the Twelve—June 1919

Rudger Clawson (1898)   Anthony W. Ivins (1907)
Reed Smoot (1900)   Joseph Fielding Smith (1910)
George Albert Smith (1903)   James E. Talmage (1911)
George F. Richards (1906)   Stephen L Richards (1917)
Orson F. Whitney (1906)   Richard R. Lyman (1918)
David O. McKay (1906)   Melvin J. Ballard (1919)

*Never ordained an apostle.
**The delay in filling the vacancy was due to the fact that Elder Clark had been serving as U.S. Ambassador to Mexico.
Note: Dates in parentheses indicate date ordained member of the Council of the Twelve.

Died	Added
1931—Orson F. Whitney	John A. Widtsoe (1921)
1933—James E. Talmage	Joseph F. Merrill (1931)
1934—Anthony W. Ivins	Charles A. Callis (1933)
1936—Alonzo A. Hinckley	Alonzo A. Hinckley (1934)
1939—Melvin J. Ballard	Albert E. Bowen (1937)
1941—Reed Smoot	Sylvester Q. Cannon (1938)
1943—Sylvester Q. Cannon	Harold B. Lee (1941)
1943—Rudger Clawson	Spencer W. Kimball (1943)
	Ezra Taft Benson (1943)
	Mark E. Petersen (1944)

Excommunicated

1943—Richard R. Lyman
    (rebaptized—1954)

April 1945

George Albert Smith (1903)	Charles A. Callis (1933)
George F. Richards (1906)	Albert E. Bowen (1937)
Joseph Fielding Smith (1910)	Harold B. Lee (1941)
Stephen L Richards (1917)	Spencer W. Kimball (1943)
John A. Widtsoe (1921)	Ezra Taft Benson (1943)
Joseph F. Merrill (1931)	Mark E. Petersen (1944)

Seventh Apostolic Presidency—May 14 to May 21, 1945 (7 days)

GEORGE ALBERT SMITH
Eighth President of the Church

Born: April 4, 1870, Salt Lake City, Utah

Died: April 4, 1951, of respiratory infection, Salt Lake City, Utah (age 81)

President of the Church: May 21, 1945, to April 4, 1951 (6 years; age 75-81)

Ancestry: English, Scottish

Education: Ward school, Brigham Young Academy, University of Utah

Occupation: Businessman

Missions: 1891: Southern Utah; 1892-94: Southern States; 1919-21: Europe

Apostle: Ordained October 8, 1903 (served 42 years; age 33-75)

President of the Council of the Twelve: July 1, 1943, to May 21, 1945

General Authority: 48 years

Church callings prior to presidency: Missionary, ward Sunday School superintendent, stake MIA superintendent, apostle, YMMIA general board, general president of YMMIA

Selective works of teachings: *Sharing the Gospel with Others*

Physical characteristics: Six feet tall, 160 pounds, slender build, beard, gray hair, hazel eyes, glasses, thin face with kindly expression

Family: Son of John Henry and Sarah Farr Smith; married Lucy Emily Woodruff, three children.

Profile of George Albert Smith

On April 4, 1951, President George Albert Smith observed his eighty-first birthday. This anniversary of his mortal life's beginning was also, appropriately, the day upon which he entered immortality. The death of President Smith stirred a sadness that spread worldwide. Telegrams of condolence began arriving almost immediately from leaders of many nations, among them President Harry S Truman, expressing his own sadness as well as the nation's great loss.

Perhaps President Smith's death was felt most deeply in his own neighborhood, where friends left their day's work to go to the home and offer help. Even a service station operator closed his station and, without stopping to change his soiled clothes, went directly to the Smith home to express his love and sorrow.

At the funeral services, President David O. McKay said of President Smith, "[He] lived as nearly as it is humanly possible for a man to live a Christ-like life." (IE, June 1951, p. 405.)

Elder Matthew Cowley also spoke at the services, and said: "God attracts the godly, and I am sure that the shortest journey this man of God ever made in all of his travels has been the journey which he has just taken." (Ibid.)

George Albert Smith, who had been president of the Church for six years, called forth all these expressions of admiration and love because of his own profound belief in brotherhood and kindness, attitudes characterizing his behavior so markedly that he was called the "Apostle of Love."

George Albert Smith around 1890

George Albert Smith's noble life was undoubtedly a reflection, in part, of his heritage. His great-grandfather was John Smith, brother of Joseph Smith, Sr., and uncle of the Prophet Joseph. John's son, the first George Albert Smith, became an apostle at the age of twenty-two and later served as a counselor to Brigham Young. George Albert's father, John Henry Smith, was an apostle and a counselor to Joseph F. Smith. George Albert and his father were the only father and son to be apostles in the Council of the Twelve at the same time, the father from 1880 to 1910, the son from 1903 to 1945.

At the time of George Albert's birth, the Saints had been in the Salt Lake Valley only twenty-three years. George Albert was born on April 4, 1870, to John Henry and Sarah Farr Smith in a home just across from Temple Square, one of fifteen children.

When he was only four years old, his father was called on a mission. When George was twelve, his father was called on another mission, and George shouldered many heavy tasks and responsibilities, thus learning early to be industrious and self-supporting.

When he was thirteen, he started school at the Brigham Young Academy and also began working at the ZCMI clothing factory, putting buttons on overalls. His $2.50 per week earnings went to support his brothers and sisters. While working at ZCMI, he was hired to accompany a salesman to Southern Utah as the driver of the team. He was responsible for feeding, washing, and currying the horses, as well as washing the wagon. His boss reported that no one had ever brought the horses and wagon back so clean.

When he was given an assignment of making boxes, he again determined to do his best and vowed to make more boxes than any other worker. He did just that, making one hundred boxes a day, compared to the sixty boxes made by his fellow workers. Because of his great industriousness, he was asked to be a grocery salesman and then advanced to higher positions. He spent one year at the University of Utah and then left school entirely to become a traveling salesman for ZCMI.

As a boy, George Albert Smith learned to work with his father, the hero of his boyhood, herding cows and driving teams of horses. He also loved being outdoors, and enjoyed swimming with friends in the Jordan River when chores were done. At age sixteen he worked in Green River, Utah, with a surveying party for the Denver and Rio Grande Western Railroad. During this tedious job, excessive heat and sunglare permanently impaired his vision, but he never let this handicap hinder his work for the Lord.

Although he was never robust, he drew upon almost unbelievable reserves of physical strength later in life as he devoted long hours to his church duties.

On May 25, 1892, he married his childhood sweetheart, Lucy Emily Woodruff, a granddaughter of Wilford Woodruff. One week later he was called to the Southern States Mission. After about four months of proselyting he was assigned to be the mission secretary, and his young bride was given permission to join him in the mission field.

As a missionary, Elder Smith was an example of courage and faith. Once, on a tour with his mission president, J. Golden Kimball, he and President Kimball were sleeping when their cabin was surrounded by an angry mob, demanding that the missionaries come out. President Kimball began to leave the cabin and asked the slumbering Elder Smith if he was planning to join him. The young missionary answered that he was going to stay in bed because he was sure the Lord would take care of them. The mob soon divided into four groups and began shooting at the cabin from all sides. President Smith later recounted: "Splinters were flying over our heads in every direction. . . . I felt absolutely no terror. I was very calm as I lay there, experiencing one of the most horrible events of my life, but I was sure that as long as I was preaching the word of God and following his teachings that the Lord would protect me, and he did." (George Albert Smith, in *A Story to Tell*, p. 156.)

At the age of fourteen he was given a patriarchal blessing in which he was told, ". . . thou shalt become a mighty prophet in the midst of the sons of Zion. And the angels of the Lord shall administer unto you, and the choice blessings of the heavens shall rest upon you." (IE, June 1951, p. 404.) That blessing truly came to pass. Nineteen years later, on October 8, 1903, at the age of thirty-three, George Albert Smith was ordained as an apostle by President Joseph F. Smith. The appointment was a complete surprise.

During his forty-two years as a member of the Twelve, he contributed significantly to many programs, especially the Boy Scout movement. He helped bring the Scouting program into the Church, and served on both church and national scouting committees. He himself exemplified the

One of the few possessions prized by George Albert Smith

spirit of Scouting in all that he did. On a camping trip, he was the first to respond if someone wanted water or if there was food to be cooked or wood to be gathered. He always took care of the horses before his own needs. If anyone needed help, he was usually there first.

In 1934, President Smith attended the national convention of the Boy Scouts of America, where he received the Silver Buffalo, the highest award in Scouting in the United States. The award for outstanding and meritorious service to boyhood included this citation: "He has been indefatigable in serving the cause of scouting, and to his enthusiasm for its program must be largely traced the fact that Utah stands above all other states in the percentage of boys who are Scouts." (IE, July 1945, pp. 430-31.)

President Smith's patriotism and love of country found expression not only in Boy Scout activities, but also as he served on various local, state, and national government committees, and as he served in the Utah National Guard as a young man.

During his apostleship he was active in preserving pioneer history, founding the Utah Trails and Landmarks Association. During the pioneer centennial in 1947, he made by car the journey that the Saints had made by covered wagon one hundred years before. When he concluded his journey in Emigration Canyon on July 24, 1947, fifty thousand Utahns were gathered to greet him and watch him lay the cornerstone for the "This Is the Place" monument.

In October 1945, at the age of seventy-five, George Albert Smith was sustained as president of the Church. He told the Saints who had just sustained him: "Today, my brethren, standing here in humility before you, I would like to express to you my gratitude that you have seen fit to promise that you will help the humble man who has been called to preside over this Church, as he strives to carry on by the inspiration of the Almighty." (Nibley, *Presidents of the Church*, p. 296.)

President Smith's special talents and great capacity to love helped him meet the challenges that the Church faced because of World War II, then reaching its conclusion. He spoke of human rights to all nations and helped destroy barriers of hate by building bridges of love. At the close of the war, he personally supervised a project to send supplies of clothes and food to Europe. He visited President Harry S Truman to get permission to send the carload of goods, and later told of the interview:

[President Truman] smiled and looked at me, and said: "Well, what do you want to ship it over there for? Their money isn't any good."

I said: "We don't want their money."

He looked at me and asked: "You don't mean you are going to give it to them?"

I said: "Of course, we would give it to them. They are our brothers and sisters and are in distress. God has blessed us with a surplus, and we will be glad to send it if we can have the co-operation of the government."

[Then he said,] "How long will it take you to get this ready?"

I said: "It's all ready." (CR, Oct. 1947, pp. 5-6.)

His secretary, Joseph Anderson, who was with him when he went to Welfare Square, where the boxes were being packed for shipment, reported: "As he stood before the open boxes . . . [President Smith] removed his coat and laid it on one of the piles. Despite the protests of his associates, he insisted and returned to the Church offices without his coat." (*Prophets I Have Known*, p. 103.)

By the end of 1947, the Church had sent more than ninety carloads of food to Europe, plus the clothing. The Church also sent forty tons of wheat to Greece, a country suffering from starvation. Because of President Smith's example, the spirit of love and concern spread throughout the Church. When President Smith called a special fast in December 1947 and asked for increased fast offerings, the Saints donated $210,000 to send to non-members in Europe.

In 1945 only 348 missionaries were serving in the field, but under President Smith's leadership the missions that had been closed in Europe were reopened, and by the end of his administration in 1951 over 5,800 missionaries were serving. Also, in 1947, President Smith reopened the Japan Mission.

During President Smith's administration another great challenge manifested itself, and again President Smith's brotherly love solved the problem. Frictions had developed in Mexico, causing a large faction of Church members to break away and form their own church. President Smith personally visited them and encouraged them to return to church activity. Some twelve hundred members who had been out of harmony pledged anew their support of the living prophet. At the meeting held by President Smith, one of the leaders of the reconciled group said, "There is only one president of The Church of Jesus Christ of Latter-day Saints, and he is here today." (Anderson, *Prophets I Have Known*, p. 107.)

For a man of such pronounced spirituality, President Smith also had a remarkably wide and varied experience in secular and civic affairs. He presided over agricultural and industrial congresses and actively participated in banking and other industrial enterprises. But his main objective was always the welfare of humanity, and throughout his life he sought out those who were ill in body, mind, or spirit to comfort and encourage. He was a frequent visitor in Salt Lake City hospitals. On his way home from work, he would frequently stop to visit a friend or neighbor who needed cheer. He never spoke of these visits, but the beneficiaries did not forget them.

George Albert Smith at about age 19

Ezra Taft Benson spoke appreciatively of his family's close association with President Smith—they had lived in the same ward—and then testified:

I shall never cease to be grateful for the visits he made to my home while I was serving as a humble missionary in the nations of war-torn Europe at the end of World War II. Particularly am I thankful for a visit in the still of the night when our little one lay at death's door. Without any announcement, President Smith found time to come into that home and place his hands upon the head of that little one, held in her mother's arms as she had been for many hours, and promise her complete recovery. This was President Smith, he always had time to help, particularly those who were sick, those who needed him most. (CR, Apr. 1951, p. 46.)

President Smith had the unique ability to enjoy the company of people from all walks of life. He occasionally entertained friends by playing his harmonica and guitar. When he performed before a group he would often wear a bold plaid suit, which, coupled with his gangly appearance, would trigger waves of laughter even before he played a note. (Glen R. Stubbs, *A Biography of George Albert Smith*, p. 15.)

He kept himself in good physical shape by exercising with Indian clubs and dumbbells, and he would sometimes give delightful exhibitions of his prowess in Lamanite villages.

It was President Smith who initiated church work among the Lamanites. At President Smith's funeral, Spencer W. Kimball, then a member of the Council of the Twelve, explained that President Smith as an apostle had asked permission from President Heber J. Grant to work among Lamanite people. President Smith visited Indian reservations and homes whenever possible. He had friends in many tribes in various parts of America who frequently visited his office and were guests in his home. He was an honorary chief among many tribes and pleaded their cause in Washington. During his administration he brought about a remarkable change in the attitude of the Saints toward the Native Americans.

Forty years before the completion of the Oakland Temple, George Albert Smith, then a member of the Council of the Twelve, was in San Francisco attending regional Boy Scout meetings. W. Aird Macdonald, president of the Oakland branch, was invited to meet with him at the Fairmont Hotel in San Francisco, atop Nob Hill. President Macdonald later related this account of the meeting:

We sat on the roof terrace . . . a wonderful panorama of the great San Francisco Bay, nestling at our feet. The setting sun seemed to set the whole eastern shore afire, until the Oakland hills were ablaze with golden light. As we admired the beauty and majesty of the scene, President Smith suddenly grew silent, ceased talking, and for several minutes gazed intently toward the East Bay hills.

"Brother Macdonald, I can almost see in vision a white temple of the Lord high upon those hills," he exclaimed rapturously, "an ensign to all the world travelers as they sail through the Golden Gate into this wonderful harbor." Then he studied the vista for a few moments as if to make sure of the scene before him. "Yes sir, a great white temple of the Lord," he confided with calm assurance, "will grace those hills, a glorious ensign to the nations, to welcome our Father's children as they visit this great city." (IE, May 1964, p. 380.)

A few years later, David O. McKay, then a member of the Council of the Twelve, came to Oakland and asked President Macdonald to accompany him to Temple Hill, the place where President Smith had envisioned a temple. Following President McKay's visit, negotiations were begun to buy the site. The land was not for sale and many problems arose, but finally, after fourteen years of negotiations, the land was purchased. In 1964 George Albert Smith's vision became a reality with the completion of the Oakland Temple. (Ibid.)

A devoted father and husband, President Smith loved his evenings with his wife and three children. His wife, Lucy, made many trips with him. Her death in 1937 saddened him greatly, and he turned to his beloved daughters to help fill the void. When his daughters were concerned about the mischievious behavior of their children, President Smith would often say, "Now girls, don't be cross with them. They're only taking after their grandfather." And he would match their offense with one of his own from his childhood.

Even in times of stress, President Smith could always see the humorous side of a situation. As an apostle, once he had an infection that the doctor decided to treat with a then-new sulfa drug that had recently come to the market. President Smith had a violent reaction to it. The family hurriedly sent for the doctor, who explained, "We have to expect this reaction at times. We have learned that one out of twelve can't tolerate sulfa." President Smith, ill as he was, looked up at the doctor with a twinkle in his eye and said, "That's right; you see I'm one of the twelve." (IE, April 1950, p. 310.)

President Smith's life was not without suffering, physical or emotional. Yet he always looked for the positive during those trials. Some of his most sacred experiences occurred during his times of greatest distress. In 1909, while an apostle, he became very ill and lay close to death. During this illness, he dreamed he was in a wooded countryside, being approached by a large man whom he recognized as his grandfather, for whom he had been named. The grandfather stopped, looked his grandson in the eye, and said, "I would like to know what you have done with my name." President Smith related: "Everything I had ever done passed before me as though it were a flying picture on a screen. . . . I smiled and looked at my grandfather and said: 'I have never done anything with your name of which you need be ashamed.' He stepped forward and took me in his arms, and as he did so, I became conscious again of my earthly surroundings. My pillow was . . . wet with tears of gratitude that I could answer unashamed." (*Sharing the Gospel*, p. 112.)

Between 1909 and 1912, President Smith was unable to serve actively in his calling because of his illness. At a general conference he remarked: "I have been in the valley of the shadow of death in recent years, so near the other side that I am sure that [except] for the special blessing of our heavenly Father I could not have remained here." (CR, Oct. 1921, p. 42.)

The Lord did preserve his life on that occasion and others, that he could become a "mighty prophet in the midst of the sons of Zion." His purpose in life was to gain a testimony of Jesus Christ, to live it, and to share it. He never departed from that mission.

Under President Smith's leadership Zion grew significantly in numbers, facilities, and spiritual strength. Many new stakes and wards were created and the build-

George Albert Smith was an avid Scouter

ing program accelerated. Over two hundred meeting houses were constructed during his six-year presidency, and the Idaho Falls Temple was dedicated. Also, in 1949, for the first time general conference was telecast, and he was the first president to appear on television.

By the end of his presidency, membership had passed the 1,100,000 mark, and the prestige of the Church in the United States and other nations had reached a new high. The love and unity within the Church were equally powerful evidence of President Smith's influence on his fellowmen.

He took upon himself a personal crusade to be a friend to the friendless and to minister to the needs of the poor.

He wrote, "I would not be an enemy to any living soul." One of his favorite phrases was, "All the people of the earth are our Father's children."

Irene Jones, a blind woman and friend, wrote after his death:

Many, many times have I heard him say, "These sightless people are God's children, and if we who can see do not help them, we are going to have to answer to our Father in Heaven." . . . Through the loving spirit of President Smith, the work for the blind in the Church has expanded. . . . Even in his illness he did not forget us, but sent messages of encouragement and inspiration by his secretary and daughters. . . .

He is not dead. Such men forever live in the boundless measure of the love they give. (Church News, Apr. 11, 1951, p. 11.)

President Smith, who had served as general superintendent of the Young Men's Mutual Improvement Association from 1921 to 1935, had especially warm feelings for the youth and gave them much of his attention. Once, as he was escorting visitors around Temple Square, he stopped to chat with a young college student who was working part-time in the Tabernacle. President Smith put his arm around the young man and chatted for a few minutes, then looked him in the eye and said, "The Lord and I want you to prepare for a mission." I was that student. I prepared—and I served a challenging and rewarding mission.

Perhaps one of the reasons President Smith gave so freely to young people was because others had helped him significantly in his youth. He never forgot the advice Karl G. Maeser of Brigham Young Academy gave him: "Not only will you be held accountable for the things that you do, but you will be held responsible for the very thoughts that you think." (Deseret News, Feb. 16, 1946.)

That inspired counsel became the foundation for his creed of life—a creed that he lived to the fullest:

I would be a friend to the friendless and find joy in ministering to the needs of the poor. I would visit the sick and afflicted and inspire in them a desire for faith to be healed. I would teach the truth to the

206

understanding and blessing of all mankind. I would seek out the er-
ring one and try to win him back to a righteous and a happy life. I
would not seek to force people to live up to my ideals but rather love
them into doing the thing that is right. I would live with the masses
and help to solve their problems that their earth life may be happy. I
would avoid the publicity of high positions and discourage the flattery
of thoughtless friends. I would not knowingly wound the feelings of
any, not even one who may have wronged me, but would seek to do
him good and make him my friend. I would overcome the tendency to
selfishness and jealousy and rejoice in the successes of all the children
of my Heavenly Father. I would not be an enemy to any living soul.
Knowing that the Redeemer of mankind has offered to the world the
only plan that will fully develop us and make us really happy here and
hereafter I feel it is not only a duty but also a blessed privilege to
disseminate this truth. (IE, Mar. 1932, p. 295.)

At the funeral of President George Albert Smith, one
of the speakers, a non-Mormon, paid him this great
tribute: "He was a man without guile, a religious man and
a spiritual leader, not only in his own Church—in any
group. Even alone with him you had a feeling of this
man's spirituality. . . . He loved to talk about the brotherhood of man, his genuine love of all mankind, which after
all is the true charity of Christ, deeper than any doctrinal
differences, that gift from above that makes for richer,
fuller understanding of man's feeling toward man." (IE,
June 1951, p. 405.)

Today his testimony is still cherished as a source of
strength to all who knew him personally and to countless
others who acknowledge that he was a man of God:

I learned when I was a boy that this is the work of the Lord. I
learned that there were prophets living upon the earth. I learned that
the inspiration of the Almighty would influence those who lived to
enjoy it. . . .

I don't know of any man in all the world who has more reason to
be grateful than I. I am thankful for my birthright, thankful for
parents who taught me the gospel of Jesus Christ and set the example
in their home. . . .

I do not have an enemy that I know of, and there is no one in the
world that I have any enmity towards. All men and all women are my
Father's children, and I have sought during my life to observe the wise
direction of the Redeemer of mankind—to love my neighbor as
myself.

I am grateful to my Heavenly Father that I was born in this land of the free, in this great nation, in this valley, among the people who have dwelt here.

I am grateful for the preservation of my life. Several times when I have been apparently ready to go to the other side, I have been kept here for some other work to be done. . . .

President Smith's rich voice made him an effective radio
speaker

I have lived a long time, as compared with the average of human beings, and I have had a happy life. It will not be many years, in the natural course of events, till the summons to the other side will reach me. I look forward to that time with pleasant anticipation. And after eighty years in mortality, traveling in many parts of the world, associating with many great and good men and women I witness to you, that I know today better than I ever knew before that God lives; that Jesus is the Christ; that Joseph Smith was a prophet of the Living God; and that the Church that he organized under the direction of our Heavenly Father, the Church of Jesus Christ of Latter-day Saints—the Church that was driven into the wilderness—is operating under the power and authority of the same priesthood that was conferred by Peter, James, and John upon Joseph Smith and Oliver Cowdery. I know this, as I know that I live, and I realize that to bear this testimony to you is a very serious matter and that I shall be held accountable by my Heavenly Father for this and all other things that I have taught in his name. Realizing this and knowing that if I were to mislead you that I would be held accountable for it, with love and kindness in my heart for all, I bear this witness in the name of Jesus Christ our Lord. (IE, Apr. 1950, pp. 263-64.)

Important Dates and Events
in Lifetime of George Albert Smith

Church Membership, 1945: 979,454   1951: 1,147,157
1951   Stakes: 191   Missions: 43   Temples: 8
          Number of General Authorities: 31
          Missionaries Serving in 1951: 5,847

1870   George Albert Smith was born in Salt Lake City, April 4.
1882-83   Attended Brigham Young Academy.
1883   Began working in ZCMI clothing factory (age 13).
1884   Received a patriarchal blessing, which foretold his future calling to the Council of the Twelve (age 14).
1887-88   Attended the University of Utah.
1888-91   Became a salesman for ZCMI.
1891   Served a mission to Southern Utah in the interests of YM-MIA.
1892   Married Lucy Emily Woodruff.
1892-94   Served a mission to the Southern States (age 22).
1903   Was ordained an apostle by President Joseph F. Smith, October 8 (age 33).
1904   Was called to the YMMIA general board.
1909-12   Illness prevented him from being active in the Council of the Twelve (age 39-42). Had a vision of his grandfather.
1912   Investigated and approved the adoption of the Scouting program in the Church.
1916   Was elected president of the International Irrigation Congress.
1917   Was elected president of the International Dry Farm Congress.
1919   Became a member of the executive board of the newly organized Salt Lake Boy Scout Council (served more than 30 years).
1919-21   Served as president of the European Mission (age 49-51).
1921-35   Was appointed general president of YMMIA (age 51).
1922   Was elected vice-president of the National Society of Sons of the American Revolution.

1930	Organized the Utah Pioneer Trails and Landmarks Association.
1931	Was elected a member of the national executive board of Boy Scouts of America.
1932	Received the Silver Beaver award in Scouting.
1934	Received his Silver Buffalo, highest award in Scouting.
1937	His wife, Lucy, died, November 5.
1938	Made a six-month tour of missions in the South Pacific.
1941	Visited the Hopi and Navajo Indians in Arizona.
1942	Was granted permission from President Grant to begin an Indian program in the Church.
1943	Was set apart as president of the Council of the Twelve, July 1 (age 73).
1945	Was sustained as president of the Church, May 21, at age 75, with J. Reuben Clark, Jr., and David O. McKay as counselors. Dedicated the Idaho Falls Temple, September 23. Directed that relief goods be sent to Saints in Europe at conclusion of World War II.
1946	Made an automobile journey over the Mormon Trail to Nauvoo. Visited Indians in Wyoming, Idaho, Utah, New Mexico. Visited the Saints in Mexico, as well as the president of Mexico.
1947	Entertained governors of 43 states and three territories at a governor's convention in Salt Lake City, July 15. Dedicated "This Is the Place" monument in Salt Lake City, July 24, at the centennial of the pioneers' arrival in the Salt Lake Valley. Church membership reached one million.
1949	Was the first Church president to appear on a telecast of general conference.
1950	Received an honorary doctor of humanities degree from the University of Utah. Dedicated the Brigham Young statue at the U.S. Capitol in Washington, D.C. Delivered the last sermon of his life, December 11.
1951	Died of respiratory infection in Salt Lake City on April 4, his eighty-first birthday.

The First Presidency and Council of the Twelve During George Albert Smith's Administration

First Counselor	President	Second Counselor
J. Reuben Clark, Jr.	George Albert Smith	David O. McKay
(1934)	(1903)	(1906)
1945-51	1945-51	1945-51

Council of the Twelve—October 1945

George F. Richards (1906) Albert E. Bowen (1937)
Joseph Fielding Smith (1910) Harold B. Lee (1941)
Stephen L Richards (1917) Spencer W. Kimball (1943)
John A. Widtsoe (1921) Ezra Taft Benson (1943)
Joseph F. Merrill (1931) Mark E. Petersen (1944)
Charles A. Callis (1933) Matthew Cowley (1945)

Died

1947—Charles A. Callis
1950—George F. Richards

Added

Henry D. Moyle (1947)
Delbert L. Stapley (1950)

April 1951

Joseph Fielding Smith (1910) Spencer W. Kimball (1943)
Stephen L Richards (1917) Ezra Taft Benson (1943)
John A. Widtsoe (1921) Mark E. Petersen (1944)
Joseph F. Merrill (1931) Matthew Cowley (1945)
Albert E. Bowen (1937) Henry D. Moyle (1947)
Harold B. Lee (1941) Delbert L. Stapley (1950)

Eighth Apostolic Presidency—Apr. 4 to Apr. 9, 1951 (5 days)

Note: Dates in parentheses indicate date ordained member of Council of the Twelve.

DAVID O. McKAY
Ninth President of the Church

Born: September 8, 1873, Huntsville, Utah
Died: January 18, 1970, of congestive heart failure, Salt
  Lake City, Utah (age 96)
President of the Church: April 9, 1951, to January 18, 1970
  (18 years, 9 months; age 77-96)
Ancestry: Scottish, Welsh
Education: Church academy (Weber), University of Utah
Occupation: Educator
Missions: 1897-99: Britain; 1920-21: World; 1922-24:
  European Mission president
Apostle: Ordained April 9, 1906 (served 45 years; age
  32-77)
President of the Council of the Twelve: September 30,
  1950, to April 9, 1951
General Authority: 64 years
Church callings prior to presidency: Missionary, stake
  Sunday School assistant, apostle, assistant and
  general superintendent of Sunday School, church
  commissioner of education, mission president,
  counselor in the First Presidency
Selective works of teachings: *Gospel Ideals; Cherished
  Experiences*
Physical characteristics: Six feet one inch tall, 195-200
  pounds, hazel-brown eyes, flowing white hair, stately
  and distinguished appearance
Family: Son of David and Jennette Evans McKay; married
  Emma Ray Riggs, seven children.

Profile of David Oman McKay

As an apostle in 1915, David O. McKay recalled his boyhood memory of a large portrait of John Taylor hanging above the pulpit in his Huntsville chapel. Beneath the portrait, in golden letters, appeared the motto: "The Kingdom of God or Nothing."

"The sentiment impressed me as a mere child years before I understood its real significance," commented President McKay. "I seemed to realize at that early date that there is no other church or organization that approaches the perfection or possesses the divinity that characterizes the church of Jesus Christ. As a child I felt this intuitively; in youth, I became thoroughly convinced of it; and today I treasure it as a firm conviction of my soul." (*Cherished Experiences*, p. 15.)

David O. McKay was born September 8, 1873, in Huntsville, Utah, the first son and third of ten children of David and Jennette Evans McKay. His home was the schoolroom for a lifetime of valiant service to the Lord. His father was called on a mission to Scotland when he was just seven. Two older sisters had recently died and Jennette was on the point of giving birth to another child that would arrive ten days after the father left for the mission field. The parents' willingness to endure sacrifices for the gospel's sake made the children willing also. Young David fed the horses and oxen, milked the cows, delivered mail and newspapers, helped care for his younger brothers and sisters, and still had time to play second base for the town baseball team.

After his father's return, the gospel training continued. David and his brothers often helped their father in the

David O. McKay at age 17

hayfield, and David told of crossing the field to load a tenth load from the lushest growth because "the best is none too good for God." (*Cherished Experiences,* p. 9.)

In his youth, David felt the hunger within to know that the Church was truly restored in its purity. Once, as his saddle horse stood by his side, he knelt by a serviceberry bush and prayed. At the completion of his prayer, he recalled, no change came. He said, "I must say I am just the same 'old boy' that I was before I prayed." (Ibid., pp. 6-7.) Later he would tell the important lesson he learned from that experience: that testimony comes, not by simple request, but by combining seeking with obedience, service, and sacrifice.

Years later, in the mission field, the elders attending an unusually spiritual meeting testified that angels were present. The mission president, James L. McMurrin, arose and added a prophecy: "Brother David, Satan has desired you that he may sift you as wheat, but God is mindful of you, and if you will keep the faith, you will yet sit in the leading councils of the Church." It was at that point that David felt he had received the answer to his boyhood prayer. (Jeanette McKay Morrell, *Highlights in the Life of President David O. McKay*, pp. 37-38.)

David attended Weber State Academy in Ogden, graduating in 1893, and taught for a year in Huntsville. In 1894 he continued his education at the University of Utah, where he played piano in the dance band, played guard on the football team, and was president of his class, still making such high grades that he graduated as valedictorian of his class. He was boarding during those years at the home of Sister Emma Robbins Riggs, and there he met her daughter Emma Ray, who would become such an important part of his life.

At the age of twenty-four, David received a call from President Wilford Woodruff to serve a mission in Great Britain. Anti-Mormon sentiment was discouragingly strong and, possibly for the first time in his life, there were people who did not like David. This was very discouraging to him. Then one day, an inscription carved in stone caught his eye: "What·E'er·Thou·Art·Act·Well·Thy·Part." From that moment on, he committed himself to be a missionary, despite the unpopularity of such a course. He was later to refer to that moment of commitment as a major source of strength through his life. (*Church News*, Sept. 21, 1957, p. 4.)

Even before he left the mission field, Weber State Academy, his first alma mater, offered him a teaching position. Three years later he was principal of the school. By that time he was also married; he had renewed his acquaintance with Emma Ray Riggs, and they were married on January 2, 1901. One of their seven children died in infancy, but their harmonious home life became a model to the Church of mutual love, respect, and security.

Much of that tone was set by President McKay's unfailing courtesy to his wife. Throughout their married life, he enjoyed opening the car door for her, offering his arm, or holding her coat. He called her "the sweetest, most helpful wife that ever inspired a man to noble endeavor. She has been an inspiration, my lifelong sweetheart, an angel of God come upon earth." (John J Stewart, *Remembering the McKays*, p. 2.) Robert Lawrence McKay, one of their sons, recalls that President McKay always rose when Emma entered the room, and later, when they were both confined to wheelchairs, they would good-humoredly challenge each other to a "race to the elevator."

In sustaining this tone of mutual affection and respect, President McKay was continuing the tradition of his own home. He once noted: "My home life from babyhood to the present time has been the greatest factor in giving me moral and spiritual standards and in shaping the courses of my life. Sincerity, courtesy, consistency in word and deed exemplified in the lives of my parents and others in the two homes have proved a safeguard and guidance." (Fred E. Schluter, *A Convert's Tribute to President David O. McKay*, p. 27.)

How did President McKay teach his children to do the right thing and allow them to use their free agency? Dr. Norman Vincent Peale illustrates the answer in an article he wrote. One day one of President McKay's sons, Llewelyn, a teenager then, came home elated because the store clerk had given him five extra dollars in change. He told his dad about the incident and after some discussion, President McKay said to his son: " 'Let us suppose that no one knows that you have the five dollars. *You* know. And you know it does not belong to you.' There was a long pause. 'It's up to you, son, to decide what is the right thing to do.' Llewelyn returned the five dollars the next day. His father could have made it a cut-and-dried matter of law, but instead he chose to respect the young personality

David O. McKay and his bride, Emma

before him, to give him principle to go on but not a command, to make the decision his." (IE, Sept. 1965, p. 768.)

In the early 1900s, while he was serving in the Weber Stake Sunday School superintendency, his great leadership ability enabled him to make many significant contributions to the Sunday School program. Through his inspired program teachers learned that their jobs involved more than presenting information: they were to have an "aim," an "illustration," and an "application." "It was not long before each teacher felt that unless every pupil left his class with a burning desire to do something as a direct result of the Sunday morning lesson, he had failed in his presentation of the subject. To David O. McKay this fulfilled the admonition 'Be ye doers of the word and not hearers only.'" (Morrell, *Highlights in the Life of President David O. McKay*, pp. 61-62.)

In 1906, at the age of thirty-two, David O. McKay was called to the apostleship. In fulfillment of his mission president's prophecy, he was sitting in the leading councils of the Church.

For twenty-eight years he served in the general superintendency of the Sunday School, and he became church commissioner of education in 1919. A teacher not only by profession but also by nature, he was a gifted speaker who loved to teach and to learn. He once said, "Teaching is the noblest profession in the world."

President Marion G. Romney tells the following story as an example of President McKay's influence as a teacher: "In the winter of 1912-13 Brother McKay came to Los Angeles to see us who had lost our homes in Mexico due to the revolution. He came to Sunday School, and he took a glass of [water and we saw] how clear and beautiful the water was, and then he dropped a drop of ink in the water, and it was clouded all through. He said to us little fellows, 'That is what sin does to a life.' I have ever since then been trying to keep that sin out of my life." (IE, Feb. 1970, pp. 72-73.)

He loved the scriptures, the works of Shakespeare, and other literary masterpieces. He had an amazing memory and could quote at will from the literary and inspirational library he had read. In his writings and speeches, he attacked pertinent issues with precision and force.

Many of his sermons and writings were compiled into books, and he was the subject of several other books during his lifetime. These included *Stepping Stones to an Abundant Life, Treasures of Life, Secrets of a Happy Life, True to the Faith, Man May Know for Himself, Highlights in the Life of David O. McKay, Ancient Apostles, Gospel Ideals, Cherished Experiences, Home Memories of President David O. McKay, A Convert's Tribute to David O. McKay,* and *Remembering the McKays.*

Under his leadership, Church education made great advances. The seminary, institute, and Church school systems were expanded worldwide; priesthood and auxiliary education improved. Brigham Young University became the largest Church-affiliated university in America; in addition to being its trustee, he also served as regent for both the University of Utah and Utah State University.

His years of apostleship were also a time of deepening spirituality for him. He experienced the healing power of the priesthood on one dramatic occasion. In March 1916 he and his brother Thomas were driving down Ogden Canyon, from Huntsville to Ogden, to catch the train to Salt Lake City. They did not realize that a watchman had stretched a rope across a canyon bridge, now unsafe because of the overflowing Ogden River. By the time David saw the rope, it was too late. The rope smashed the window, threw back the top of the car, and "caught me just in the chin, severing my lip, knocking out my lower teeth, and breaking my upper jaw." Thomas had had time to duck and could therefore render aid to his brother, but David's face was so badly lacerated that doctors warned him he would be disfigured for life. Heber J. Grant, then president of the Council of the Twelve, gave him a blessing and promised him that he would not be scarred. "Several months later at a General Authorities' banquet, President Grant looked at David and commented, 'David, from where I am sitting I cannot see a scar on your face!' David answered, 'No, President Grant, there are no scars—your blessing was realized completely!' " (*Cherished Experiences*, p. 140.)

On December 4, 1920, President Grant called Elder McKay on a year-long tour of the world's missions—one of the most unusual assignments given to a General Authority and another occasion for great outpourings of the Spirit. He began the tour by dedicating China for missionary work; he then traveled to the South Sea islands, Australia, and Europe before returning home. This tour gave him the worldwide perspective that would shape his own presidency years later. One particularly special experience occurred in New Zealand at a members' conference, where hundreds of Maoris had gathered to hear their first apostle. President McKay, recognizing "the great expectations" of these members and stricken at the thought of "how inadequately I might satisfy the ardent desires of their souls," remembered the gift of tongues of pioneer and ancient times and, for the first time in his life, "wished with all my heart, that I might be worthy of that divine power. . . . From the depth of my soul, I prayed for divine assistance." He rose to speak, telling the interpreter, Stuart Meha, that he would speak without sentence-by-sentence translation, and then addressing the congregation:

David O. McKay as a young man

"I wish, oh, how I wish I had the power to speak to you in your own tongue, that I might tell you what is in my heart; but since I have not the gift, I pray, and I ask you to pray, that you might have the spirit of interpretation, of discernment, that you may understand at least the spirit while I am speaking, and then you will get the words and the thought when Brother Meha interprets."

My sermon lasted forty minutes, and I have never addressed a more attentive, a more respectful audience. My listeners were in perfect rapport—this I knew when I saw tears in their eyes. Some of them at least, perhaps most of them, who did not understand English, had the gift of interpretation. (*Cherished Experiences*, pp. 54-55.)

If the effect on President McKay of seeing these world-wide Saints was lasting, so was his effect on the Saints. Many of them had prayed for years for the privilege of seeing an apostle. For them, David O. McKay was an answer to their prayers, and his words to them were scripture. At Sauniatu, Samoa, the moment of parting was so intensely spiritual that the Saints erected a monument on the spot and have since gathered annually on the anniversary of his departure "to review those events and the prayer given by the apostle." (IE, Feb. 1970, p. 15.)

After serving for twenty-eight years on the Council of the Twelve, David O. McKay was called as a counselor to Heber J. Grant; he also served as counselor to George Albert Smith. In solemn assembly at general conference on April 9, 1951, he was sustained as president of the Church, forty-five years to the day since he had been ordained an apostle. In addressing the congregation, he testified movingly:

When that reality [the death of President George Albert Smith] came, as I tell you, I was deeply moved. And I am today, and pray that I may, even though inadequately, be able to tell you how weighty this responsibility seems.

The Lord has said that the three presiding high priests chosen by the body, appointed and ordained to this office of presidency, are to be "upheld by the confidence, faith, and prayer of the Church." No one can preside over this Church without first being in tune with the head of the Church, our Lord and Savior, Jesus Christ. He is our head. This is his Church. Without his divine guidance and constant inspiration, we cannot succeed. With his guidance, with his inspiration, we cannot fail. . . .

Today you have by your vote placed upon us the greatest responsibility, as well as the greatest honor, that lies within your power to bestow as members of the Church of Jesus Christ of Latter-day Saints. Your doing so increases the duty of the First Presidency to render service to the people. (IE, June 1951, pp. 406-7.)

It is characteristic that he saw the calling in terms of

service, a characteristic that lasted throughout his administration. Each president of the Church has been greatly loved, but President McKay seemed to draw forth the love of the members in special measure because of his interest, his tenderness, and his unfailing kindness.

Elder Richard L. Evans of the Council of the Twelve, shortly after President McKay became president, wrote of his long hours in the office, beginning early in the morning and lasting until long after five on almost any afternoon; "his delightful laugh and his quick and keen and always kindly humor"; his pleasure in the poetry of Robert Burns; his Scottish dialect stories; "his steady and appraising gaze, and the light in his eyes and the changes in his ever-expressive face; the broad shoulders and the long, firm stride as he purposefully walks from place to place; the wonderful head of silvered hair; his encouragement, his confidence, and his consideration; and his faith and his firmness." Elder Evans noted that, despite pressures, President McKay was never "impatient at interruption" but was always as "gracious to the humble as to the great." (IE, June 1951, p. 458.)

The conference talks that he gave as president of the Church featured Jesus Christ as the Messiah and Savior as his most frequent theme. The scripture he quoted most frequently was Acts 4:12: "Neither is there salvation in any other: for there is none other name under heaven given among men, whereby we must be saved."

His second most frequent theme was the importance of home and family. "Home is the nearest image of heaven," he taught, and "No other success can compensate for failure in the home." He encouraged all members to hold weekly family home evenings.

Other favorite mottos were "Character is greater than intellect" (Gospel Ideals, p. 443), and "To be trusted is a greater compliment than to be loved." (Treasures of Life, p. 379.) He taught that the greatest dangers come from within, not without, and urged the Saints to understand the nature of true spirituality. "Man's chief concern in life," he said, "should not be the acquiring of gold, or of fame, or of material possessions. It should not be development of physical powers, nor of intellectual strength, but his aim, the highest in life, should be the development of a Christ-like character. . . . The true purpose in life is perfection of humanity through individual effort under the guidance of God's inspiration. Real life is response to the best about us." (Morrell, *Highlights in the Life of President David O. McKay*, p. 240.)

The most frequent expressions used to describe President McKay were "kind," "a complete gentleman," "a noble individual," "a man of God," "a great teacher," "a great organizer," "the temple builder," and "beloved leader."

President McKay loved the youth of the Church. He paid them great tributes. Many times he spoke directly to youth and counseled them. One adult remembers vividly one particular teaching he heard as a youth that he never forgot. It was the story of "Dandy," President McKay's impulsive colt. President McKay told of how he had trained the well-bred colt—which was a "choice equine possession." But he commented that "Dandy resented restraint." Dandy was a curious animal and loved to explore.

> One day, however, somebody left the gate unwired. Detecting this, Dandy unlatched it, took Nig, his companion, with him, and together they visited the neighbor's field. They went to an old house used for storage. Dandy's curiosity prompted him to push open the door. There was a sack of grain. What a find! Yes, and what a tragedy! The grain was poisoned bait for rodents! In a few minutes Dandy and Nig were in spasmodic pain, and shortly both were dead.
>
> How like Dandy are many of our youth! They are not bad, they do not intend to do wrong; but they are impulsive, full of life, full of curiosity, and long to do something. They, too, are restive under restraint, but if they are kept busy, guided carefully and rightly, they prove to be responsive and capable; but if left to wander unguided, they all too frequently find themselves in the environment of temptation and too often are entangled in the snares of evil. (*Gospel Ideals*, pp. 518-19.)

He challenged every member of the Church to be a missionary and set the example himself. He traveled on

David O. McKay as general superintendent
of the Sunday School

foot, by horse and buggy, and by jet airliner—covering over two million miles—and made numerous television and radio addresses. The number of missions under his administration more than doubled, to a total of eighty-eight; the number of missionaries zoomed from 2,000 to 13,000. He instituted three language training schools for missionaries and held seminars for newly called mission presidents. He was the first president to visit—as president—South Africa, Asia, South America, Australia, New Zealand, and Central America.

In Montevideo, Uruguay, in January 1954, many spiritual events accompanied his visit. After the mission conference, he asked to shake hands with the members. As a Sister Bighen approached, President McKay took her gloved hand in both of his and murmured something to her. It was the last day Sister Bighen was planning to shake hands with anyone—she had been diagnosed as having cancer, and amputation of her hand had been scheduled for the following day. "But when she returned to the doctors, after President McKay's visit, they found no vestige of the disease. The doctors were so surprised that they redid all the tests and analysis but everything was negative." (Lyman S. Shreeve, "History of the Uruguayan Mission," unpublished typescript in possession of author.)

President McKay's tours among the members prompted him to give local members full priesthood leadership; stakes with local leadership were organized throughout the world, bringing the total from 184 to 500. During his administration, more than 3,750 Church buildings were constructed, including 2,000 ward and branch chapels, many of them in mission areas. Eight temples were built or announced during his administration, in Switzerland, Los Angeles, New Zealand, London, Oakland, Ogden, Provo, and Washington, D.C. President McKay evidently saw the Swiss Temple in a vision, for he described it so vividly to Church architect Edward O. Anderson that Brother Anderson was able to draw it. As the drawings developed through several stages, some alterations were made; and when President McKay saw

President McKay loved to take his family sleigh riding

the drawings again, he observed: "Brother Anderson, that is not the temple that you and I saw together." The original concept was promptly restored in the drawings. (*Church Almanac*, 1979, p. 268.)

Major world conflicts—the Korean and Vietnam wars—erupted while he was president; social and moral problems increased. By word and action, President McKay testified to the need for universal brotherhood and faith in Christ. It was a message sorely needed, and the Church grew from one million to nearly three million members. By President McKay's ninetieth birthday in 1963, fifty percent of the membership of the Church had been baptized since 1951 and thus had known no other president.

Church administration changed creatively to meet the new demands on it. The Church correlation program was instituted, concentrating member responsibility into four areas: home teaching, missionary work, the welfare program, and genealogy. Regional Representatives were called to aid coordination and administration.

As he grew older, President McKay's faith and warmth did not slacken, nor did his sense of humor. Norman Vincent Peale remembers "a heart-stopping moment when as the aged President McKay mounted the platform to address a group, he tripped on the stairs. There was a gasp from the people. But he stood up and faced the audience with that irrepressible smile. 'It's awful to grow old,' he said ruefully, 'but I prefer it to the alternative.' " (IE, Feb. 1970, p. 24.)

One day, while he was in his early nineties, he was "climbing a hill to inspect a site for a new chapel. Two local church officers thought to assist him, one on either arm. Part way up the hill President McKay stopped and said, 'Brethren, I don't mind helping one of you climb this hill, but I can't carry you both.' " (Stewart, *Remembering the McKays*, p. 34.)

On still another occasion, when he was still driving, a highway patrolman stopped him for speeding. President McKay quipped that he was glad of it since some people thought that he was slowing down in his old age.

A man of great personal warmth and charm, he numbered several presidents of the United States among his personal friends: Harry S Truman, Dwight D. Eisenhower, John F. Kennedy, Lyndon B. Johnson, and Richard M. Nixon. Movie director Cecil B. DeMille once said, "David McKay, almost thou persuadest me to be a Mormon." (IE, Feb. 1970, p. 24.)

Arch L. Madsen, president of Bonneville International Corporation, recalled the influence President McKay had on one individual in a chance encounter:

I remember being in New York when President McKay returned from Europe. Arrangements had been made for pictures to be taken, but the regular photographer was unable to go, so in desperation the United Press picked their crime photographer—a man accustomed to the toughest type of work in New York. He went to the airport, stayed there for two hours, and returned later from [the] dark room with a tremendous sheaf of pictures. He was supposed to take only two. His boss immediately chided him, "What in the world are you wasting time and all those photographic supplies for?"

The photographer replied very curtly, saying he would gladly pay for the extra materials, and they could even dock him for the extra time he took. It was obvious that he was very touchy about it. Several hours later the vice-president called him to his office, wanted to learn what happened. The crime photographer said, "When I was a little boy, my mother used to read to me out of the Old Testament, and all my life I have wondered what a prophet of God must really look like. Well, today I found one." (IE, Feb. 1970, p. 72.)

As President McKay moved into his ninth decade, he became seriously ill on several occasions, and many thought that there was no hope for his life, but each time he fought the illness off until January 18, 1970, when he died of a heart attack on a Sunday morning in Salt Lake City at the age of ninety-six. He had served for seventeen years as a counselor in the First Presidency and for almost nineteen years as president—nearly thirty-six years in the First Presidency, a record exceeded only by Joseph F. Smith's thirty-eight years. Only Heber J. Grant and Brigham Young had served longer as president, and no one had served longer than his sixty-four years as a General Authority.

All major newspapers in the United States carried obituaries. The *New York Times* announced his death on the front page and continued for a full page inside, space equalled or exceeded only by the passing of the nation's former presidents.

At the funeral, President McKay's counselor Hugh B. Brown paid him eloquent tribute:

President McKay in Huntsville, Utah

President McKay was a symbol of moral strength to the people of many nations. His life was an inspiration, his memory a benediction.

He was a man who was tall in character as well as physically. He stood out, head and shoulders, above the crowd—a measuring standard for manhood. He was known for his largeness of spirit and the grace with which he lived.

The "God-image" quality of President McKay's nature was the root of his dignity. Those who listened to him felt there was something finer in the man than anything that he said.

. . . President McKay has lived as nearly as it is humanly possible for any man to live a Christ-like life. (IE, Feb. 1970, p. 88.)

John Taylor's motto "The Kingdom of God or Nothing," so often regarded by President McKay as a child, contemplated as a young man, and superbly acted upon as an adult, gave him the irresistible energy of one deeply committed to one prime goal. He testified:

[A] truth that I have cherished from childhood is that God is a personal Being and is, indeed, our Father whom we can approach in prayer and receive answers thereto. I cherish as one of the dearest experiences in life the knowledge that God hears the prayer of faith.

It is true that the answer may not come as direct and at the time or in the manner we anticipate; but it comes, and at a time and in a manner best for the interests of him who offers the supplication. On more than one occasion, I have received direct and immediate assurances that my petition has been granted. At one time particularly, the answer came as distinctly as though my father stood by my side and spoke the words. These experiences are part of my being and must remain so as long as memory and intelligence last. They have taught me that "heaven is never deaf but when man's heart is dumb."

I have an abiding testimony that the Father and the Son appeared to the Prophet Joseph Smith and revealed through him the gospel of Jesus Christ, which is, indeed, "the power of God unto salvation." I know, too, that a knowledge of the truth of the gospel may be obtained only through obedience to the principles thereof. In other words, the best way to know the truth of any principle is to live it. (Cherished Experiences, pp. 15-16.)

"If any man will do his will, he shall know of the doctrine, whether it be of God, or whether I speak of myself." Test it from any source you wish, and you will find that there is not one phase of the gospel of Jesus Christ which will not stand that test. And in your weakness, if you will undertake to embrace the principles of life everlasting, you will find it instilling upon your soul a benediction of the Holy Ghost which will give you a testimony beyond any possibility of doubt that God lives, that he is indeed our Father, and that this is his work established through the Prophet Joseph Smith. That is my testimony—the most precious thing in life. (Treasures of Life, p. 232.)

Important Dates and Events
in Lifetime of David O. McKay

Church Membership, 1951: 1,111,314   1970: 2,811,092
1970   Stakes: 499   Missions: 88   Temples: 13
         Number of General Authorities: 40
         Missionaries Serving in 1970: 14,387

1873   David O. McKay was born in Huntsville, Utah, September 8.
1897   Graduated from the University of Utah. Served as president and valedictorian of his class.
1897-99 Served a mission to Scotland (age 24-26).
1899   Joined the faculty of Weber State Academy (now Weber State College) at Ogden, Utah.
1901   Married Emma Ray Riggs.
1902   Served as principal of Weber Academy.
1906   Was ordained an apostle by President Joseph F. Smith, April 9. Served on Church board of education. Was named second assistant president of Deseret Sunday School Union (DSSU) (age 32).
1909   Became first assistant president of DSSU.
1917   Published his first book, *Ancient Apostles.*
1918-34 Became general president of DSSU.
1919-21 Became Church commissioner of education.
1920-21 Made a world tour of Church missions, traveling 65,500 miles.
1921   Dedicated China for the preaching of the gospel.
1921-22 Served as a member of the board of regents, University of Utah.
1922-24 Served as president of the European Mission (age 49-51).
1932   Became chairman of the Utah Council for Child Health and Protection.
1934   Was sustained as second counselor to President Heber J. Grant in the First Presidency, October 6 (age 61).
1938-47 Served as chairman of the Utah State centennial commission.

1940-41   Served on the board of trustees of Utah State Agricultural College (now Utah State University).

1942   Became chairman of the Utah State Advisory Committee of the American Red Cross and of the Utah Council for Child Health and Protection.

1945   Was sustained as second counselor to President George Albert Smith (age 72).

1950   Was sustained as president of the Council of the Twelve, September 30 (age 77). Received an honorary doctor of laws degree from Utah State Agricultural College.

1951   Was sustained as president of the Church, April 9, with Stephen L Richards and J. Reuben Clark, Jr., as counselors. Received honorary doctorate degrees from Brigham Young University, University of Utah, and Temple University in Philadelphia (age 78).

1952   Toured nine missions of Europe.

1953   Received the Silver Buffalo award from the Boy Scouts of America.

1954   Toured South Africa, South America, Central America. Dedicated the David O. McKay Building on BYU campus. Received the Cross of the Commander of the Royal Order of Phoenix from the government of Greece.

1955   Toured Tahiti, Tonga, New Zealand, and Australia. Dedicated the Swiss Temple.

1956   Dedicated the Los Angeles Temple. Received the Silver Beaver Scouting Award.

1958   Toured the missions of the South Seas. Dedicated the New Zealand Temple, Church College of New Zealand, the London Temple, and Church College of Hawaii.

1960   Gave the initial message in a Churchwide youth fireside series—about 200,000 persons assembled in 170 places.

1961   Presided at the first mission president's seminar, where a uniform method of teaching the gospel was presented.

1962   Was honored by business and civic leaders at a dinner in Salt Lake City.

1963   Dedicated a new Salt Lake Temple annex.

1964   Was hospitalized with a heart ailment. Dedicated the Oakland Temple.

1965   Received an honorary doctorate degree from Weber State College. Two counselors were added in the First Presidency. Family home evenings were inaugurated, January 1.

1966   Mormon students gathered in the Salt Lake Tabernacle for a special tribute to President McKay, sponsored by the institute of religion at the University of Utah.

1967   Regional Representatives of the Council of the Twelve were appointed.

1968   President McKay added one counselor to the First Presidency. Received the Exemplary Manhood award from BYU students, and the Distinguished American award from the National Football Foundation and Hall of Fame.

1969   Attended dedicatory ceremonies for the David O. McKay Hospital in Ogden.

1970   Died of congestive heart failure, January 18, in Salt Lake City (age 96).

The First Presidency and Council of the Twelve During David O. McKay's Administration

First Counselor	President	Second Counselor
Stephen L Richards (1917) 1951-59	David O. McKay (1906) 1951-70	J. Reuben Clark, Jr. (1934) 1951-59
J. Reuben Clark, Jr. (1934) 1959-61		Henry D. Moyle (1947) 1959-61
Henry D. Moyle (1947) 1961-63		Hugh B. Brown (1958) 1961-63
Hugh B. Brown (1958) 1963-70		N. Eldon Tanner (1962) 1963-70

Additional Counselors

Hugh B. Brown (1958)
June-October 1961

Joseph Fielding Smith (1910)
1965-70

Thorpe B. Isaacson*
1965-70

Alvin R. Dyer**
1968-70

Council of the Twelve—April 1951

Joseph Fielding Smith (1910)
John A. Widtsoe (1921)

Ezra Taft Benson (1943)
Mark E. Petersen (1944)

---

*Not ordained an apostle.
**Ordained an apostle but not a member of the Council of the Twelve.
Note: Dates in parentheses indicate date ordained member of the Council of the Twelve.

Joseph F. Merrill (1931)   Matthew Cowley (1945)
Albert E. Bowen (1937)   Henry D. Moyle (1947)
Harold B. Lee (1941)   Delbert L. Stapley (1950)
Spencer W. Kimball (1943)

Died   **Added**

1952—Joseph F. Merrill   Marion G. Romney (1951)
1952—John A. Widtsoe   LeGrand Richards (1952)
1953—Albert E. Bowen   Adam S. Bennion (1953)
1953—Matthew Cowley   Richard L. Evans (1953)
1958—Adam S. Bennion   George Q. Morris (1954)
1962—George Q. Morris   Hugh B. Brown (1958)
                                  Howard W. Hunter (1959)
                                  Gordon B. Hinckley (1961)
                                  N. Eldon Tanner (1962)
                                  Thomas S. Monson (1963)

October 1969

Joseph Fielding Smith (1910)   Marion G. Romney (1951)
Harold B. Lee (1941)   LeGrand Richards (1952)
Spencer W. Kimball (1943)   Richard L. Evans (1953)
Ezra Taft Benson (1943)   Howard W. Hunter (1959)
Mark E. Petersen (1944)   Gordon B. Hinckley (1961)
Delbert L. Stapley (1950)   Thomas S. Monson (1963)

Ninth Apostolic Presidency—Jan. 18 to Jan. 23, 1970 (5 days)

JOSEPH FIELDING SMITH
Tenth President of the Church

Born: July 19, 1876, Salt Lake City, Utah

Died: July 2, 1972, of a heart attack, Salt Lake City, Utah
(age 95)

President of the Church: January 23, 1970, to July 2, 1972
(2½ years; age 93-95)

Ancestry: English, Scottish

Education: Public and ward schools, LDS Business College

Occupation: Genealogist, historian

Mission: 1899-1902: Britain

Apostle: Ordained April 7, 1910 (served 60 years; age 33-93)

President of the Council of the Twelve: April 9, 1951, to
January 23, 1970

General Authority: 62 years

Church callings prior to presidency: Missionary, YMMIA
general board, high councilor, apostle, assistant and
church historian, president of Genealogical Society,
temple president, First Presidency

Selective works of teachings: *Doctrines of Salvation* and
Answers to Gospel Questions

Physical characteristics: Five feet ten inches tall, 165
pounds, medium build, gray hair, blue eyes

Family: Son of Joseph Fielding and Julina Lambson Smith.
Married: Louie E. Shurtliff, Ethel G. Reynolds, Jessie
Ella Evans. Had total of 11 children.

Profile of Joseph Fielding Smith

It was April of 1910. Joseph R. Winder of the First Presidency had died, and the First Presidency and the Council of the Twelve had been meeting for more than an hour in the Salt Lake Temple. They had reached easy accord on a decision to call Elder John Henry Smith to the presidency, but finding a successor to fill his seat in the council was another matter. At least one member felt uncomfortable with each name suggested.

Finally, President Joseph F. Smith went to a private room and prayed for guidance. When he returned, he had another name but he offered it somewhat hesitantly. Would the other brethren consider his son Joseph Fielding Smith for the position? His son Hyrum was already a member of the council and a second son, David, was a counselor in the Presiding Bishopric. Might it cause ill feelings among the members to have a third son ordained as a General Authority? Yet that had been the inspiration that had come to him.

The council "seemed immediately receptive to the suggestion" and promptly sustained their prophet in his action. (Smith and Stewart, *The Life of Joseph Fielding Smith*, p. 174.) Their action was timely. General conference was only a few days away. Joseph Fielding Smith, then only thirty-three years old, walked through the gates with the usual throng of visitors to enter the Tabernacle for the concluding session. One of the gatekeepers asked him, "Well, who is going to be called to fill the vacancy in the Council of the Twelve today?" With a good-humored smile, young Joseph responded, "I don't know, but there is one thing I do know—it won't be me and it won't be you."

He listened to his father welcome the congregation and announce the opening hymn, "We Thank Thee, O God, for a Prophet." We do not know what thoughts passed through the son's mind as he sang the hymn, bowed his head for the invocation by Elder B. H. Roberts, listened to the choir sing "The Spirit of God Like a Fire Is Burning,"

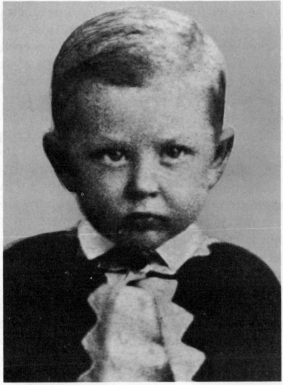

Joseph Fielding Smith as a child

and then heard Elder Heber J. Grant present the names of the General Authorities for a sustaining vote. (In those days it was not the common practice to interview in advance the person to be called.) "About thirty seconds before he got to the point where he would read the name of the new apostle, Joseph Fielding suddenly knew that the name that would be read was his." (Joseph F. McConkie, *True and Faithful,* p. 35.)

Joseph Fielding Smith would spend the next sixty-two years of his life in the leading councils of the Church, dying as its president on July 2, 1972. He was a member of the Council of the Twelve longer than any man in this dispensation—sixty years—and served as president of that council for nineteen years. He was one of the oldest men to serve as president of the Council of the Twelve, beginning at age seventy-four. In 1964 he became a counselor to President McKay, and was the first man to serve concurrently as president of the Council of the Twelve and a counselor in the First Presidency. When he was sustained as president of the Church at age ninety-three on January 23, 1970, he was the oldest man to fill that position as well.

During the two and one-half years of his administration he laid the cornerstone for the Ogden Temple and presided over the laying of the cornerstone for the Provo Temple. He offered the dedicatory prayer for the Ogden Temple and spoke at the services in Provo. Under his administration, much of the work begun in the 1960s came to fruition: members of the Church in need of psychological help could turn to Church Social Services; the education system of the Church was reorganized; the Church magazines were unified into three: the *Ensign* for adults, the *New Era* for the youth, and the *Friend* for children. Meetinghouse library facilities took a jump forward. His beloved Historical Department was organized for the first time on a professional basis. A bishops' training program was inaugurated. The teacher development program spread churchwide. Fourteen new missions were opened. And by his instructions, Monday nights were reserved for the family, with no other Church activities allowed on that evening.

He toured the European missions in 1939, just before the outbreak of World War II, and dedicated Korea for the preaching of the gospel in 1955. As chairman of the first Missionary Committee in 1954, he was sensitive to the internationalization of the gospel. He presided over the Church's first area general conference, held in Manchester, England, in August 1971, and planned

Joseph Fielding Smith as a missionary—age 23

another for Mexico. At Manchester he announced: "We are coming of age as a church and as a people. . . . The Church is not an American church except in America. In Canada it is a Canadian church; in Australia it is an Australian church; and in Great Britain it is a British church. It is a world church; the gospel is for all men." (*Ensign*, Sept. 1971, p. 3.) It is somehow suitable that this man, so firmly rooted in Utah's history and culture, should have been the prophet who, in some important ways, made the Church truly international.

Joseph Fielding Smith turned his considerable scholarly and logical ability to defending the Church as part of strengthening the faith of members. In 1905, the Toronto *Daily Star* published an interview with R. C. Evans, a member of the First Presidency of the Reorganized Church of Jesus Christ of Latter Day Saints. Feeling that the Church had been misrepresented, President Smith responded. A public exchange of letters and a formal response in an RLDS publication, the *Saints Herald*, ensued, and the complete correspondence was reprinted in a pamphlet, *Blood Atonement and the Origin of Plural Marriage.* (Smith and Stewart, *Life of Joseph Fielding Smith,* p. 135.)

A summary of his activities as president is dizzying, but he took them in his stride. His life had always been a balance of continuity and change—the changes that anyone sees in his own family and in society at large, the continuity of love and faith and unchanging values.

One of these values was his heritage. Named for his father, Joseph F. Smith, who would preside over the Church from 1901 to 1918, he was also the the grandson of Hyrum Smith. He was born in Salt Lake City on July 19, 1876, the year before Brigham Young died. Thus, Joseph Fielding Smith's life touched all of the presidents of the Church except his great-uncle, Joseph Smith.

He grew up on the family farm in Taylorsville, Utah, herding cows near the Jordan River and diving off its banks. More studious than his brothers, he hurried through his chores to have more time to spend in his father's library. He had read the Book of Mormon twice before the age of ten. To his mother, Julina Lambson Smith, he credits much of his spiritual training. She guided his reading, taught him to pray, and encouraged him in his priesthood duties as each advancement came along. As a result, even as a child young Joseph knew that God lived, and he could say with telling understatement: "I have tried to be obedient, always with some measure of success." (Smith and Stewart, *Life of Joseph Fielding Smith,* pp. 56-57.)

When he was twenty, he received his patriarchal blessing from his uncle John Smith, the Church patriarch. It promised him that he would live to "a good old age" and become a "mighty man in Israel" and "preside" among the people.

For those who wonder what it takes to become "mighty" in Israel, President Smith's life is instructive.

Joseph Fielding Smith in 1910

Two years after receiving this blessing, on April 26, 1898, he married Louie E. Shurtliff, and a year later he was called on a mission to England. The same thing had happened to his father in 1860, and, like his father, he accepted the mission with mixed emotions. He and Louie had two daughters before she died of complications with a third pregnancy in March 1908.

Joseph Fielding Smith was the only son of a Church president to serve as president as well

Eight months after Louie's death, on November 2, 1908, he married Ethel G. Reynolds, his wife for the next twenty-nine years. She was a devoted mother to his two daughters as well as to their four daughters and five sons. A year after her death, he married Jessie Ella Evans on April 12, 1938. For the next thirty-three years, until her death of a heart ailment on August 3, 1971, they were inseparable. Jessie was a contralto soloist with the Tabernacle Choir, and her duets with President Smith at conferences and other gatherings delighted the Saints.

To his family, President Smith was unquestionably mighty. As he had been willing to sacrifice his own desires to serve the Lord, so he was willing to sacrifice his own convenience for his children. His second wife, Ethel, paid him a tender tribute after twenty-four years of marriage:

> The man I know is a kind, loving husband and father whose greatest ambition in life is to make his family happy. . . . He is the man that lulls to sleep the fretful child, who tells bedtime stories to the little ones, who is never too tired or too busy to sit up late at night or to get up early in the morning to help the older children solve perplexing school problems. When illness comes the man I know watches tenderly over the afflicted one and waits upon him. It is their father for whom they cry, feeling his presence a panacea for all ills. (IE, June 1932, p. 459.)

When one of the children needed correction, he would discuss the problem, then look earnestly into the child's eyes, rest his hands on the young one's shoulders, and say softly, "I do wish my kiddies would be good!" (Smith and Stewart, *Life of Joseph Fielding Smith*, p. 234.) All five of his sons served missions. All of his children who grew to maturity married in the temple. All received some college education, and three received master's degrees.

Part of being mighty was being unconcerned about his own dignity. He enjoyed sports of all kinds and encouraged his children in any kind of recreation but hunting. Their Salt Lake City home had a tennis court and a horseshoe pit. An ardent baseball player as a young man, he prided himself on unnerving a batter by pitching with either hand. Until his doctor made him give up handball at the age of seventy, he excelled at the strenuous game, once beating two of his sons with one hand—their choice—behind his back.

And he raised his family on the modest salary of a church employee. Shortly after his mission, he turned down a high-paying position to begin work in the Church Historian's Office. In 1906 he became assistant Church historian, and in 1921 was made Church historian, a position he held for nearly half a century. He finished off his own long day's work by helping his father with his correspondence until his father died in 1918. And he sandwiched in long service as president of the Salt Lake Temple and director of the Genealogical Society.

In 1960 he was honored with a service award from

Brigham Young University, which read in part: "He is unquestionably one of the greatest scripturians of this dispensation, one who knows whereof he speaks." Elder Bruce R. McConkie of the Council of the Twelve has said this of him: "Joseph Fielding Smith is the leading gospel scholar and the greatest doctrinal teacher of this generation. Few men in this dispensation have approached him in gospel knowledge or surpassed him in spiritual insight." (*Doctrines of Salvation* 1:v.)

He was also mighty in writing. An ardent lover of the scriptures, he soon found himself explaining his gospel understanding to others. He was perhaps the most prolific writer on doctrinal subjects that the Church has yet produced. He published twenty-five books and dozens of articles to define, clarify, and explain doctrine. His answers to the questions of Latter-day Saints, which appeared monthly in the *Improvement Era*, fill five volumes. His published books include: *Blood Atonement and the Origin of Plural Marriage, Essentials in Church History, Elijah the Prophet and His Mission and Salvation Universal, The Way to Perfection, The Progress of Man, The Life of Joseph F. Smith, Signs of the Times, The Restoration of All Things, Church History and Modern Revelation* (two volumes), *Doctrines of Salvation* (three volumes), *Answers to Gospel Questions* (five volumes), *Take Heed to Yourselves, Asael Smith of Topsfield Massachusetts, Origin of the Reorganized Church and the Question of Succession, Seeking After Our Dead, Seek Ye Earnestly,* and *Man: His Origin and Destiny.* He also compiled *Teachings of the Prophet Joseph Smith.*

He wrote numerous articles for the *Utah Genealogical Magazine*, always returning the author's royalties to the magazine itself. Not so well known is the fact that he wrote words to several hymns, including "The Best Is Not Too Good for Me," "Come, Come My Brother, Wake! Awake!," "Does the Journey Seem Long?," and "We Are Watchmen of the Tower of Zion."

He was a man of sound understanding and keen intellect, yet it was love and faith that fired his pen, not knowledge alone. One of his sons remembers that he never spoke of the atonement of the Savior without tears in his eyes, saying with tender yearning, "If only the people in the world would understand the trials, the tribulations, the sins our Lord took upon himself for our benefit."

The clarity of his understanding and the staunchness of his faith gave the impression of rigidity and sternness. But more than one of his friends has been identified as the source of this spontaneous tribute: "If I were to be judged by any of my fellowmen, let it be by Joseph Fielding Smith." Once, when ordaining a bishop, he advised, "If you ever make a mistake in judgment, let it be on the side of mercy."

As a speaker he was known as a defender of the faith. When he stood behind the pulpit, he taught the word of God as it was found in the scriptures. In public meetings he was not a storyteller or an entertainer. Without question, Joseph Fielding Smith will be quoted extensively in years to come.

His deep reverence for holy things and his unquestioning obedience did not make him grim. He had a delicious sense of humor and delighted in jokes. Once he announced to some interested listeners, "My first assignment in the Church was to go with Brigham Young down to St. George to dedicate the temple there." While they nodded, then made some astonished mental calculations, he beat them to it: "I was one year old then."

When his sister dropped by the office after lunch and found him continuing to work at his usual energetic pace, she scolded him for not taking a nap. She checked off half a dozen of his predecessors who had long made a habit of doing so and he retorted briskly, "Yes, and where are they today? All dead!" (Smith and Stewart, *Life of Joseph Fielding Smith*, p. 4.)

His third wife, Jessie Evans Smith, had a keen sense of humor herself and delighted to draw out that side of him.

There was a direct line of sight between their apartment and his office in the church headquarters building, half a block away. One day as he sat at his desk he received a phone call from Jessie. "Joseph," she demanded, "who is that woman in your office?" "There is no woman in my office," he protested. "Oh, yes, there is!" she insisted. "I have my spy glasses focused on you and I know she's there!" President Smith glanced around his office. Near one wall on a pedestal sits a bust of his great-grandmother, Lucy Mack Smith, mother of the Prophet Joseph Smith. "Jessie, I must confess," he said. "You've caught me cold!" He afterward delighted in telling of his guardian angel with binoculars keeping a close watch over him. (Smith and Stewart, *Life of Joseph Fielding Smith*, p. 13.)

His secretary of fifty years, Ruby Egbert, found him far from stern. Both shy and independent, she recalled, "he wouldn't think of asking you to do something for him that he could do himself," and he would never be deliberately brusque or withdrawn. "He shakes hands with everyone on the elevator and on the floor where his office is. And the door to his office has always been open to anyone who needed his help. He loves children. He has a special voice for them, and will often go out in the hall to play with them or chat with them when they pass." (McConkie, *True and Faithful*, pp. 70-71.)

At one of President Smith's last general conferences, a little girl left her parents and ran up to him. He picked her up and held her close. Reproved later by her parents who feared she might have become lost in the crowd, the child replied, "I wasn't lost; I was in the arms of the Prophet." (*Church News*, July 8, 1972, p. 7.)

Deeply in love with history, he represented the last leader of the Church who could introduce a quotation by saying, "I want to read to you something I heard President Woodruff say." Yet he did not turn back to the past. One of his favorite hobbies was flying. When one visitor called at his office, the secretary invited him to step to the window and see if he could find President Smith. He was riding in a jet that was climbing, looping, diving, and rolling over Salt Lake. He frequently went flying with a friend in the National Guard—President Smith was an honorary brigadier general with the Utah National Guard—and loved to take the controls himself. His secretary marveled that he "flew down to Grand Canyon and back last week,

*Joseph Fielding Smith served for 62 years as a General
Authority*

400 miles an hour." (Smith and Stewart, *Life of Joseph Fielding Smith,* pp. 1-2.)

Being "mighty" to President Smith clearly held its true
scriptural meaning. He saw himself as a humble servant of
the Lord and took literally his temple covenants of consecration. Somehow he always had enough time to play with
his children, to speak a kindly word to a co-worker, to
prepare a soundly researched sermon, and to keep himself
healthy. But there was not a second to waste in idleness.
He wore two watches, one on each wrist, and kept another
pair in reserve. He was up every morning before six and
worked hard all day long. One of his sons recalls,
"Somehow it seemed immoral to lie in bed after 6. Of
course, I only tried it once. Father saw to that." (Smith and
Stewart, *Life of Joseph Fielding Smith,* p. 3.) One of President

Smith's maxims was "People die in bed. And so does ambition." It is somehow appropriate that President Smith died very gently, sitting up, after a conversation with his family.

When people asked him how he accomplished so much, he answered, "It's in the bag," and pointed to his lunch sack. For years, he took his lunch to the office so he could keep working through the day. He once estimated, "That gives me an extra 300 hours per year." (Smith and Stewart, *Life of Joseph Fielding Smith,* pp. 3-4.)

His strength came from his simplicity. He found his greatest pleasures in the simple circle of his family. Rather than living in the church-owned Beehive House, he lived in a modest apartment across the street. Instead of riding to work in the church limousine, he preferred taking his own compact car or, better yet, walking. Even his eating habits were simple; a bowl of bread and milk was his favorite evening meal. And his greatest strength was the great simplicity of his faith. An aged, but far from weak, man when he was sustained to preside over the Church, he unflinchingly warned members and nonmembers alike:

These are the last days. They are days of trouble and sorrow and desolation. They are days when Satan dwells in the hearts of ungodly men, when iniquity abounds, and when the signs of the times are being shown forth.

And there is no cure for the ills of the world except the gospel of the Lord Jesus Christ. Our hope for peace, for temporal and spiritual prosperity, and for an eventual inheritance in the kingdom of God is found only in and through the restored gospel. There is no work that any of us can engage in that is as important as preaching the gospel and building up the Church and kingdom of God on earth. (*Conference Report,* April 1972, p. 13.)

This, then, was Joseph Fielding Smith: crusader for righteousness, lifelong scholar, tender husband and father, concerned neighbor and devoted friend, strict but loving spiritual leader, prophet of God. He lived a life that reflected honor and credit on his parentage, and on the Church that shaped him and that he, in turn, helped shape.

To those who gathered to sustain him in April 1970, as he began his short presidency, he bore a moving and eloquent testimony:

As I stand now, in what I might call the twilight of life, with the realization that in a not-far-distant day I shall be called upon to give an account of my mortal stewardship, I bear testimony again of the truth and divinity of this great work.

I know that God lives and that he sent his beloved Son into the world to atone for our sins.

President Smith reading with one of his granddaughters

I know that the Father and the Son appeared to the Prophet Joseph Smith to usher in this final gospel dispensation.

I know that Joseph Smith was and is a prophet; moreover, that this is the Lord's church, and that the gospel cause shall roll forward until the knowledge of the Lord covers the earth as the waters cover the sea.

I am sure that we all love the Lord. I know that he lives, and I look forward to that day when I shall see his face, and I hope to hear his voice say unto me: "Come, ye blessed of my Father, inherit the kingdom prepared for you from the foundation of the world." (Matt. 25:34.) (*Ensign,* December 1971, p. 136.)

All of his life was shaped toward that blessed end.

Important Dates and Events
in Lifetime of Joseph Fielding Smith

Church Membership, 1970: 2,807,456   1972: 3,090,053
1972   Stakes: 58   Missions: 101   Temples: 15
         Number of General Authorities: 41
         Missionaries Serving in 1972: 16,357

1876	Joseph Fielding Smith was born in Salt Lake City, Utah, July 19.
1895	Worked at ZCMI.
1898	Married Louie E. Shurtliff. Was appointed to the Salt Lake Stake YMMIA board.
1899-1901	Served a mission to the British Isles (age 22-24.)
1901	Began working in the Church Historian's Offce. His father was sustained as president of the Church.
1901-10	Became a home missionary in the Salt Lake Stake.
1903-19	Became a member of the YMMIA general board.
1904	Became a member of the Salt Lake Stake high council.
1906	Was appointed assistant Church historian.
1907	Began work with the Genealogical Society. Was commissioned by the U.S. Department of Commerce and Labor to collect statistics of the Church for religious census being compiled at that time.
1908	Was appointed director and librarian of Genealogical Society. His wife, Louie, died, March. Married Ethel G. Reynolds, November.
1909	Was appointed to general board of religion classes. Was named librarian and treasurer of Genealogical Society.
1910	Was ordained an apostle by Joseph F. Smith, April 7. Became first associate editor and business manager of *Utah Genealogical and Historical Magazine* (age 33).
1910-22	Was named Secretary of Genealogical Society.
1912	Was appointed to board of trustees, Brigham Young University.
1915-35	Was named counselor in Salt Lake Temple presidency.
1917	Was appointed to Church Board of Education.

1921   Was named Church Historian (age 44).

1934   Was named president of Genealogical Society.

1937   His wife, Ethel, died.

1938   Married Jessie Ella Evans. Toured the California Mission.

1939   Toured the European missions and supervised evacuation of American LDS missionaries throughout Europe except the British Isles.

1945-49 Became president of the Salt Lake Temple (age 68).

1950   Toured the Texas-Louisiana Mission. Was sustained as acting president of the Council of the Twelve, September 30.

1951   Became president of the Council of the Twelve, April. Received an honorary doctor of letters degree from Brigham Young University (age 75).

1955   Toured the Japanese Mission. Dedicated Korea, Okinawa, Guam, and Philippines for the preaching of the gospel, and divided the Japanese Mission to form the Northern Far East and Southern Far East missions.

1959   Visited stakes and missions in New Zealand and Australia.

1960   Was named honorary brigadier general of the Utah National Guard. Visited missions in South America.

1963   Dedicated historical landmarks at Liberty and Kansas City, Missouri. Officiated at the laying of the cornerstone of the Oakland Temple.

1965   Was named counselor in the First Presidency, October 29 (age 89).

1966   A collection of books and materials on American church history was named in his honor at Brigham Young University.

1970   Joseph Fielding Smith was sustained as president of the Church, January 23, with Harold B. Lee and N. Eldon Tanner as counselors. Visited Mexico City. Greeted President and Mrs. Richard M. Nixon. Visited Hawaii. Family home evening was uniformly designated for Monday nights throughout Church.

1971   President Smith spoke to nearly 10,000 youths at Utah State University institute of religion and to 13,000 youths in Southern California. Gave the baccalaureate sermon at Ricks College, May 7. Presided and spoke at the first area general conference at Manchester, England. Three new Church magazines—*Ensign, New Era,* and *Friend*—began publication.

1972   Dedicated the Ogden and Provo temples. Addressed MIA June Conference, Sunday, June 25—his last public address. Died of a heart attack at 9:25 P.M. on Sunday, July 2, in Salt Lake City (age 95).

The First Presidency and Council of the Twelve
During Joseph Fielding Smith's Administration

First Counselor	President	Second Counselor
Harold B. Lee	Joseph Fielding Smith	N. Eldon Tanner
(1941)	(1910)	(1962)
1970-72	1970-72	1970-72

Council of the Twelve—April 1970

Spencer W. Kimball (1943)   Richard L. Evans (1953)
Ezra Taft Benson (1943)   Hugh B. Brown (1958)
Mark E. Petersen (1944)   Howard W. Hunter (1959)
Delbert L. Stapley (1950)   Gordon B. Hinckley (1961)
Marion G. Romney (1951)   Thomas S. Monson (1963)
LeGrand Richards (1952)   Boyd K. Packer (1970)

Died   **Added**

1971—Richard L. Evans   1971—Marvin J. Ashton

July 1972

Spencer W. Kimball (1943)   Hugh B. Brown (1958)
Ezra Taft Benson (1943)   Howard W. Hunter (1959)
Mark E. Petersen (1944)   Gordon B. Hinckley (1961)
Delbert L. Stapley (1950)   Thomas S. Monson (1963)
Marion G. Romney (1951)   Boyd K. Packer (1970)
LeGrand Richards (1952)   Marvin J. Ashton (1971)

Tenth Apostolic Presidency—July 2 to July 7, 1972 (5 days)

Note: Dates in parentheses indicate date ordained member of the Council of the Twelve.

HAROLD B. LEE
Eleventh President of the Church

Born: March 28, 1899, Clifton, Idaho
Died: December 26, 1973, of heart and lung failure, Salt
    Lake City, Utah (age 74)
President of the Church: July 7, 1972, to December 26,
    1973 (1½ years; age 73-74)
Ancestry: English, Irish, Scottish
Education: Public schools, University of Utah
Occupation: Educator, businessman
Mission: 1920-22: Western States
Apostle: Ordained April 10, 1941 (served 31 years; age
    42-73)
President of the Council of the Twelve: January 23, 1970,
    to July 7, 1972
General Authority: 32 years
Church callings prior to presidency: Missionary, ward
    Sunday School superintendent, high councilor, stake
    presidencies, manager of Church welfare program,
    apostle, counselor in the First Presidency
Selective works of teachings: *Stand Ye in Holy Places* and
    Ye Are the Light of the World
Physical characteristics: Five feet eleven inches tall, 175
    pounds, medium build, hazel eyes, gray hair
Family: Son of Samuel Marion and Louisa Bingham Lee.
    Married: Fern Lucinda Tanner, Freda Joan Jensen.
    Had total of two children.

Profile of Harold Bingham Lee

On Friday, July 7, 1972, in the council room of the Salt Lake Temple, Harold B. Lee was set apart as the eleventh president of the Church. His years of preparation for this calling had included twenty-five months as a missionary, seven years as a stake president, thirty-one years as an apostle serving under the direction of Heber J. Grant, George Albert Smith, David O. McKay, and Joseph Fielding Smith, and two and a half years as first counselor in the First Presidency and as president of the Council of the Twelve simultaneously.

He was the youngest president in forty years, since President Heber J. Grant; he would have the shortest term of service—eighteen months—of any president. At seventy-four, he died younger than any other president except Joseph Smith.

One of his most important teachings and possibly the single sentence by which he is best known is: "The most important of the Lord's work that you will ever do will be the work you do within the walls of your own home." (*Decisions for Successful Living*, p. 248.) In addition to prescribing for Church members, he was also describing the conditions of his own homes. He was born, one of six children, to Samuel Marion Lee and Louisa Emeline Bingham on March 27, 1899, in Clifton, Idaho. His heritage in the Church went back to his great-grandfather and great-grandmother, Frances Lee and Jane Vail Johnson, who had been baptized in Indiana, suffered through the attempted settlement of Missouri and of Nauvoo, and

Five-year-old Harold B. Lee (left) with his brother, Perry

reached the Salt Lake Valley in 1850. Samuel and Louisa, pioneers in their own right, were colonists in Idaho. His grandmother, Margaret McMurrin Lee, lost eleven children. The twelfth was premature and so tiny that a finger ring could be slipped on his arm. His mother died and he was raised by an aunt. He was named after his father, Samuel.

The family's economic life was not easy—a round of hand-me-downs, hard physical labor, thrift, sharing, and the help of the Lord and good neighbors. President Lee later would say:

I have thought of the discipline of the boy and girl of my youthful days in a rural community. We began to "do chores" shortly after daybreak so we could "start" with the day's work by sun-up. When

261

the day's work was finished, we had yet to do our evening "chores," usually by aid of a lantern. Despite the fact that there were no wages and hours regulations or child labor laws, we did not seem to be stunted from our exertions. Sleep requirements did not admit of too frequent frivolities. Returns from our labors were small and usually came on a once-a-year basis at harvest time. Homes of that day went throughout the summer with but very little ready money but from our cows we were provided milk, butter and cheese; in our granaries there was usually sufficient wheat to be taken to the mill for flour and cereals. We had our own chickens and garden and fruits in season. Large families required mother to remodel the suits and dresses of the eldest to meet the needs of the youngest who rarely had a "boughten" suit from the store. (*Youth and the Church*, pp. 11-12.)

In wry understatement, he also said, "We had everything that money could not buy"—an education in spirituality. (Preston Nibley, *Presidents of the Church*, p. 431.) He told of watching a violent lightning storm from the

Harold B. Lee (standing, right) was active in school sports

doorway when his mother suddenly pushed him so vigorously that he went sprawling backwards into the yard. At that very instant, lightning struck the house and shot through the doorway. If he had been standing there, he would almost certainly have been killed. (*Friend,* Nov. 1971, p. 12.)

On another occasion, his mother sent his father out in a storm to look for young Harold. His horse had stumbled and had thrown him into a pool of half-frozen mud, out of which his father had to pull him. As a child he was playing on the farm, waiting for his father, when he saw in the neighbor's yard some abandoned outbuildings. Tempted to explore them, he started to climb through the fence when "I heard a voice as distinctly as you are hearing mine: 'Harold, don't go over there.' I looked in every direction to see where the speaker was. I wondered if it was my father, but he couldn't see me. There was no one in sight. I realized that someone was warning me of an unseen danger . . . whether the rotting timbers would fall on me and crush me, I don't know. But from that time on, I accepted without question the fact that there were processes not known to man by which we can hear voices from the unseen world, by which we can have brought to us the visions of eternity." (*Ensign,* Nov. 1971, p. 17.)

On another occasion he shared an experience of his mother's faith and vibrant spirituality, a model for his own:

"As just a high school boy I went away on a high school debating team. We won the debate. I came back and called mother on the telephone only to have her say: 'Never mind, Son. I know all about it. I will tell you when you come home at the end of the week.' When I came home she took me aside and said: 'When I knew it was just time for this performance to start I went out among the willows by the creek side, and there, all by myself, I remembered you and prayed God you would not fail.'" Elder Lee added, "I have come to know that that kind of love is necessary for every son and daughter who seek to achieve in this world." (CR, Apr. 1941, p. 120.)

Harold attended the local elementary school and went fifteen miles to the Church-owned Oneida Academy for his secondary education. At Albion State Normal School he qualified as a teacher at age seventeen, and for sixty dollars a month he taught in the Weston, Idaho, one-room Silver Star School. The next year he became principal of the four-room school at Oxford, Idaho. In choosing education as his profession, he was following the examples of two other Church presidents—Lorenzo Snow and David O. McKay.

In 1920, at age twenty-one, he was called to serve in the Western States Mission, and he spent sixteen months of that mission as president of the Denver Conference. Honorably released in December 1922, he returned to his teaching duties in Idaho and then, the next summer, moved to Salt Lake City. He was looking to the future: in Denver he had met a sister missionary, Fern Lucinda Tanner, a native of Salt Lake City and a skilled organist. They were married in the Salt Lake Temple on November 14, 1923. Doubling his efforts, Harold served as principal of two schools in Salt Lake City—Whittier, then Wilson— from 1923 to 1928 while he completed his university education through correspondence courses and extension classes from the University of Utah.

During one summer he took a selling job with Foundation Press, a library service, and eventually became its intermountain manager. He and Fern became the parents of two daughters, Maurine (Mrs. Ernest J. Wilkins) and Helen (Mrs. L. Brent Goates) and worked faithfully at their church callings. Harold served as stake Sunday School superintendent, ward M-Men leader, stake religion class superintendent, member of the high council, and counselor in the stake presidency. In 1930 he was called as president of the Pioneer Stake, and he spent eighteen months of his service time as a seminary teacher for South High.

Then he had to rechannel his efforts. The United States was entering the Depression's darkest phase. In 1932 he reported to his stake officers that one-third of

Pioneer Stake's members were unemployed. Deeply concerned, he struggled with the problem and worked so successfully to bring the city commission's attention to needed improvements on the west side that that year he was appointed to the city commission by the mayor, with the unanimous approval of the commission. From then on he worked for the well-being of the whole city, though his concern for members of his stake did not slacken. Under his direction, some members found employment by recycling the materials from a demolished business building into a stake gymnasium. In 1934 the stake negotiated with farmers and fruit-growers to exchange labor for produce. His stake built a warehouse to store and distribute food; a variety of production projects and rehabilitation work began.

The First Presidency asked him to resign from the city commission, accept release from his current Church calling, and head up a Churchwide movement that would help the Saints without forcing them to rely on government relief. Later, in describing that meeting on April 20, 1935, he remembered:

I left there about noontime and drove . . . to the head of City Creek Canyon. I got out, after I had driven as far as I could, and I walked up through the trees. I sought my Heavenly Father.

As I sat down to pore over this matter, wondering about an organization to be perfected to carry on this work, I received a testimony, on that beautiful spring afternoon, that God had already revealed the greatest organization that ever could be given to mankind, and that all that was needed now was that that organization be set to work, and the temporal welfare of the Latter-day Saints would be safe-guarded. (*Church News*, Jan. 31, 1970, p. 6.)

With this spiritual assurance, he gave his letter of resignation to the city and in 1937 became the managing director of the Church security program, which was later called the Church welfare program. He became known as the "Father of the Welfare Program."

Five years later this man who had hardly been outside the boundaries of Utah and Idaho was called, at age forty-two, to fill the vacancy left by Reed Smoot in the Council of the Twelve. He was sustained on April 10, 1941, and set apart by President Heber J. Grant. In his first address to the Saints, he humbly and eloquently said:

"Since nine o'clock last night I have lived an entire lifetime in retrospect and in prospect. . . . Throughout the night, as I thought of this most appalling and soul-stirring assignment, there kept coming to me the words of the Apostle Paul, 'Let us therefore come boldly unto the throne of grace, that we may obtain mercy, and find grace to help in time of need.' . . . Therefore I shall take the word of the Apostle Paul. I shall come boldly unto the throne of grace and ask for mercy and his grace to help me in my time of need. With that help I cannot fail. Without it I cannot succeed." (IE, July 1953, p. 504.)

After President Lee's death, Elder Gordon B. Hinckley of the Council of the Twelve summarized his life: "President Lee was frequently knocked down by circumstances during his long odyssey from farm to the office of church president. But, he stood up again where he had fallen and then moved on to greater achievement . . . for out of that chastening process there came a refinement, a patience, a polish, an understanding, a grace beautiful to witness and marvelous in its expression." (*Deseret News,* December 29, 1973.)

And during his life, his colleague in the Council of the Twelve, President Marion G. Romney, claimed:

Humility before God—and fearlessness before men—is the key to his character. His ministry is characterized by an uncommon originality and daring. He is not hampered and restricted by the learning of the world and the forms of men. We, who sit with him daily, are frequently startled by the scope of his vision and the depth of his understanding. With forthrightness, he separates the wheat from the chaff and comes directly to the truth. . . . The source of his strength is in his knowledge that he lives in the shadow of the Almighty. To him, his Heavenly Father is a senior partner, daily giving him guidance. His contacts with heaven are direct and regular. (IE, July 1953, p. 504.)

During his next thirty-one years as an apostle, Harold B. Lee was unstinting in his labors. During World War II he traveled extensively to visit LDS servicemen in his capacity as chairman of the Church's Servicemen's Committee, and toured missions in Japan, Korea, Okinawa, the Philippines, Guam, South Africa, and throughout South and Central America. He organized two missions in South America and the first stake in England. When he toured Japan in 1954, the U.S. Army made him an honorary

Harold B. Lee in the mid-1930s

major general and provided his transportation. One soldier, Paul K. Winward, recalled that Elder Lee visited each LDS soldier on each base he reached. Referring affectionately to this tour later, Elder Lee joked:

> One of the commanding generals, when I was introduced to him in Korea, said, "Well, you have a lot of relatives in this country." The

267

five most prominent names in Korea are Yi, Chang, Kim, Pak, and Lee. In China I discovered that there were over five hundred thousand Chinese who have the surname of Li (Lee), and actually, some of the immigration authorities, when I signed my name, or they saw my name on my passport, would ask: "Chinese?" and I answered, "No, American." Then the comment, "You look Chinese." So, I was accepted . . . as almost a native. My coloring as to hair and eyes and skin seem to fit the general terrain. (IE, Dec. 1954, p. 926.)

Concerned about the success and happiness of the Church's youth, he gave numerous radio talks in the series *Youth and the Church.* These were later compiled into a successful book. He also delivered a trio of youth firesides in 1960 to about 120,000 persons assembled in 170 locations, and spoke repeatedly at seminaries and institutes, and on college and university campuses.

As adviser to the Primary and the Relief Society, he became well acquainted with the needs and goals of the women and children of the Church. By assignment from President McKay, he became executive director of the new Correlation Committee, which was designed to examine the Church's entire curriculum and tailor it to teach most effectively the necessary principles to the Saints through the auxiliaries and Church educational system. It also worked to train bishoprics in their duties, to oversee a simple and standard plan of teacher development, and to encourage more effective home teaching and family home evenings. As president of the Church, Harold B. Lee would continue these efforts by restructuring the general auxiliary boards and priesthood organizations at ward, stake, and regional levels; by creating the internal and public communications departments; and by bringing the MIA programs "under the umbrella of the priesthood," giving the young people themselves more responsibility for planning and directing activities with emphasis on service. He also spearheaded the development of the Melchizedek Priesthood MIA, a churchwide organization for single adults that included the never-married, the divorced, and the widowed. In his own words, this program was "potentially one of the most significant changes in the Church in our lifetime."

As an apostle Elder Lee also served on the General Music Committee, as a member of the executive committee of BYU's board of trustees, and on the General Appropriations Committee.

In addition to the volume on his radio talks, *Youth and the Church,* President Lee published a later revision of that book, titled *Decisions for Successful Living.* After his death many of his sermons and writings were published in *Stand Ye in Holy Places* and *Ye Are the Light of the World.* When he had time, he enjoyed music, the theater, football and basketball games, hunting, fishing, walking in the country, or adding to his art collection. He ate simple food and tried to exercise his body as much as he exercised his mind and spirit. In his younger days he had learned to play the baritone, trombone, mandolin, and piano, and had both given piano lessons and played in a dance band. As his daughters grew up, they eagerly followed his lead, and he enjoyed playing duets with Maurine and accompanying Helen's violin. As an apostle, he frequently played the piano for the General Authorities as they sang in their council meetings.

For someone who loved and appreciated family life as he did, the bitterest tests came with the death of his wife on September 21, 1962; and of their daughter Maurine in 1965. He met these trials faithfully, testifying: "I have come to learn that only through heartbreak and a lonely walk through the valley of the shadow of death do we really begin to glimpse the path that Jesus walked. Only then can we come to claim kinship with Him who gave His life that men might be." (*BYU Speeches of the Year,* 1963, p. 11.)

On June 17, 1963, he married Freda Joan Jensen in the Salt Lake Temple. A member of the Primary General Board, she was director of elementary education in Salt Lake County's Jordan School District.

President Lee was a great instrument for the Lord in touching countless thousands of lives. He was not only a man dedicated to the Lord, but also a man who loved people and life. He touched people's lives in many ways:

shaking hands, putting a loving arm around a shoulder to give reassurance, uttering a strengthening word, giving a prophetic blessing upon someone called to a new assignment, listening to problems, and visiting the hospital to bless and comfort the sick.

An unfailing Church worker and tender family man, he was also a hard-working contributor to the community. He served on the board of directors for the Union Pacific Railroad Company, on the American Red Cross's board of governors, and as chairman of the board for many businesses, including Zion's First National Bank, Hotel Utah, the Utah-Idaho Sugar Company, Bonneville International, ZCMI, and Deseret Management Corporation. He also served as president of the Salt Lake Oratorio Society.

His state and community honored him by making him an honorary lifetime member of the sons of the Utah Pioneers and an honorary colonel of the Utah National Guard. BYU's students awarded him the Exemplary Manhood Award for 1973. More than twenty years earlier, he had been awarded an honorary Master M-Man award for outstanding leadership, and received the Silver Buffalo—Scouting's highest award—for involvement that went back to his days in Idaho as a Scoutmaster. All three of Utah's major universities—Utah State University, Brigham Young University, and the University of Utah, awarded him honorary doctorate degrees. BYU renamed its library after him only months before his death.

Though he was successful as a businessman and an administrator, Harold B. Lee was most intensely concerned with the spirituality of the Saints. As a counselor in the First Presidency, he counseled at conference on October 5, 1970: "Don't try to live too many days ahead." He went on to tell of a father who was gradually and painfully dying of an incurable disease. After a particularly agonizing night, this man told his wife with great feeling: " 'I am so thankful today.' 'For what?' she asked. He replied, 'For God's giving me the privilege of one more day with you.' "

President Lee continued: "Today I could desire with all my heart that all within the sound of this broadcast would likewise thank God for one more day! For what? For the opportunity to take care of some unfinished business. To repent; to right some wrongs; to influence for good some wayward child; to reach out to someone who cries for help—in short, to thank God for one more day to prepare to meet God."

He himself had paid the price of spirituality. As

Harold B. Lee as the newest member of the Council of the Twelve

president of the Church, relating an experience that had taken place earlier, he told of an aggravated ulcer that had flared upon on a mission tour. He made arrangements to get home "as quickly as possible, although we had planned to stay for some other meetings."

On the way across the country, we were sitting in the forward section of the airplane. Some of our Church members were in the next section. As we approached a certain point en route, someone laid his hand upon my head. I looked up; I could see no one. That happened

271

again before we arrived home, again with the same experience. Who it was, by what means or what medium, I may never know, except I knew that I was receiving a blessing that I came a few hours later to know I needed most desperately.

As soon as we arrived home, my wife very anxiously called the doctor. It was now about 11 o'clock at night. He called me to come to the telephone, and he asked me how I was; and I said, "Well, I am very tired. I think I will be all right." But shortly thereafter, there came massive hemorrhages which, had they occurred while we were in flight, I wouldn't be here today talking about it.

I know that there are powers divine that reach out when all other help is not available. (*Ensign,* Feb. 1974, p. 16.)

On another occasion Fenton L. Williams, patriarch in the Sacramento (California) Stake, testified to President Lee's spiritual gifts:

Our stake had just been divided, and Elder Lee, then one of the Twelve, conducted a special Sunday afternoon meeting to set apart the high councilors, bishoprics, and other officers.

I knew these men well. . . . However, our visiting apostle knew none of them personally. . . . As a member of the older stake presidency I was invited to join in the laying on of hands. . . . After the first two or three blessings, I found myself thinking, "He surely has read these men correctly—almost seems to know them."

As the blessings continued I began listening intently to every word, tears welling in my eyes, as I began to realize that the pronouncements had not been by chance but by prophetic inspiration.

Here was a new bishop's counselor who would need to "always be on guard" to "honor his priesthood and calling." How well I knew it. Then followed one who had been having a tithing and coffee problem. His blessing contained specific warnings against those weaknesses.

By this time, my tears flowed freely and I personally did some intense soul-searching about my worthiness to participate in that humbling hour. . . . I bear witness that not in one instance did the servant of the Lord fail to strike home. Several of the men who received blessings that day have since borne witness, in my hearing, of the prophetic utterances of our inspired visitor. They were from God. (*Ensign,* Feb. 1974, pp. 27-28.)

Elder Marion D. Hanks of the presidency of the First Quorum of the Seventy witnessed, on one occasion, President Lee's ability to bring the Spirit of the Lord into a gathering. In December 1969 President Lee spoke at the concluding devotional of a three-day conference of Latter-day Saint Student Association representatives from some three hundred colleges and universities. For an hour he spoke eloquently about the relevance of the scriptures to our everyday conditions, then bore a powerful, moving testimony. At the end of the closing prayer, said Elder Hanks,

Everyone sat in absolute silence. No one moved. Several minutes passed. The room was charged with a perceptible and almost tangible spirit that brought almost everybody to tears.

President Lee was then escorted from the stand. The students arose. About midway down the aisle, the congregation began to sing "The Spirit of God Like a Fire is Burning." As the students left there was no conversation. Everyone knew we had been greatly blessed with a deep spiritual experience which would not be forgotten.

Not a single one of the students attending the conference felt inclined to attend a dance in their honor that evening. All returned to their rooms to ponder the significant events they had experienced.

No clearer evidence could exist of the Lord's acceptance of His chosen servant than this great outpouring of the spirit, participated in by hundreds of people. (*Church News*, Jan. 31, 1970, p. 6.)

On July 7, 1972, Harold B. Lee was ordained president of the Church. On the following day, in his first meeting with newsmen, he repeated one simple and direct message for members of the Church: "The safety of the church lies in the members keeping the commandments. There is nothing more important that I could say. As they keep the commandments, blessings will come." (*Church News*, July 15, 1972.)

That urgency was carried on the wings of love. As a member of the Council of the Twelve, he had related an earlier experience that shaped the entire course of his life: "I know there are powers that can draw close to one who fills his heart with . . . love. . . . I came to a night, some years ago, when on my bed, I realized that before I could be worthy of the high place to which I had been called, I must love and forgive every soul that walked the earth, and in that time I came to know and I received a peace and a direction, and a comfort, and an inspiration, that told me

273

Harold B. Lee as an apostle (1960s)

things to come and gave me impressions that I knew were from a divine source." (IE, July 1953, p. 504.)

This love, which drew forth the unstinting love of others in return, did not make him proud. "Never think of me as the head of this Church," he taught. "Jesus Christ is the head of this Church. I am only a man, his servant." When a business leader once confessed, "I believe in the Lord, but I do not have a testimony of the living Lord," President Lee reassured him, "Then you lean on my testimony while you study and pray until your own is strong enough to stand alone." (*Ensign,* Feb. 1974, p. 90.) He continued, "My whole soul pleads that I may so live that if the Lord has any communication that he would wish me to receive for my beloved people that I could be a pure vessel through which that message could come." (Ibid., p. 89.)

He would pack into the next eighteen months even more intensive service. He presided over the continued correlation of the Church. One month after his ordination he spoke at the Church's second area general conference in Mexico City, August 1972; the 17,000 devoted Saints in attendance made up the largest indoor conference ever held in the Church. He also presided at the third area general conference in Munich, Germany, in August 1973, and reminded members that "no longer might this church be thought of as the 'Utah Church' or as an 'American church,' but the membership of the Church is now distributed over the earth in 78 countries, teaching the gospel in 17 different languages at the present time." (*Ensign,* July 1973, p. 5.) Dr. Norman Vincent Peale, minister of Marble Collegiate Church in New York and a personal friend of President Lee, called him "one of the most enlightened and creative religious leaders in the world."

The great intensity with which he addressed the Saints during the time he spent as president of the Church may have been premonitory. On December 26, 1973, came the stunning news that he had died at 8:58 p.m. in the LDS Hospital in Salt Lake City of lung and cardiac failure. He had earlier told his wife, "God is very near." President Spencer W. Kimball, his successor, paid him poetic tribute: "A giant redwood had fallen and left a great space in the forest."

Harold B. Lee was sensitive to the needs and problems of others. A peacemaker and a man of God, he enriched, blessed, and healed innumerable lives. He was a persuader of people, a resolver of problems, a builder of confidence, the possessor of unusual spiritual insight and understanding. To journey with him was to be strengthened, challenged, inspired, and changed. He bore a strong personal witness to the divinity of the Lord Jesus Christ and the restoration of the gospel:

The Lord and Savior, Jesus Christ, is the head of this Church. I happen to be the one who has been called to preside over his church at the present time here upon the earth.

There is no more powerful weapon that can be forged than the powerful teaching of the gospel of Jesus Christ.

There are two things that, when fully applied, would save the world. The first is to put the full might of the priesthood of the

275

kingdom of God to work, and the second is the powerful teachings of the gospel of Jesus Christ.

No truly converted Latter-day Saint can be immoral; no truly converted Latter-day Saint can be dishonest, nor lie, nor steal. That means that one may have a testimony as of today, but when he stoops to do things that contradict the law of God, it is because he has lost his testimony, and he has to fight to regain it again. Testimony isn't something that you have today and you keep always. Testimony is either going to grow to a brightness of certainty or it is going to diminish to nothingness, depending on what we do about it. The testimony that we recapture day by day, is the thing that saves us from the pitfalls of the adversary. . . .

Now, more than ever, I sense the great import of the Lord's revelation relative to the First Presidency. Three things are required of those who are called to this position. They must be ordained, they must be chosen by the Twelve, and third, to me one of the most significant things, they must be upheld by the confidence, faith and prayers of the church. That means by the faith of the total individual membership of the church.

With all sincerity I bear my witness to you that by a witness of the spirit, more powerful than I have ever experienced before, I know that the Savior lives. As I have sought to live as close as I know how, to know His mind and will concerning matters, and to take the first steps during this last change in the presidency of the church, I need your faith and prayers. Pray for me . . . I plead with you to pray for me. (*Church News*, August 19, 1972, pp. 3, 5.)

Important Dates and Events
in Lifetime of Harold B. Lee

Church Membership, 1972: 3,090,053   1973: 3,360,190
1973   Stakes: 630   Missions: 109   Temples: 15
Number of General Authorities: 44
Missionaries Serving in 1973: 17,258

1899	Harold B. Lee was born in Clifton, Idaho, March 28.
1912-16	Enrolled in Oneida Stake Academy, Preston, Idaho.
1916	Entered Albion State Normal College in Idaho; began teaching in a one-room school at Silver Star, Idaho (age 17).
1917	Taught school near Weston, Idaho; later became principal of a school at Oxford, Idaho, at age 18.
1920-22	Served a mission to the Western States.
1922	Attended summer sessions at the University of Utah.
1923	Married Fern Lucinda Tanner.
1923-28	Continued his education at University of Utah by correspondence and extension classes while serving as a principal in the Granite School District, Salt Lake County.
1926-29	Served as Pioneer Stake religion class superintendent, Sunday School superintendent, high councilor, and counselor in the stake presidency.
1928-32	Became intermountain manager for Foundation Press, Inc.
1930-37	Served as president of Pioneer Stake (age 31-38).
1931-34	Served as a seminary teacher at South High School, Salt Lake City.
1932	Was appointed to the Salt Lake City commission (won reelection in 1933). Established, with his counselors, a Pioneer Stake welfare program, with a warehouse for storing and distributing food and other commodities.
1937	Was called as managing director of the Church welfare program (age 38).
1941	Was ordained an apostle by President Heber J. Grant on April 10 (age 42).
1941-45	Traveled extensively to visit Latter-day Saint servicemen on

military duty in World War II; served as chairman of the Church's Servicemen's Committee.

1945   Gave radio sermons titled *Youth and the Church,* later published as a book.

1946   Met with President Harry S Truman to discuss plans for sending aid to the Saints in Europe.

1953   Received an honorary doctor of humanities degree from Utah State Agricultural College (now Utah State University).

1954   Taught seminary and institute teachers at summer school at BYU. Visited the Orient—Japan, Korea, Okinawa, the Philippines, Guam.

1955   Received an honorary doctor of Christian service degree from BYU.

1956   Toured Mexican missions.

1957   Was elected to the board of Union Pacific Railroad (reelected in 1960).

1958   Became a member of the board of directors of Equitable Life Assurance Society. Toured the South Africa Mission.

1959   Visited missions in South and Central America.

1960   Became a member of the board of Zion's National Bank. Delivered three talks in a Churchwide youth fireside series, with about 120,000 persons assembled in 170 locations.

1961   Became chairman of the executive committee of the Church's new correlation program.

1962   His wife, Fern, died. Visited American servicemen in Germany.

1963   Married Freda Joan Jensen. Was elected to the national board of directors, American Red Cross. Received the Silver Buffalo award from Boy Scouts of America.

1964   Became vice-chairman of the board of Beneficial Life Insurance Company. Received an honorary doctor of humanities degree from the University of Utah.

1967   Was named chairman of the board, Zion's First National Bank.

1968   Was appointed supervisor of the mid-American missions.

1970   Was sustained as first counselor in the First Presidency under President Joseph Fielding Smith and as president of the Council of the Twelve, January 23 (age 70).

1971   Received a distinguished service award from LDS Student Association. Became chairman of the board of Utah-Idaho Sugar Company. Visited the Far East. Spoke at the first area general conference in Manchester, England, August.

1972   Attended the dedications of the Ogden Temple and the Provo Temple. Was ordained as president of the Church, July 7 (age 73), with N. Eldon Tanner and Marion G.

Romney as counselors. Spoke at the second area general conference in Mexico City. Was elected as chairman of the boards of ZCMI, Beneficial Life Insurance Company, and Hotel Utah. Was named director of Zion's Utah Bancorporation. MIA program was restructured into Aaronic Priesthood MIA and Melchizedek Priesthood MIA. Visited England, Switzerland, Italy, Germany, Greece, and the Holy Land. Spoke to 3,000 Young Adults in Mesa, Arizona.

1973   Received the Exemplary Manhood Award presented by BYU Associated Students. Was awarded the Utah Army National Guard Minuteman Award for significant contributions to state, nation, and National Guard. Was awarded honorary life membership in the Sons of Utah Pioneers. Published *Decisions for Successful Living,* a revision of the book *Youth and the Church.* Presided and spoke at the third area general conference in Munich, Germany. Delivered his last sermon to Church employees and families on December 13. Died of heart and lung failure at 8:58 P.M. on Wednesday, December 26, in Salt Lake City (age 74).

The First Presidency and Council of the Twelve During Harold B. Lee's Administration

First Counselor	President	Second Counselor
N. Eldon Tanner	Harold B. Lee	Marion G. Romney
(1962)	(1941)	(1951)
1972-73	1972-73	1972-73

Council of the Twelve—October 1972 to December 1973

Spencer W. Kimball (1943)	Howard W. Hunter (1959)
Ezra Taft Benson (1943)	Gordon B. Hinckley (1961)
Mark E. Petersen (1944)	Thomas S. Monson (1963)
Delbert L. Stapley (1950)	Boyd K. Packer (1970)
LeGrand Richards (1952)	Marvin J. Ashton (1971)
Hugh B. Brown (1958)	Bruce R. McConkie (1972)

Eleventh Apostolic Presidency—Dec. 26 to Dec. 30, 1973 (5 days)

Note: Dates in parentheses indicate year ordained member of the Council of the Twelve.

SPENCER W. KIMBALL
Twelfth President of the Church

Born: March 28, 1895, Salt Lake City, Utah
President of the Church: December 30, 1973
Ancestry: English
Education: Public schools, University of Arizona
Occupation: Businessman
Mission: 1914-16: Central States
Apostle: Ordained October 7, 1943 (served 30 years; age
    48-78)
President of the Council of the Twelve: July 7, 1972, to
    December 30, 1973
Church callings prior to presidency: Missionary, stake
    clerk, stake counselor, stake president, apostle
Selective works of teachings: *Miracle of Forgiveness* and
    Faith Precedes the Miracle
Physical characteristics: Five feet six and one-half inches
    tall, 165 pounds, medium build, brown eyes, gray
    hair
Family: Son of Andrew and Olive Woolley Kimball;
    married Camilla Eyring, four children.

Profile of Spencer Woolley Kimball

It is difficult to evaluate a prophet while he is still among us or to single out one feature as perhaps his most important contribution. But, unquestionably, President Spencer W. Kimball's acceleration of missionary work, his great personal compassion, and the quietly intense spirituality of his personal life are three characteristics that leapt into sharp focus on June 9, 1978, when a letter was released to Church leaders throughout the world. The letter itself is quietly eloquent, its joy and thanksgiving phrased in dignified sentences; and while all three members of the First Presidency put their pens to this historic document, the spirit behind it is President Kimball's. It reads in part:

"We have pleaded long and earnestly . . . spending many hours in the Upper Room of the Temple. . . . He has heard our prayers, and by revelation has confirmed that . . . the long promised day has come when every faithful, worthy man in the Church may now receive the holy priesthood, with power to exercise its divine authority . . . without regard for race or color." (*Ensign,* July 1978, p. 75.)

The revelation was accepted as "the word and will of the Lord to the Church" by a vote of general conference, September 30, 1978, and is now Official Declaration 2 in the Doctrine and Covenants.

After that revelation was given, President Kimball saw the fruits of it when he dedicated the Sao Paulo Temple in Brazil. A black member had been called to the stake presidency within those intervening months, and President

Kimball noted: "I don't know when I have ever been as touched as I was to see that man and his wife in the congregation . . . and to see them wipe their eyes all through the session. They were so thrilled to be permitted to have the blessings." (*Church News*, Jan. 6, 1979, p. 4.)

Three sons of Andrew Kimball: Andrew Gordon, Spencer W., and Delbert G., in about 1906

The intense compassion that had led President Kimball to the temple to seek an answer to the question of so many faithful members of the Church was part of the compassionate pattern of his life. Any human being, member or nonmember, was a child of God and he reached out willingly to fulfill Paul's admonition: "Bear ye one another's burdens, and so fulfil the law of Christ." (Gal. 6:2.)

One example is that of Dr. Norman Vincent Peale, a well-known minister in another church, who shared with his radio audience in 1975 an experience he had had with President Kimball. Dr. Peale told of struggling with a problem for weeks, praying and searching in vain for an answer. During that period, he traveled to Salt Lake City for a speaking engagement and, while there, met privately with the First Presidency. He felt impressed to ask President Kimball for a blessing. The three brethren placed their hands on his head and, states Dr. Peale: "President Kimball in his quiet, sincere, loving manner prayed for me by name. He asked the Lord to be near to me and love me and to take care of me and to guide me. As he prayed, I began to be very broken up and touched, and then of a sudden I had a wondrous feeling of the Presence and I said to him, 'Sir, He is here; I feel His presence.' "

Dr. Peale said that as he left and walked out into the "crisp, sunkissed morning," he suddenly felt "the burden lift." He said, "I saw the answer to the difficulty and I felt the victory. I had called upon the Lord and he had answered me; I had cried to him and he said, 'Here I am.' " (Quoted in *Ensign,* Feb. 1977, p. 84 from a radio address, WOE Radio, New York City, April 27, 1975. Used with permission.)

President Kimball is truly a man who shares love wherever he goes and with whomever he meets. He epitomizes compassion and service to all people. Often he will change his schedule to be with a person in need, ofttimes a stranger.

Once a non-Latter-day Saint neighbor of the Kimballs

who was dying of lung cancer asked President Kimball for a blessing. President Kimball gave him one with love and understanding. The dying man's wife commented that during the blessing she felt the Spirit of the Lord pass from the crown of her head to the tip of her toes. From that time on, the family has called President Kimball the "Good Shepherd."

Another time an acquaintance called President Kimball's office to ask him to pray for a family member who was ill. President Kimball not only said a prayer, but left his office in midday and spent more than an hour with the sick person.

The Kimballs' next-door neighbor describes how President Kimball and his wife are among the first to visit them in times of sickness to see if they can help. The same neighbor also recounts this story: "Having arrived at sacrament meeting early one Sunday, my son and I were sitting waiting for church to begin when President Kimball came into the chapel. Seeing us, he came over and said in his familiar deep voice, 'May I sit down?'

"We moved over, happy to enjoy his company. My son sat between us, and the prophet put his arm around the boy, squeezing him affectionately. We chatted for a few minutes, then just before he left to take his place on the stand, he turned to my ten-year old son and said, 'My boy, you will be one of the finest missionaries in the Church.' Needless to say, this has been one of my son's loftiest goals—to fulfill the words of the prophet."

President Kimball is devoted to "reaching the one." His public sermons give practical, inspiring advice to help people find joy and fulfillment in life. His private conversations are filled with understanding, compassion, and words of encouragement and comfort. Indeed, President Kimball is a mouthpiece for the Lord. He is the one the Saints depend upon to reveal new truths, new solutions, and new programs. He is a man of humility. He radiates spiritual fervor. He is a great teacher of truth, and has gained love and respect throughout the world.

Spencer W. Kimball was born with a rich heritage: his

paternal grandfather was Heber C. Kimball, apostle and counselor to Brigham Young; his maternal grandfather, Edwin D. Woolley, served forty years as a bishop in Salt Lake City and was business manager for President Brigham Young; his father, Andrew Kimball, served for many years as a stake president in Arizona.

Spencer Woolley Kimball was born March 28, 1895, in Salt Lake City, a son of Andrew and Olive Woolley Kimball; he was the sixth of eleven children. Three years after Spencer was born, his father was called to be a stake president in the Gila Valley of Arizona. He had previously served ten years as president of the Indian Territory Mission. While listening to Indian stories and songs at his father's knee, young Spencer developed a great love for the Indian people, which later sustained him through twenty-five years as head of the Church Indian Affairs Committee. He later said:

> My patriarchal blessing, given at age 11, told me I would preach to men, but especially to the Indians. When my mission call was to the Swiss-German Mission I could not see how I would be teaching the Indians. Then because of World War I I was sent to the Central States Mission, but not to the Indians. This worried me a little, until I was called to the Council and was asked to work with President George Albert Smith, then a member of the Twelve, as he labored to revive the Indian work. I have always loved those people and I know that the day of the Lamanite has come. (*Church News*, Feb. 26, 1972, p. 13.)

Even as a youth, Spencer loved the Lord and his work. His father, who had received the gift of prophecy, once said to a neighbor: "That boy, Spencer, is an exceptional boy. He always tries to mind me, whatever I ask him to do. I have dedicated him to be one of the mouthpieces of the Lord—the Lord willing. You will see him someday as a great leader. I have dedicated him to the service of God, and he will become a mighty man in the Church." (CR, Oct. 1943, p. 17.)

As a boy, Spencer demanded much of himself. He excelled in all his school and church activities. He was president of his deacons quorum and filled leadership positions throughout his growing-up years—always serv-

Young Spencer and his sweetheart, Camilla

ing with steadfastness and devotion. At nine years of age he systematically memorized scriptures and hymns, and at age fourteen he read the Bible from cover to cover.

D. Arthur Haycock, secretary to President Kimball, has shared some of President Kimball's own recollections of his childhood:

"He used to milk nine cows every morning and night, the old-fashioned way. And as he milked the cows he learned the Articles of Faith, he learned the hymns, and he learned the Ten Commandments. He wrote them down on a little card and put them on the ground where he could look as he milked the cows. . . .

"He had made up his mind just once to say no, and after that it was easy always to say no to the bad things." (*New Era*, May 1979, p. 7.)

In his school days at Thatcher, Arizona, Spencer was a class leader, honor student, and athlete. In the Church-sponsored high school he played on the basketball team and was studentbody president. He also enjoyed handball as an adult.

During his high school years he worked in dairying and farming to meet his school and mission expenses. He sold his black horse to help support himself on his mission.

President Kimball described his mission to the Central States as "a great character builder." He said, "My mission was a stabilizer and an organizer and a spiritualizer. It strengthened my testimony. It solidified my character and my life. It was a great experience. It was a time of personal growth." (*Church News,* Jan. 5, 1974, p. 4.)

Shortly after his mission, Spencer acquired summer work, mining water for a large ranch. He and a co-worker camped in a tent on a mountain, cooked their own food, and once a week got the local newspaper. One week the paper told about Camilla Eyring, a new teacher at Gila Academy. Spencer read about her with great interest. He

LDS chapel in Thatcher, Arizona

had met her just before his mission. He recalled the situation: "As soon as I got back down in the valley and was finished with the well work, I looked her up and a courtship was started. I was in the military service, waiting to be called, so my courtship was mostly in a khaki uniform. But she seemed not to be too much offended by my appearance. We were married in November, 1917." (*Church News,* Jan. 5, 1974, p. 4.)

He was not called up for active duty, and two months later his father, the stake president, called him as stake clerk. He served for six and a half years under his father. When his father died, Spencer, still in his twenties, was called by Heber J. Grant to be a counselor in the new stake presidency, a position he held for ten years.

He recounts that, unbeknown to him, some of his relatives went to President Grant and told him it was a mistake to call a young man like that to a position of responsibility and make an old man of him. Finally, after some discussion, President Grant said very calmly, but firmly, "Spencer has been called to this work, and he can do as he pleases about it." (Edward L. and Andrew E. Kimball, *Spencer W. Kimball,* p. 111.)

President Kimball says that of course he gladly accepted the call, and he served twelve years as counselor in the stake presidency, two years again as stake clerk, and then five and a half years as the first president of the newly created Mt. Graham Stake. While in this position he directed the rather spectacular rehabilitation efforts of members of the Church after a disastrous flood in the upper Gila Valley at Duncan in 1938.

Spencer and Camilla Kimball are the parents of one daughter and three sons: Olive Beth (Mrs. Grant M. Mack), Spencer LeVan, Andrew Eyring, and Edward Lawrence. They have twenty-seven grandchildren and twenty-eight great-grandchildren. For President and Sister Kimball, their family remains a central concern in their life.

The Kimballs have the highest regard for the benefits of education. As the children grew up they expected to go to college. All four children earned college degrees—a total of ten degrees among them. President Kimball took some time to play, but his children learned most of their lessons from him by watching him work or by working with him or for him.

"To encourage his children to work and save, Spencer paid them for working around the home—Eddie's account book as a child shows ten cents for catching a mouse, twenty-five cents for a gopher, five cents for each half-hour practicing the piano (and a deduction of ten cents for missing daily practice). . . . What the children did not need for gifts or movies or other personal pleasures Spencer encouraged them to invest in the business. . . . Over the years this money, compounded with its earnings, added up to a considerable sum. The boys saved enough in this way to cover a large share of their mission expenses." (*Spencer W. Kimball*, pp. 148-49.)

President Kimball had a reputation for his keen abilities to organize. He began his business career as a teller and bookkeeper in a bank, then progressed to branch manager and assistant cashier. After eight years he resigned to venture into business with a partner as half-owner and manager of an insurance and realty company.

During those early years of laboriously building up a new business, he also bought a small farm, where a neighbor raised cotton and alfalfa on shares, and the family kept some livestock. He also found time for civic, professional, and community work. He helped organize the Gila Broadcasting Company and the Gila Valley Irrigation Company, and served in important leadership assignments in these ventures. Other positions he held included district governor of Rotary International, president of the Safford Rotary Club, member of the Gila Junior College board of trustees, member of the Arizona Teachers Retirement Board, vice-chairman of the United War Fund campaign in Graham County, and director of the Association of Arizona Insurance Agents.

He was working in the insurance and realty business when he was called to be a member of the Council of the

Twelve on July 8, 1943. He remembers, as a boy, the almost reverential awe in which he held many of the General Authorities who stayed in the Kimball home when his father was stake president. Little did he know that years later President J. Reuben Clark, Jr., would greet him on the telephone with the words, "Spencer, this is Brother Clark speaking. The brethren have just called you to fill one of the vacancies in the Quorum of the Twelve Apostles." (CR, Oct. 1943, p. 15.) At age 48, he was the oldest man to be ordained an apostle and then become president; he served the second shortest period of time as an apostle—thirty years—before becoming president. (Brigham Young served as an apostle for only twelve years before becoming president.)

For most of his thirty years as an apostle, Elder Kimball was in charge of conference assignment schedules; he also headed the Church Indian Affairs Committee, the Church Missionary Committee, and the Budget Committee. Because of his great work with the Lamanites, many Church members came to link his name with the Indian Student Placement program.

President Kimball has always been admired for his powerful and persuasive speaking, his frank, wise, and relevant messages. His son Edward describes well his father's speaking and purpose:

> In the many sermons he has delivered over the years there are several repeated strains. One is the Church Indian program. Another reflects his feeling of responsibility to speak forthrightly to members of the Church about sexual sins, warning of the approaches to them, emphasizing the seriousness of succumbing to the near-universal temptations, and pointing out the road back for those who have erred and yearn for reconciliation with the Lord. This is a difficult and unpleasant task, but one he has not shirked. His objective has not been to be popular, or to please the ear, but to preach repentance. It is true, however, that his directness, his earnestness, his careful statement of the problem and solution, and his obvious love and concern for those to whom he speaks have made him one of the most respected speakers of his generation. What he says is not intended to be entertaining, but almost always is worth hearing and rehearing. (*Faith Precedes the Miracle,* p. xx.)

Watching Spencer W. Kimball at work, one would never know of the trials that have filled his life. When he was seven he nearly drowned. At ten he suffered a facial paralysis. His mother died when he was eleven. At twelve he had typhoid fever. In adulthood he was stricken with Bells palsy, smallpox, scores of boils, a major heart attack,

Spencer W. Kimball in 1933

and cancer of the throat, which resulted in the removal of most of his vocal cords. Forced to redevelop his ability to speak, he talks today with a deep, deliberate voice.

In April 1972 he had open heart surgery, and he has suffered from a number of other health problems. But in overcoming these obstacles and going through these severe tests, he has found a stronger faith in and greater closeness to his Heavenly Father.

When he is called a "modern miracle," President Kimball replies, "Haven't you read in the scriptures that men will be strengthened even to the renewing of their bodies if they are doing the work of the Lord?"

In his first general conference address as an apostle, he reported that just as Jacob wrestled all night "until the breaking of the day" for a blessing, so he went through that experience for eighty-five nights, "praying to the Lord to help me and strengthen me and make me equal to this great responsibility that has come to me." (CR, Oct. 1943, p. 16.)

Similarly, as the mantle of president and prophet came upon him, he said, "I doubt if anyone in the Church has prayed harder and more consistently for a long life and the general welfare for President Lee than my Camilla and myself. . . . I have expected that I would go long before he would go." (*Ensign,* Feb. 1974, p. 86.)

He has been accurately portrayed by one of his fellow apostles as "a man of strength and dignity, of personableness and persuasion—and of faith. He believes that the impossible is possible with the help of God. He knows the profound importance of his calling, and devotes himself to it with a kind of dedication that is rare among men." (IE, Nov. 1966, p. 992.)

Today, he is perhaps the most widely traveled General Authority in the Church. He has visited almost every country in the world, toured most missions, visited most stakes, and created many new stakes and missions. He has interviewed thousands of missionaries. His years as a stake clerk have made him sensitive to pertinent details and the importance of follow-through.

One recurring theme in his talks is the importance of family worship. "We would go a long way to curing the world's ills," he promises, "if the families could follow the same pattern of living as that laid down by my father." His father's pattern was to have family prayer morning and night, hold family home evening at least once a week, and go to church meetings as a family. President Kimball has said:

I was fortunate that I grew up in a good home. My father was sent into the Arizona territory to preside there when I was only three. As long as I can remember, my father was stake president. . . .

My father was kind; he took me with him to conferences in the stake, and once I came to Salt Lake City with him to attend general conference. I think closeness with your children pays off. My mother died when I was eleven, but I always had a mother to come home to. My second mother was very special. . . .

I was one of eleven children in the family, and this meant everyone had to help on our small family farm.

I feel that's the problem today. Young people don't have enough to do to keep out of mischief, and in many cases the mothers are not home to guide the children. (*Church News,* July 15, 1972, p. 10.)

President Kimball is a builder of character in youth and is well aware of their needs and problems. He is well known for his talks concerning dating, morals, modesty, temple marriage, and missionary work. He counsels with those who need help the most, and as he talks, he draws diagrams to illustrate his ideas. He listens, he comforts, he occasionally reprimands, but always his display of love is apparent.

Many years ago as Church members came to President Kimball for advice and counsel, he would write down a scriptural reference or a little note to help them remember the counsel. The little note became a list, and then a sheet of information. Soon he was duplicating several sheets of scriptural references and direction. "I thought I would write a little message of encouragement, and counsel," he said. "That message became twenty-three chapters in a book." The book is *The Miracle of Forgiveness* (Bookcraft, 1969), which has sold more than half a million copies. It is common occurrence to receive letters of appreciation from members who have read the book. Many bishops even use it as a text in working with transgressors. President Kimball, referring to the book, says:

I have had many experiences in dealing with transgressors, especially those involved in sexual sins, both inside and outside of marriage. . . . To cure spiritual diseases which throttle us and plague our lives, the Lord has given us a sure cure—repentance. . . . Having come to recognize their deep sin, many have tended to surrender hope, not having a clear knowledge of the scriptures and of the redeeming power of Christ. . . . Man can be literally transformed by his own repentance and by God's gift of forgiveness which follows for all except unpardonable sins. It is far better not to have committed the sin;

the way of the transgressor is hard; but recovery is possible. (*The Miracle of Forgiveness*, pp. ix-xi.)

One of that book's solid contributions was President Kimball's understanding of the nature of repentance. Those who mistake mercy for softness were surprised to hear him explain in detailed clarity that one must repent, as the scriptures state, "with all his heart." (See D&C 42:25.) President Kimball explains:

Obviously this rules out any reservations. Repentance must involve an all-out, total surrender to the program of the Lord. That transgressor is not fully repentant who neglects his tithing, misses his meetings, breaks the Sabbath, fails in his family prayers, does not sustain the authorities of the Church, breaks the Word of Wisdom, does not love the Lord nor his fellowmen. A reforming adulterer who drinks or curses is not repentant. The repenting burglar who has sex play is not ready for forgiveness. God cannot forgive unless the transgressor shows a true repentance which spreads to all areas of his life. (*The Miracle of Forgiveness*, p. 203.)

Another outstanding book, *Faith Precedes the Miracle*, published by Deseret Book in 1972, has been equally helpful and inspiring.

Through his writings on marriage, President Kimball has inspired thousands of people to seek for eternal marriages by choosing proper companions or by improving existing marriage relationships. Temples have a special meaning to President Kimball. He has said: "Wouldn't it be wonderful if every Latter-day Saint home had in the bedroom of each boy and each girl, or on the mantle of the living room, a fairly good-sized picture of a temple which would help them recall, frequently, the purpose of these beautiful edifices. I believe there would be far more marriages in the temple than there are today, because the children would have as a part of their growing experience the picture of one of our temples constantly before them as a reminder and a goal." (*Ensign*, Jan. 1977, p. 7.)

President Kimball dedicated the temples in Washington, D.C., and Sao Paulo, Brazil, and rededicated remodeled temples in Mesa, Arizona; St. George, Utah; Laie, Hawaii; and Logan, Utah. These are the first temples in the

Spencer W. Kimball as an apostle

history of the Church to be rededicated. And he has announced the building of temples in Mexico, Seattle,
Samoa, Japan, and the Salt Lake Valley.

Never before in the history of the Church have so
many Church members had such direct contact with the
prophet. Not only have they had the opportunity of reading and hearing his words, but of actually being in his
presence. He has placed great emphasis on area
conferences, and has emphasized the importance of taking
the Church programs to the various parts of the free
world. In the first five years of his administration he
conducted thirty-eight area conferences in South and
Central America, Australia, the South Pacific, the British
Isles, the Far East, and Europe. At these conferences, he

has stressed the importance of strengthening the family and keeping the commandments of God. He has taken time to mingle with the Saints, shaking hands and bearing his testimony. It is a common sight at these conferences to see faces of people, young and old, streaming with tears as they touch and embrace the prophet of God.

After the final session of an area conference in Brazil, the Saints some 8,000 strong rose to their feet and, waving white handkerchiefs, sang in Portuguese "We Thank Thee, O God, for a Prophet."

President Kimball's administration may be characterized as an administration of accomplishment. He has overseen the restructuring of the First Quorum of the Seventy (October 1976), a series of solemn assemblies throughout the United States and Canada, and the shifting of administrative responsibilities to local leaders abroad. In the general conference of April 1976, Church members voted to canonize two important revelations received by former presidents concerning the state of the dead. During his presidency there has been simplification of Church programs and procedures; general conference has been shortened from three days to two days; stake conferences are now held only twice a year instead of quarterly. General auxiliary conferences have been discontinued, and regional auxiliary meetings are now held. The youth program has been restructured. Responsibilities of General Authorities have been clarified and redefined. The names of stakes and missions now reflect their geographic locations.

President Kimball has called for an increase in missionary activity, not only in increasing the number of missionaries serving, but also in sending them out better prepared. He proclaims an urgency in spreading the gospel, and declares that every worthy young man should fulfill a mission. As president he has seen the missionary force expanded from 17,500 to over 28,000 missionaries, and the number of missions increase from 110 to 175 (1974 to June 1979).

President Kimball constantly reminds the Saints to purify themselves and find true happiness. He talks in specifics—from gardening and home beautification to building strong marriages and families. He has firmly decried divorce, abortion, pornography, drugs, and immorality.

President Kimball's challenge is "Lengthen Your Stride," an admonition he applies to members of all ages. He has stated: "We have great works to perform on this earth, and I suppose the whole program of the Church could be put in one of three categories: missionary work, temple work, and keeping Church members active and faithful." (*Ensign*, Jan. 1977, p. 3.)

Above his desk is a card with the simple motto "Do it!" President Kimball is a model of energy and vigor. He thrives on hard work, often arriving at the office at 6:45 A.M. He stays at the office until 5:30 or 6:00 in the evening, then takes two or three briefcases full of material home and often spends the evening working until 9:30 or 10:00.

His trip to England, South Africa, and South America in November 1978 is illustrative of his activity. During that time he traveled 24,000 miles, attended numerous meetings and banquets, gave 26 major addresses, dedicated a temple (repeating the dedicatory prayer nine times in subsequent sessions), installed two temple presidents on two different continents, and greeted thousands of people. Upon arriving home, he went directly to his office for a while, then returned early the next morning for his usual business affairs.

Sister Kimball, who accompanies him on the majority of his trips, commented, "I am glad he isn't any younger! I just hope I can keep up with him!"

Shortly after he became president, he was asked what he did for entertainment. He replied with a twinkle, "Sleep!"

In spite of President Kimball's responsibilities and demands, he is never too busy to alter his schedule to accommodate people. When he meets with someone he never appears rushed, but creates a calm and unhurried atmosphere. He also realizes the need for relaxation. In

Arizona he served as a choir director, organist, and member of a chorus or quartet. For many years he sang with a popular quartet called the Conquistadores. He was also in great demand to sing at funerals until 1957, when part of his vocal cords were removed. Today he still enjoys playing the piano, especially for children. He has enjoyed the theater and participating in sports, and also likes to walk in the hills, woods, or on a seaside.

President Kimball's work schedule has not permitted time-consuming hobbies. But one of the things he has done is to write faithfully in his journal. He believes that every person should keep a personal journal, so posterity can know about ancestors. He himself has kept some sort of journal since he was a very young man. His journal was the major source for the popular and well-written biography brought out by his son Edward and grandson Andrew in 1977.

President and Sister Kimball with their children

He is keenly perceptive and has a lively sense of humor. As a visitor in Washington, he was invited to open a U.S. Senate session with prayer and arrived to find only six Senators present. The person introducing him apologized but President Kimball quipped, "That's all right. I was not going to pray to them, anyway." (*Spencer W. Kimball*, p. 419.)

His keen appreciation for a pun showed up on another occasion. He disliked any kind of medication but had to take heavy doses of anticoagulants and diuretics after heart surgery. When he developed some muscular aches in his leg, his son Ed suggested that he take some aspirin. With a twinkle, President Kimball said he didn't want to take *anything* else "because he was already 'the piller' of the Church." (Ibid., p. 425.)

Once while speaking with a lifelong friend who had been in a serious car accident, President Kimball was asked how he retained such a wonderful attitude toward life in spite of his own personal health trials. He responded: "We have to expect difficulties, as they are an abrasive to prove our faith in Him. I do not question God's wisdom, but believe blessings will follow if I continue to love him and keep all of his commandments. I am trying to do just that and I am having fun doing it!"

Junius E. Driggs, president of the Mesa Temple, is a personal friend of President Kimball, and they have shared many sacred spiritual experiences together. He knows and understands President Kimball's health problems and bears witness of the blessings the Lord has given to this great man so he can lead the Church. President Driggs bears this testimony: "The vigorous, forceful, effective leadership of President Kimball is ample evidence of the plan the Lord had to continue to use him and to literally 'renew his body' with fresh vigor and strength to perform the great responsibilities of prophet, seer and revelator and president of The Church. This is full and fervent testimony that Spencer W. Kimball is the man the Lord has chosen to lead his Church in this particular time of need for his specific talents and strengths."

President Kimball shakes hands with general conference visitors outside Salt Lake Tabernacle

President Kimball, prophet for all the world, projects a vibrant spirituality and is determined to make the Church an increasingly visible force for good. He has charged members to prepare and to pray for the day when the doors of all nations are opened to the preaching of the gospel. Indeed, Spencer W. Kimball is an example to all. He is dedicated to building brotherhood among members and nonmembers alike, as he teaches the world to "quicken your pace" and "lengthen your stride."

One of his greatest strengths as the leader of the restored church is his unflinching dedication to the Lord. He sings with true commitment his favorite hymn, "I Need Thee Every Hour."

Perhaps one of the most fitting tributes to this beloved prophet comes from his closest associates, the Council of the Twelve, who echo the feelings of millions of people throughout the world:

> We, his associates, are continually stirred to better performance through watching our leader unwearily at work—from directing a worldwide missionary effort to remembering a visit with a woman in pain in a wheelchair or a tearful child in Chile.
>
> The restored Church under President Kimball's inspired leadership is expanding around this challenging, changing world as never before.
>
> We honor President Kimball as our valiant leader, chosen of the Lord. We love him as our warm and selfless associate. We esteem him as a pure, noble, guileless exemplar of the teachings of Jesus the Christ, whose noble representative he is in the building of God's Kingdom here on earth. (*Church News*, Jan. 6, 1979, p. 2.)

Today Spencer W. Kimball is the voice of the Lord, his spokesman on earth, a beloved prophet-president. His testimony is heard on radio and television throughout the world, and it resounds in the hearts of millions who diligently follow his counsel and believe on his words:

> Recently a prominent doctor, knowing of my surgeries and cancer treatments, exhibited a little surprise at my assuming this great responsibility of presidency. He was not a member of the Church and evidently had never known the pull and pressure one feels who has a positive assurance that the Lord is not playing games, but has a serious program for man for his glory. The Lord knows what he is doing, and all his moves are appropriate and right. And I was surprised also that any man would wonder and question the work of the Lord. We who have the positive assurance and testimony of the divinity of this work do not question the ways or determinations of the Lord.
>
> I know without question that God lives, and I have a feeling of sorrow for those people living in the world of doubt who do not have such assurance.
>
> I know that the Lord Jesus Christ is the Only Begotten Son of our Heavenly Father and that he assisted in the creation of man and all that serves man, including this earth and all that is in the world, and that he was the Redeemer of mankind and the Savior of this world, the author of the plan of salvation for all men, and the exalter of all who live all the laws he has given.
>
> He it is who organized the true vehicle, this church, and called it after his own name: The Church of Jesus Christ of Latter-day Saints,

and in it are all the saving graces. I know that there is contact between the Lord with his prophets and that he reveals the truth today to his servants as he did in the days of Adam, Abraham, Moses, and Peter, and numerous others throughout time. God's messages of *light* and *truth* are as surely given to man today as in any other dispensation. Since Adam and Eve were placed in the garden, the Lord has been eager to reveal truth and light to his people, but there have been many times when man would not listen, and, of course, "where there is no ear there is no voice." I know that the gospel truths will save and exalt mankind if men will accept the truths and fully live up to their commitments and covenants.

I know this is true, and I bear this testimony to all the world. I urge all men to seriously accept and conform their lives totally to the precepts of the gospel. I bear this witness in all soberness and in the name of Jesus Christ. Amen. (Written for publication in this volume, February 1974.)

Important Dates and Events
in Lifetime of Spencer W. Kimball

Church Membership, 1979: 4.3 million (est.)
1979   Stakes: 1090   Missions: 175   Temples: 17
       Number of General Authorities: 69
       Missionaries Serving in 1979: 28,847

1895	Spencer W. Kimball was born in Salt Lake City, Utah, March 28.
1898	Moved to Thatcher, Arizona, where his father had been called as president of the St. Joseph Stake.
1906	Received his patriarchal blessing from Samuel Claridge, which said he would one day preach the gospel to the Lamanites (age 11).
1914	Graduated from Gila Academy (Church-operated high school) with highest honors and as studentbody president.
1914-16	Was called to the Swiss-German Mission, but served in the Central States because of World War I.
1917	Attended the University of Arizona at Tucson. While waiting for his World War I military contingent to be called up, he married Camilla Eyring. He was never called to active duty.
1917-26	Started his career in banking as a teller and bookkeeper, then branch manager, and assistant cashier.
1918	Was called as clerk of St. Joseph Stake, serving under his father. Was sealed to his wife, Camilla, in the Salt Lake Temple.
1924	Was called as second counselor in the St. Joseph Stake presidency, and continued to serve for several years as stake clerk. Became a member of the Gila College board of education.
1927	Became half-owner and manager of Kimball-Greenhalgh Insurance and Realty Co.
1935	Became secretary of the Gila Valley Irrigation Co. Organized and became part-owner of Gila Broadcasting Co., station KGLU.

1938-43   Served as president of the newly organized Mt. Graham Stake (age 42-48).

1943   Was called to the Council of the Twelve, July 8. Was ordained an apostle by President Heber J. Grant, October 7 (age 48).

1946   Was called by President George Albert Smith on special assignment to work with Lamanites, thus fulfilling in part his patriarchal blessing. Was named to serve as chairman of the Church Indian Affairs Committee.

1952   Traveled to Mexico and Central America; dedicated the land for proselyting; divided the Mexican Mission; organized the Central American Mission.

1954   Toured missions in Canada.

1955   Toured missions of Europe, visiting cities in the Norwegian, Swedish, Danish, Finnish, British, Netherlands, French, Swiss-Austrian, East German, and West German missions; attended the dedication of the Swiss Temple.

1957   Underwent surgery for malignancy in his throat. Lost one vocal cord and part of another; also temporarily lost his voice.

1958   Received an honorary Master M-Men award, and his wife received an honorary Golden Gleaner award during June MIA Conference. Toured the Spanish-American West Mission.

1959   Toured missions in South America.

1960   Delivered talks in a Churchwide youth fireside series, with about 120,000 persons assembled in 170 locations.

1961-62   Traveled to the Holy Land and to European stake conferences, December to February.

1964   Toured missions in Brazil and Uruguay.

1965   Was named Council of the Twelve supervisor for South American missions.

1966   Toured Chile, Argentina, Uruguay, and Brazil.

1967   Received "The Gardener of Souls" award from the institute of religion studentbody at Snow College, Ephraim, Utah.

1968   Was named Council of the Twelve supervisor for the British Mission.

1969   Received an honorary doctor of laws degree from Brigham Young University. His book *The Miracle of Forgiveness* was published.

1970   Was sustained as acting president of the Council of the Twelve, January 23 (age 75). Was honored by Indian students at BYU.

1971   Was presented with the Pursuit of Excellence award at the sixth annual conference of the Latter-day Saints Student

Association at the University of Utah Institute of Religion. Spoke at the first area conference in Manchester, England, August.

1972   Underwent open heart surgery, April. Was sustained as president of the Council of the Twelve, July 7 (age 77). His book *Faith Precedes the Miracle* was published. Spoke at the second area conference in Mexico City.

1973   Spoke at the third area general conference in Munich, Germany (August). Visited Church members in South Africa (September). Was sustained as president of the Church on December 30, with N. Eldon Tanner and Marion G. Romney as counselors (age 78).

1974   Spoke at BYU graduation, an area conference for Lamanite youth in Salt Lake, a Young Adult fireside in the Salt Lake Tabernacle, the Snow College graduation, a meeting of Church members in Spokane, Washington, youth conferences in Colorado, and before the BYU studentbody. Received the student-given Exemplary Manhood award at BYU. Spoke at the Stockholm area conference. Dedicated the Washington Temple. Spoke to the Saints in Mexico City.

1975   Rededicated the Arizona Temple at Mesa. Dedicated the New York City Visitor's Center. Resigned as chairman of various businesses so he would have more time for religious matters. Announced the organization of the First Quorum of the Seventy. Spoke at area conferences in Brazil, Argentina, Japan, the Philippines, Hong Kong, Taiwan, and Korea. Held solemn assemblies in the U.S. and Canada; these continued in subsequent years of his administration. Auxiliary general conferences were replaced with regional meetings.

1976   Two revelations received by presidents Joseph Smith and Joseph F. Smith were added to the Pearl of Great Price. President Kimball visited the scene of a disastrous flood in Idaho to reassure flood victims. Dedicated the Visitor's Center at the Washington Temple. Spoke to 23,000 gathered in a Church-sponsored bicentennial meeting in Landover, Maryland. Announced that Assistants to the Twelve would now serve as members of the First Quorum of the Seventy. Spoke at 17 area conferences in American Samoa, Western Samoa, New Zealand, Fiji, Tonga, Australia, Tahiti, England, Scotland, France, Finland, Denmark, the Netherlands, and Germany (age 81).

1977   Was presented with the Silver World award, International Scouting's highest honor. Was chosen as one of 40 distinguished Americans who each received a Golden Plate award for "extraordinary accomplishment" at Orlando, Florida. Spoke at the twelfth annual priesthood genealogy seminar. Dedicated the land of Poland for missionary work and visited Switzerland, Austria, Italy, England, and Germany. Spoke at area conferences in Mexico, Guatemala, Costa Rica, Peru, Chile, Bolivia, and Colombia. Spoke to thousands of seminary students in the Salt Lake Tabernacle. His biography, *Spencer W. Kimball,* was published. General conference was changed to two days. The Church's youth program was restructured.

1978   Rededicated temples in St. George, Utah, and Laie, Hawaii, and dedicated the temple in Sao Paulo, Brazil. Announced a revelation that priesthood is to be granted to worthy men of all races. Spoke to women in a special Churchwide fireside. Spoke at area conferences in Hawaii, Uruguay, Argentina, Brazil, and South Africa. Presented to U.S. President Jimmy Carter a family statuette at a special program in the Salt Lake Tabernacle, culminating National Family Week in the United States. Spoke to 14,000 youths in Southern California and 11,000 students at a fireside at Utah State University. A new genealogy program was announced.

1979   Rededicated the Logan Temple. Dedicated the temple site for the Jordan River Temple in South Jordan, Utah. Spoke at area conferences in Texas, Wisconsin, Canada, Washington, D.C., Georgia, Michigan, California, New Zealand, and Australia. Joseph Smith's Vision of the Celestial Kingdom and Joseph F. Smith's Vision of the Redemption of the Dead were transferred from the Pearl of Great Price to the Doctrine and Covenants. The revelation extending priesthood to "all worthy male members of the Church" was also added to the Doctrine and Covenants as Official Declaration 2. Underwent a successful operation for removal of fluid from the brain. Traveled to the Holy Land with a BYU tour and dedicated the Orson Hyde park in Jerusalem.

The First Presidency and Council of the Twelve During Spencer W. Kimball's Administration

First Counselor	President	Second Counselor
N. Eldon Tanner	Spencer W. Kimball	Marion G. Romney
(1962)	(1943)	(1951)
1973-	1973-	1973-

Council of the Twelve—April 1974

Ezra Taft Benson (1943)	Gordon B. Hinckley (1961)
Mark E. Petersen (1944)	Thomas S. Monson (1963)
Delbert L. Stapley (1950)	Boyd K. Packer (1970)
LeGrand Richards (1952)	Marvin J. Ashton (1971)
Hugh B. Brown (1958)	Bruce R. McConkie (1972)
Howard W. Hunter (1959)	L. Tom Perry (1974)

Died	Added
1975—Hugh B. Brown	David B. Haight (1976)
1978—Delbert L. Stapley	James E. Faust (1978)

December 1979

Ezra Taft Benson (1943)	Boyd K. Packer (1970)
Mark E. Petersen (1944)	Marvin J. Ashton (1971)
LeGrand Richards (1952)	Bruce R. McConkie (1972)
Howard W. Hunter (1959)	L. Tom Perry (1974)
Gordon B. Hinckley (1961)	David B. Haight (1976)
Thomas S. Monson (1963)	James E. Faust (1978)

Note: Dates in parentheses indicate year ordained member of the Council of the Twelve.

Appendix 1

PROFILES OF THE PRESIDENTS

Name	Born	Birthplace	Date Ordained Apostle	President Council of Twelve	Age & Date Sustained as Pres.
Joseph Smith 1805-1844	Dec. 23, 1805	Sharon, Vermont	May 1829 (age 23)	First Elder	24 Apr. 6 26 Jan. 25
Brigham Young 1801-1877	June 1, 1801	Whitingham, Vermont	Feb. 14, 1835 (age 33)	Apr. 14, 1840	46 Dec. 27
John Taylor 1808-1887	Nov. 1, 1808	Milnthorpe, England	Dec. 19, 1838 (age 30)	Oct. 6, 1877	71 Oct. 10
Wilford Woodruff 1807-1898	Mar. 1, 1807	Avon (now Farmington), Connecticut	April 26, 1839 (age 32)	Oct. 10, 1880	82 Apr. 7
Lorenzo Snow 1814-1901	April 3, 1814	Mantua, Ohio	Feb. 12, 1849 (age 34)	April 7, 1889	84 Sept. 13
Joseph Fielding Smith 1838-1918	Nov. 13, 1838	Far West, Missouri	July 1, 1866 (age 27)	No record	62 Oct. 17
Heber Jeddy Grant 1856-1945	Nov. 22, 1856	Salt Lake City, Utah	Oct. 16, 1882 (age 25)	Nov. 23, 1916	62 Nov. 23
George Albert Smith 1870-1951	April 4, 1870	Salt Lake City, Utah	Oct. 8, 1903 (age 33)	July 1, 1943	75 May 21
David Oman McKay 1873-1970	Sept. 8, 1873	Huntsville, Utah	April 9, 1906 (age 32)	Sept. 30, 1950	77 Apr. 9
Joseph Fielding Smith 1876-1972	July 19, 1876	Salt Lake City, Utah	April 7, 1910 (age 33)	April 9, 1951	93 Jan. 23
Harold Bingham Lee 1899-1973	Mar. 28, 1899	Clifton, Idaho	April 10, 1941 (age 42)	Jan. 23, 1970	73 July 7
Spencer Woolley Kimball 1895-	Mar. 28, 1895	Salt Lake City, Utah	Oct. 7 1943 (age 48)	July 7, 1972	78 Dec. 30

Source: Church Historical Department

Served as President	Years as Pres.	Years as General Authority	Died	Age at Death	Church Membership	Stakes Missions Temples		
1830-1832 1832-1844	1 + 9 mos. 12½	14	June 27, 1844	38	1844 35,000 (est.)	9	3	2
1847-1877	30	42	Aug. 29, 1877	76	1877 155,000 (est.)	20	9	1
1880-1887	6 + 9 mos.	49	July 25, 1887	78	1887 192,000 (est.)	31	12	3
1889-1898	9½	59	Sept. 2, 1898	91	1898 228,032	40	20	4
1898-1901	3	52	Oct. 10, 1901	87	1901 278,645	50	21	4
1901-1918	17	52	Nov. 19, 1918	80	1918 495,962	75	22	4
1918-1945	26½	63	May 14, 1945	88	1945 979,454	155	38	7
1945-1951	6	48	April 4, 1951	81	1951 1,147,157	191	43	8
1951-1970	18 + 9 mos.	64	Jan. 18, 1970	96	1970 2,930,910	499	88	13
1970-1972	2½	62	July 2, 1972	95	1972 3,277,790	581	102	15
1972-1973	1½	32	Dec. 26, 1973	74	1973 3,321,556 (est.)	631	110	15
1973-								

Appendix 2

Line of Authority
for Presidents of the Church
(Their Apostleship)

(Dates in parentheses indicate years served as president)

THE LORD JESUS CHRIST

PETER, JAMES, AND JOHN

were ordained apostles by the Lord Jesus Christ (John 15:16).

JOSEPH SMITH, JR. (1830-1844)

received the Melchizedek Priesthood and apostleship in 1829 (age 23) under the hands of Peter, James, and John (see D&C 20:2; 27:12). 1830-32, First Elder; 1832-44, president. Served three years as an apostle (1829-1832; age as an apostle 23-26).

THE THREE WITNESSES

Oliver Cowdery, David Whitmer, and Martin Harris were called by revelation to choose the Twelve Apostles, and on February 14, 1835, they were "blessed by the laying on of hands of the Presidency," Joseph Smith, Jr., Sidney Rigdon, and Frederick G. Williams, to ordain the Twelve Apostles. (HC 2:187-88.)

BRIGHAM YOUNG (1847-1877)

was ordained an apostle Feb. 14, 1835 (age 33) by the Three Witnesses. Apostle no. 3; served 12 years as an apostle (1835-1847; age as an apostle 33-46).

JOHN TAYLOR (1880-1887)

was ordained an apostle Dec. 19, 1838 (age 30) by Brigham Young and Heber C. Kimball (ordained by the Three Witnesses). Apostle no. 14; served 41 years as an apostle (1838-1880; age as an apostle 30-71).

WILFORD WOODRUFF (1889-1898)

was ordained an apostle April 26, 1839 (age 32) by Brigham Young.

Apostle no. 15; served 50 years as an apostle (1839-1889; age as an apostle 32-82).

LORENZO SNOW (1898-1901)

was ordained an apostle Feb. 12, 1849 (age 34) by Heber C. Kimball. Apostle no. 22; served 49½ years as an apostle (1849-1898; age as an apostle 34-84).

JOSEPH F. SMITH (1901-1918)

was ordained an apostle July 1, 1866 (age 27) by Brigham Young. Apostle no. 26; served 35 years as an apostle (1866-1901; age as an apostle 27-62).

HEBER J. GRANT (1918-1945)

was ordained an apostle Oct. 16, 1882 (age 25) by George Q. Cannon (ordained by Brigham Young. Apostle no. 33; served 36 years as an apostle (1882-1918; age as an apostle 25-62).

GEORGE ALBERT SMITH (1945-1951)

was ordained an apostle Oct. 8, 1903 (age 33) by Joseph F. Smith. Apostle no. 43; served 42 years as an apostle (1903-1945; age as an apostle 33-75).

DAVID O. McKAY (1951-1970)

was ordained an apostle April 9, 1906 (age 32) by Joseph F. Smith. Apostle no. 47; served 45 years as an apostle (1906-1951; age as an apostle 32-77).

JOSEPH FIELDING SMITH (1970-1972)

was ordained an apostle April 7, 1910 (age 33) by Joseph F. Smith. Apostle no. 49; served 60 years as an apostle (1910-1970; age as an apostle 33-93).

HAROLD B. LEE (1972-1973)

was ordained an apostle April 10, 1941 (age 42) by Heber J. Grant. Apostle no. 61; served 31 years as an apostle (1941-1972; age as an apostle 42-73).

SPENCER W. KIMBALL (1973-   )

was ordained an apostle Oct. 7, 1943 (age 48) by Heber J. Grant. Apostle no. 62; served 30 years as an apostle (1943-1973; age as an apostle 48-78).

Bibliography

Books and Pamphlets

Allen, James B., and Leonard, Glen M. *The Story of the Latter-day Saints.* Salt Lake City: Deseret Book Co., 1976.

Anderson, Edward H. *The Life of Brigham Young.* Salt Lake City: George Q. Cannon and Sons, 1893.

Anderson, Joseph. *Prophets I Have Known.* Salt Lake City: Deseret Book Co., 1973.

Andrus, Hyrum L. *Joseph Smith: The Man and the Seer.* Salt Lake City: Deseret Book Co., 1960.

Arrington, Leonard J., Fox, Feramorz Y., and May, Dean L. *Building the City of God.* Salt Lake City: Deseret Book Co., 1976.

Ashton, Marvin J. *What Is Your Destination?* Salt Lake City: Deseret Book Co., 1978.

Backman, Milton V., Jr. *American Religions and the Rise of Mormonism.* Salt Lake City: Deseret Book Co., 1965.

_____. *Joseph Smith's First Vision.* Salt Lake City: Bookcraft, 1971.

Barrett, Ivan J. *Joseph Smith and the Restoration: A History of the Church to 1846.* 2nd ed. Provo, Utah: Brigham Young University Press, 1973.

Bennion, M. Lynn, comp. *Oil for Their Lamps.* Salt Lake City: The Church of Jesus Christ of Latter-day Saints Department of Education, 1943.

Benson, Ezra Taft. *God, Family, Country: Our Three Great Loyalties.* Salt Lake City: Deseret Book Co., 1970.

Brigham Young: Prophet, Statesman, Pioneer. Pamphlet. Salt Lake City: Deseret News Press, 1968.

Brooks, Melvin R. *LDS Reference Encyclopedia.* Salt Lake City: Bookcraft, 1960.

Burton, Alma P., and Burton, Clea M. *Stories from Mormon History.* Salt Lake City: Deseret Book Co., 1976.

Cannon, George Q. *The Life of Joseph Smith, The Prophet.* Salt Lake City: Deseret Book Co., 1958.

Carter, Kate B. *Unique Story—President Brigham Young.* Salt Lake City: Utah Printing Co., 1975.

Cheesman, Paul R. *The Keystone of Mormonism.* Salt Lake City: Deseret Book Co., 1973.

Clark, James R., comp. *Messages of the First Presidency of The Church of Jesus Christ of Latter-day Saints.* 6 vols. Salt Lake City: Bookcraft, 1965-75.

Conkling, J. Christopher. *A Joseph Smith Chronology.* Salt Lake City: Deseret Book Co., 1979.

Cornwall, J. Spencer. *Stories of Our Mormon Hymns.* Salt Lake City: Deseret Book Co., 1963.

Cowley, Matthias F. *Wilford Woodruff.* Salt Lake City: Bookcraft, 1964.

Day, Robert B. *They Made Mormon History.* Salt Lake City: Deseret Book Co., 1973.

Deseret News Church Almanac. Salt Lake City: Deseret News, 1974-79.

Doxey, Roy W. *Latter-day Prophets and the Doctrine and Covenants.* 4 vols. Salt Lake City: Deseret Book Co., 1963-65.

_____. *Zion in the Last Days.* 2nd ed. Salt Lake City: Bookcraft, 1968.

Durham, G. Homer. *Joseph Smith: Prophet-Statesman.* Salt Lake City: Bookcraft, 1944.

Durham, Reed C., Jr., and Heath, Stephen H. *Succession in the Church.* Salt Lake City: Bookcraft, 1970.

Evans, John Henry. *Joseph Smith, An American Prophet.* New York: The Macmillan Co., 1933.

Flake, Lawrence R. *Mighty Men of Zion.* Salt Lake City: Karl D. Butler, 1974.

Gates, Susa Young, and Widtsoe, Leah D. *The Life Story of Brigham Young.* New York: The Macmillan Co., 1930.

Gibbons, Francis M. *Heber J. Grant: Man of Steel, Prophet of God.* Salt Lake City: Deseret Book Co., 1979.

_____. *Joseph Smith: Martyr, Prophet of God.* Salt Lake City: Deseret Book Co., 1977.

Grant, Heber J. *Gospel Standards.* Compiled by G. Homer Durham. Salt Lake City: Deseret Book Co., 1969.

Heslop, J.M., and Van Orden, Dell R. *A Prophet Among the People.* Salt Lake City: Deseret Book Co., 1971.

Hill, Donna. *Joseph Smith: The First Mormon.* Garden City, New York: Doubleday and Co., 1977.

Hinckley, Bryant S. *The Faith of Our Pioneer Fathers.* Salt Lake City: Deseret Book Co., 1956.

_____. *Heber J. Grant: Highlights in the Life of a Great Leader.* Salt Lake City: Deseret Book Co., 1951.

Hunter, Milton R. *Brigham Young, the Colonizer.* Salt Lake City: Deseret News Press, 1940.

Jenson, Andrew. *Latter-day Saint Biographical Encyclopedia.* 4 vols. Salt Lake City: Andrew Jenson Historical Co., 1901-36.

Jesse, Dean C. *Letters of Brigham Young to His Sons.* Salt Lake City: Deseret Book Co., 1974.

Journal of Discourses. 26 vols. London: Latter-day Saints Book Depot, 1855-86.

Kimball, Edward L., and Kimball, Andrew E., Jr. *Spencer W. Kimball.* Salt Lake City: Bookcraft, 1977.

Kimball, Spencer W. *Faith Precedes the Miracle.* Salt Lake City: Deseret Book Co., 1972.

_____. *The Miracle of Forgiveness.* Salt Lake City: Bookcraft, 1969.

Lee, Harold B. *Decisions for Successful Living.* Salt Lake City: Deseret Book Co., 1973.

_____. *Stand Ye in Holy Places.* Salt Lake City: Deseret Book Co., 1974.

_____. *Youth and the Church.* Salt Lake City: Deseret Book Co., 1970.

Ludlow, Daniel H. *Latter-day Prophets Speak.* Salt Lake City: Bookcraft, 1948.

McConkie, Bruce R. *Mormon Doctrine.* Salt Lake City: Bookcraft, 1966.

McConkie, Joseph F. *True and Faithful.* Salt Lake City: Bookcraft, 1971.

McKay, David O. *Cherished Experiences From the Writings of President David O. McKay.* Compiled by Clare Middlemiss. Salt Lake City: Deseret Book Co., 1976.

_____. *Gospel Ideals.* Salt Lake City: Deseret Book Co., 1953.

_____. *Man May Know for Himself.* Compiled by Clare Middlemiss. Salt Lake City: Deseret Book Co., 1967.

_____. *Treasures of Life.* Compiled by Clare Middlemiss. Salt Lake City: Deseret Book Co., 1962.

McKay, Llewelyn R., comp. *Home Memories of President David O. McKay.* Salt Lake City: Deseret Book Co., 1956.

Mormon Temple—Oakland California. Pamphlet. Salt Lake City: The Church of Jesus Christ of Latter-day Saints, 1964.

Morrell, Jeanette McKay. *Highlights in the Life of President David O. McKay.* Salt Lake City: Deseret Book Co., 1966.

Madsen, Truman G. *Joseph Smith Among the Prophets.* Salt Lake City: Deseret Book Co., 1966.

Nibley, Preston. *Brigham Young, the Man and His Work,* 6th ed. Independence, Missouri: Zion's Printing and Publishing Co., 1970.

_____. *Presidents of the Church.* 13th ed. Salt Lake City: Deseret Book Co., 1974.

Oaks, Dallin H., and Hill, Marvin S. *Carthage Conspiracy.* Chicago: University of Illinois Press, 1975.

Pratt, Parley P. *Autobiography of Parley Parker Pratt.* Salt Lake City: Deseret News Press, 1938.

Presidents of the Church. Institute of religion manual. Salt Lake City: The Church of Jesus Christ of Latter-day Saints, 1979.

Quincy, Josiah. *Figures of the Past.* Boston, 1883.

Rich, Russell R. *Ensign to the Nations.* Provo, Utah: Brigham Young University Publications, 1972.

Richards, Stephen L. *Contributions of Joseph Smith*. Pamphlet. Salt Lake City: Deseret News Press.

Roberts, B.H. *A Comprehensive History of the Church of Jesus Christ of Latter-day Saints*. 6 vols. Provo, Utah: Brigham Young University Press, 1957.

_____. *The Life of John Taylor*. Salt Lake City: Bookcraft, 1963.

Romney, Thomas C. *The Life of Lorenzo Snow*. Salt Lake City: Deseret Book Co., 1955.

Schluter, Fred E. *A Convert's Tribute to President David O. McKay*. Salt Lake City: Deseret News Press, 1964.

Schreeve, Lyman S. *History of the Uruguayan Mission*. Provo, Utah: Brigham Young University (unpublished manuscript), 1978.

Smith, Eliza R. Snow. *Biography and Family Record of Lorenzo Snow*. Salt Lake City: Deseret News Co., 1884.

Smith, George Albert. *Sharing the Gospel with Others*. Compiled by Preston Nibley. Salt Lake City: Deseret Book Co., 1948.

Smith, Joseph. *History of the Church of Jesus Christ of Latter-day Saints*. 7 vols. Salt Lake City: The Church of Jesus Christ of Latter-day Saints, 1932-51.

_____. *Teachings of the Prophet Joseph Smith*. Compiled by Joseph Fielding Smith. Salt Lake City: Deseret Book Co., 1938.

Smith, Joseph F. *Gospel Doctrine*. Edited by John A. Widtsoe et al. Salt Lake City: Deseret Book Co., 1939.

Smith, Joseph Fielding. *Answers to Gospel Questions*. 5 vols. Salt Lake City: Deseret Book Co., 1954-66.

_____. *Doctrines of Salvation*. 3 vols. Compiled by Bruce R. McConkie. Salt Lake City: Bookcraft, 1954-56.

_____. *Essentials in Church History*. 27th ed. Salt Lake City: Deseret Book Co., 1950.

_____. *The Life of Joseph F. Smith*. 2nd ed. Salt Lake City: Deseret Book Co., 1938.

_____. *Seek Ye Earnestly*. Salt Lake City: Deseret Book Co., 1970.

Smith, Joseph Fielding, Jr., and Stewart, John J. *The Life of Joseph Fielding Smith*. Salt Lake City: Deseret Book Co., 1972.

Smith, Lucy Mack. *History of Joseph Smith by His Mother*. Salt Lake City: Bookcraft, 1958.

Smith, William. *William Smith on Mormonism*. Lamoni, Iowa: Herald Steam and Job Office, 1883.

Spencer, Clarissa Young, and Harmer, Mabel. *Brigham Young at Home*. Salt Lake City: Deseret Book Co., 1947.

Stewart, John J. *Remembering the McKays*. Salt Lake City: Deseret Book Co., 1970.

Story to Tell. Compiled by the Primary Association general board and Deseret Sunday School. Salt Lake City: Deseret Book Co., 1945.

Stubbs, Glen R. "A Biography of George Albert Smith 1870-1951." Ph.D. dissertation, Brigham Young University, 1974.

Talmage, James E. *Jesus the Christ*. 38th ed. Salt Lake City: Deseret Book Co., 1970.

Taylor, John. *Gospel Kingdom*. 4th ed. Compiled by G. Homer Durham. Salt Lake City: Bookcraft, 1943.

_____. *Mediation and Atonement*. Salt Lake City: Deseret News Co., 1882.

Taylor, Samuel W. *The Kingdom of God or Nothing*. New York: Macmillan Publishing Co., Inc., 1976.

Tullidge, Edward. *Life of Brigham Young or Utah & Her Founders*. New York: Tullidge and Crandall, 1877.

Tyler, Daniel. *A Concise History of the Mormon Battalion in the Mexican War, 1846-1847*. Chicago: Rio Grande Press, Inc., 1964.

West, Emerson R. *Vital Quotations*. Salt Lake City: Bookcraft, 1968.

Widtsoe, John A. *Evidences and Reconciliations*. Compiled by G. Homer Durham. Salt Lake City: Bookcraft, 1960.

_____. *Joseph Smith: Seeker After Truth, Prophet of God*. Salt Lake City: Bookcraft, 1957.

_____. *Priesthood and Church Government*. Revised ed. Salt Lake City: Deseret Book Co., 1939.

Woodruff, Wilford. *The Discourses of Wilford Woodruff*. Edited by G. Homer Durham. Salt Lake City: Bookcraft, 1946.

_____. *Journal of Wilford Woodruff*. Salt Lake City: Church Historical Department.

_____. *Leaves From My Journal*. Salt Lake City: Juvenile Instructor Office, 1882.

Young, Brigham. *Discourses of Brigham Young*. Compiled by John A. Widtsoe. 1961 ed. Salt Lake City: Deseret Book Co., 1954.

Zimmerman, Dean R., comp. *The Living Prophet*. Salt Lake City: Hawkes Publishing Co., 1974.

Periodicals

Brigham Young University *Speeches of the Year*, Provo, Utah, 1954-1979.

BYU Quarterly, Brigham Young University, Provo, Utah.

Church News, section of the *Deseret News*, Salt Lake City, Utah, 1931-1979.

Conference Report, Salt Lake City, Utah.

Deseret News, Salt Lake City, Utah, 1850-1979.

Ensign, Salt Lake City, Utah, 1971-1979.

The Friend, Salt Lake City, Utah, 1971-1979.

Historical Record, Salt Lake City, Utah, 1886-1890.

Improvement Era, Salt Lake City, Utah, 1897-1970.

Instructor, Salt Lake City, Utah, 1866-1970.

Juvenile Instructor, Salt Lake City, Utah, 1866-1929.

Liahona, or Elders' Journal, Chattanooga, Tennessee, and Independence, Missouri, 1907-1945.

Millennial Star, Manchester, Liverpool, and London, England, 1840-1970.

New Era, Salt Lake City, Utah, 1971-1979.

Relief Society Magazine, Salt Lake City, Utah, 1915-1970.

Utah Genealogical and Historical Magazine, Salt Lake City, Utah, 1910-1940.

Utah Historical Quarterly, Salt Lake City, Utah.

Young Women's Journal, Salt Lake City, Utah, 1889-1929.

Index